Richard Brautigan

Richard Brautigan
An Annotated Bibliography

by
John F. Barber

McFarland & Company, Inc., Publishers
Jefferson, North Carolina, and London

British Library Cataloguing-in-Publication data are available

Library of Congress Cataloguing-in-Publication Data

Barber, John F.
    Richard Brautigan : an annotated bibliography / by John F. Barber.
      p. cm.
    Includes index.
    ISBN 0-89950-525-2 (lib. bdg. : 50# alk. paper) ∞
    1. Brautigan, Richard—Bibliography. I. Title.
Z8115.9.B37   1990
[PS3503.R2736]
016.813'54—dc20   89-43698
                                                                CIP

©1990 John F. Barber. All rights reserved

Manufactured in the United States of America

McFarland & Company, Inc., Publishers
  Box 611, Jefferson, North Carolina 28640

My thanks to Grier Weeks, owner of Dogwood Publishing and Design in Asheville, North Carolina, for all his efforts in the production of this book. Grier spent the better part of a year embroiled with "the Big B," as he called it, massaging, manipulating, and mangling the manuscript into its finished form. I appreciate his time, efforts, and frustrations. Now that this project is completed, I hope he'll have more time to spend with his wife and family.

TABLE OF CONTENTS

PROLOGUE 1

INTRODUCTION 7

CRITICAL/BIOGRAPHICAL OVERVIEW 9

CHRONOLOGY 17

KEYS TO ABBREVIATIONS AND SHORT TITLES 21

WORKS BY BRAUTIGAN
Poetry 25
Novels 41
Short Stories 51
Collection 54
Essays and Articles 55
Letters/Papers 56
Recordings 56

GENERAL COMMENTARY ABOUT BRAUTIGAN
Book-Length Studies 57
Bibliographies 59

Theses and Dissertations 60
Parodies 62
Censorship Litigation 63
Teaching Experiences 64

CRITICISM OF BRAUTIGAN
General Criticism 67
General International Criticism 92

REVIEWS OF WORKS BY BRAUTIGAN
Poetry 99
Novels 109
Short Stories 164
Collection 169

MYSTERIOUS AND ERRONEOUS CITATIONS 173

OBITUARIES AND EULOGIES 175

SOURCES 187

INDEX 195

PROLOGUE

I met Richard Brautigan in the spring of 1982. I was a student in his creative writing course at Montana State University in Bozeman, Montana. We became friends and started meeting at the Eagles Club downtown after class. The Eagles Club was the VFW outpost in Bozeman. It was dark and cool inside, a welcome relief from the hot streets. Chrome and vinyl tables and chairs ringed the bar which stood alone like an island in a pool of alcoholic light that filtered through the various bottles above. Beyond the tables and chairs and the bar was a small dance floor where, on weekend nights, a three-piece country western band sawed out the favorites.

The Eagles Club was frequented by shadowy figures drinking to forget the past, or to build fortitude to deal with the present. Richard thought it was the best bar in Montana and we spent a lot of time there drinking together. We joked about our time in the Eagles Club as searching for "The Great American Good Time." We joked about it but Richard was quite serious. Richard often said that life was horrible and cruel and that people often suffered and lamented. But that didn't have to happen because all that mattered was having fun. I never knew, until much later, and even then not completely, how desperately lonely Richard was, how unhappy he was, how unsatisfied and unfulfilled he was, and how much he needed and wanted the attention and notoriety that holding court at the Eagles Club brought him.

The search for "The Great American Good Time" was a diversion, an escape from the specter of meaninglessness that Richard felt in and around his life. If he didn't find it at the Eagles Club he went to another bar, or another, all night, drinking heavily and looking for people or conversational fisticuffs.

He never quit until all the bars were closed and every last opportunity for serious drinking was exhausted. Richard often bought a bottle of George Dickel Tennessee Whiskey from the last bar and took it back to his motel room. He stayed at the Alpine Motel, a low rent place just on the eastern outskirts of Bozeman, unless he met a woman who took him home for the night. Wherever he ended up for the night, and no matter how much George Dickel he had consumed, first thing the next morning Richard would call and say, "Meet me for breakfast. I'll buy and then you can give me a ride home."

He had a house he called "Rancho Brautigan" in Paradise Valley, about 50 miles southeast of Bozeman. Richard liked to go there after finishing his weekly creative writing class at the university and work on his own writing projects. That summer he told me he wrote two novels, but never told me anything about them. He also published So the Wind Won't Blow It All Away.

Richard and I enjoyed each other's company but there was also an understood mutual usage of one another. Richard never learned to drive and never, until that summer, owned a car. He bought an old car and parked it in his barn, intending to learn how to drive. We discussed my teaching him. In the meantime he used me for rides back and forth between Rancho Brautigan and Bozeman and for non-threatening companionship while in search of "The Great American Good Time." I used him as a possible outlet for my writing. He was complimentary of a manuscript I was working on and promised to show it to his literary agent when I completed it. I thought that was fair enough compensation for the one hundred mile shuttle whenever Richard wanted a ride.

And there were special times that only friendship that has taken the time to earn the trust can provide.

"My friend just died," Richard said from the other end of the telephone. "Why don't you come over. Bring a bottle of whiskey."

He had mentioned his "friend" several times that summer, saying she was dying of cancer in Japan. He had been waiting for the final telephone call.

I arrived about an hour later. Richard was sitting in the small guest house off to the side of the main ranch house. It was the first time I had ever seen that little house opened up. He was in good spirits and with a sweep of his hand showed me the one room of the little house. "This used to be a smokehouse," he said, "and one time, when I had some money, I hired a master carpenter to do the remodeling work you see here. Some day I want to put in a bathroom, a small kitchen, and a hot tub with a roof which slides back exposing the sky. Think what it would be like to soak in a hot tub during a rain storm, or while it is snowing!"

The remodeling already done included a redwood floor, redwood trim around the room, and a triangular, free-standing closet in one corner. A painting hung on one wall. It was a painting of the view once seen out a window filled in during the remodeling. A wood cook stove stood in the middle of the room, its chimney bottom boxed in with wood painted a rich shade of raspberry. It served as an effective dividing point between the sitting and sleeping portions of the room.

Most of the sleeping area was taken by an old swayback brass bed. Behind the bed, a large window looked out to the decaying chicken coops. Richard was proud of the shade he had installed on the window. It was a full-length roll-down plastic shade with a silvery, metallic coating on one side that allowed one to see out but prevented anyone on the outside from seeing in.

"You can lie here in bed with people all around in the backyard and make love," he said. "No one can see in, no one knows what you are doing."

A mound of sheets and blankets lay on the bed. I thought of his friend. Who was she? They had been lovers. Had she shared this room with him?

We left the smokehouse love-nest and walked around the main ranch house, onto the back porch. I sat at the green table in a spindly wooden lawn chair. Richard sat on the porch railing, leaning against a pillar. For a long time neither of us said anything. Lost in our own thoughts, we watched the pods on the cottonwood trees explode and release their feathery seeds. They snowed down around us and gathered on the porch floor where gentle puffs of air rolled them into balls and swirled them into the corners.

We watched mosquitoes land on our arms and then take off later, burdened with blood. We watched storms, trailing lightning and veils of rain, boil up over the mountains. As twilight lengthened we watched lithe brown ghost deer jump the fences of the old corral and float into the backyard. One whitetail buck stood for several minutes silhouetted on the side of the hill by the barn watching us watch him.

Richard broke the silence. "She's gone now. It's all done."

It was the first time he had mentioned the death of his friend since our telephone conversation. That had been hours ago. I didn't know what to say in return. I said, "She's gone, but not forgotten," and immediately felt stupid for having said it.

"I have no pictures of her, none of her letters, nothing. She's gone."

"But you have memories and you can write them down and preserve them," I retorted.

"I don't write for therapy, or to eulogize. But, then again..."

Richard stood up, stretched, walked across the porch, and into the house. The cottonwood seed fluffs swirled in his wake. He returned with a poem written on a scrap of paper. He read the poem to me, and the deer, and the cottonwood seeds, and the rain storms over the mountains.

Rendezvous

Where you are now
I will join you.

"Come inside." Richard said, "Hunger has visited us. Let's eat." He left the poem on the green table, fluttering in the puffs of cottonwood air.

We prepared noodles with smoked oysters, green peas, and chopped fresh onion shoots gathered from the backyard. Richard taught me how to eat the noodles with chopsticks and how to suck the noodles into my mouth. He said that sucking the noodles into my mouth helped to cool them and make them taste better. He said that in Japan, it was quite acceptable to make a sound while sucking noodles into your mouth. He taught me to make the correct sound.

"Someday, if we are still friends, I will have Japanese friends over for dinner, make noodles, and invite you to join us. They will compliment you on your sound."

After dinner we talked of writing, mutual friends, and of other times spent together. The night grew older and the whiskey died a lingering death. We decided to make the forty-mile trip into town for another bottle.

We drove down the valley, following the moonlit meanderings of the Yellowstone River. The stars shone like points of radium on a cosmic clock and we both stared out the windows, neither of us talking. It wasn't that there was nothing to say, but rather that we couldn't think of a way to say it. It was a long, quiet, thoughtful trip for a bottle of whiskey.

Back at the ranch, bottle of whiskey half consumed during the return trip, Richard said, "My friend was Japanese. She was a Buddhist. The Buddhists believe that one can send things to the dead by burning them. I have two books of hers and the poem. I will burn them and you can help if you don't think it's too heavy."

We gathered the books, some matches, and lighter fluid. Passing through the kitchen Richard said, "She loved white wine." He poured some white wine into a delicate tulip-shaped wine glass. "She loved white wine and she loved to drink it from a glass like this. We will burn this also."

We waded through the waist high grass in the backyard guided by the brief flare of matches. On a pile of rocks we placed the two books, the poem, and the delicate tulip glass of white wine. Richard gathered a handful of white and yellow columbine and placed them on top of the books and the poem.

I soaked the shrine with lighter fluid and lit a match. As the flames erupted Richard said, "She always had great style."

We stood with our arms around each other, watching until the books, the poem, and the wildflowers were only ashes. The wine glass broke apart and lay atop the remains.

"She's gone," he said. "It's done."

"Yes," I answered.

Outside these moments, our friendship was an uneasy one. I noticed an undercurrent in Richard, a violent one, seemingly waiting to explode. He often talked of being able to kill someone very quickly, so quickly that they wouldn't be able to do anything to prevent him from culminating their life in some dark and dirty manner. I was always afraid that this undercurrent would burst out. I was afraid that he wasn't talking idly, but that he was instead telling the truth, and that he would indeed live up to his boast. I was afraid that he would go for me sometime after the heavy drinking and the philosophical meanderings over the cups that our evenings together often were. I was afraid that indeed I wouldn't be able to do anything to stop him. Only later did I realize that by talking about how quickly he could end <u>my</u> life, Richard was actually talking about the desire to end <u>his</u>. He said that he felt like he had seen and done everything. He kept looking for meanings in his life and could find none.

He was, I believe, fatally disappointed over the lack of acclaim for his books, especially his most recent, <u>So the Wind Won't Blow It All Away</u>. He said that novel had been in his head for 17 years and that he had worked very hard to write it. When it was not accepted and acclaimed by the critics or the reading public he felt misunderstood and alienated.

Richard impressed me as a very lonely man. He seemed incapable of upholding an enduring relationship with anyone. He deplored the breakdown of the American family but was twice divorced and barely on speaking terms with his daughter Ianthe. He had "boycotted" her marriage because he didn't like her husband, and said that he would like her second husband "a helluva" lot better. He said that he didn't like children.

Although he never said it directly, I often surmised that Richard didn't like people who got too close to him. Toward the end of summer, we had a disagreement and Richard told me to go away and never speak to him again. I saw him on the street shortly afterwards and asked if we couldn't talk the disagreement through. I told him that I was sorry, and asked if we couldn't save our friendship. He said, "I don't know. We'll see. I'll let you know."

In 1983 I moved away from Bozeman and never saw Richard again. The following year I wrote him, apologizing again for my part in the disagreement. He wrote back from Japan. "Forget the past. It ain't worth it," he said. He wrote that he didn't know when he would be in Montana again, but when he was, he would like to see me. "I'd like that," he said.

I never heard from him again. With a strange sort of premonition though I expected to hear about his death and watched the obituaries for the announcement. Richard often said that the obituaries were his favorite part of the paper. He said that an obituary was what was left of a person after they died, a summation of their life. He enjoyed reading the obituaries and wondered what his would say.

When I saw the article about Richard's death in October of 1984 it was an expected shock; I had waited for it. And then it seemed like relief; I wouldn't have to watch for his obituary anymore.

In his last novel, So the Wind Won't Blow It All Away, Brautigan wrote:

> "If ever I got pneumonia, I wanted whoever was there to tie a very long string on my finger and fasten the other end of the string to their finger and when they left the room, if I felt like I was dying, I could pull the string and they'd come back. I wouldn't die if there was a long piece of string between us" [52-53].

In the end there was no long piece of string between Brautigan and the world and he died alone, vulnerable, lonely, and disconnected in his house north of San Francisco, not of pneumonia, but of a self-inflicted gunshot wound. He lived a troubled and weary life and felt that proper fame and notoriety had eluded him. In the end, like Ernest Hemingway, to whom he was so often compared, he took his own life.

INTRODUCTION

Richard Brautigan's novels, poetry, and short stories were reviewed and criticized in both the popular and scholarly press. His writing was the subject of several dissertations. Brautigan himself was the subject of several book-length studies. The one area where Brautigan has not been comprehensively investigated is bibliography.

Outside the listings of "other publications" in each of his books and the "primary works" and "sources" cited in various literary biography articles, only three incomplete and dated bibliographies concerning Richard Brautigan exist.

James Wanless and Christine Kolodziej entitle their primary and secondary bibliography "A Working Checklist " (*Critique* 16(1) 1974: 41-52). They freely admit being unable to verify some bibliographical information and to excluding other material.

Gary M. Lepper's primary bibliography (A Bibliographical Introduction to Seventy-Five Modern American Authors. Berkeley, CA: Serendipity Books, 1976. 81-85) covers Brautigan's work only through 1975.

Stephen B. Jones introduces his primary and secondary bibliography (*Bulletin of Bibliography and Magazine Notes* 33 1976: 53-59) by saying, "I have attempted to collect entries through late 1975. Emendation and fugitive information will be welcomed" (53).

Since Brautigan was productive up until his death in 1984, there is obviously much bibliographical information that can and must be collected and organized. As scholars of contemporary American literature begin to look more and more closely at the significance of the writers of the 1960s and 1970s, and especially at Richard Brautigan, the deficiencies of the existing bibliographies become increasingly frustrating.

This bibliography's inclusion dates range from 1956 through June 1989. It includes all of Brautigan's publications and all those publications concerning Brautigan that can be identified during this time period. Because Brautigan's early work was often published in broadside form and given away, or published in "underground" newspapers which were never indexed or collected, I cannot confidentially state that this bibliography includes everything ever published by or about Brautigan but every effort has been made to be as inclusive as possible.

This bibliography is divided into six parts. "Works By Brautigan" is a primary bibliography listing, chronologically, the publication of poems, novels, short stories, collections, essays, letters/papers, and recordings by Brautigan. Annotations concern first editions (United States and England), special publications, reprints, translations, previously published portions, published excerpts, and where copies of out-of-print works are held.

"General Commentary about Brautigan" collects book-length studies, bibliographies, theses and dissertations, parodies, and articles concerning censorship litigation and teaching experiences.

"Criticism of Brautigan" is a secondary bibliography and collects general United States criticism and general international criticism. Criticism and reviews of poetry, novels, short stories, and collections are listed in "Reviews of Works by Brautigan."

The remaining parts deal with "Mysterious and Erroneous Citations," "Obituaries and Eulogies," and "Sources." Annotations concerning the nature or content of the citations in each part are provided.

A modified Modern Language Association (MLA) style for citations is used herein. Book titles are <u>underlined</u>. Journal and periodical titles are *italicized*. Curly brackets and question marks ({?}) are used to indicate unknown or questionable information. Such a notation indicates an area for continuing bibliographical research.

Square brackets are used to insert words intended to make the annotations easier to read.

CRITICAL/BIOGRAPHICAL OVERVIEW

Richard Gary Brautigan (1935-1984), American novelist, short story writer, and poet has been called one of the major writers of "New Fiction" and was considered the literary representative of the 1960s era known variously as "the hippie generation," "the counterculture movement," and "the Age of Aquarius." He is generally considered to be the "voice" of this time of tremendous social change, the voice representing the developing values of the youth of this period.

Brautigan's early novels were offbeat autobiographical pastorals, and were widely acclaimed. His later works experimented with different genres like gothic, science fiction, mystery, and detective, resisted classification, and were generally considered less successful by critics.

Save for a campus/underground cult following, and a growing popularity abroad, Brautigan all but disappeared from the arena of literary attention in America in the 1970s when critics began accusing him of relying too heavily on whimsy and being disconnected from reality.

This sense of disconnection was a prevalent theme in his writing. He often used an autobiographical "I" figure as his narrator, a figure who wandered through the world as an observer, who seemed "of" the world but not "in" it, a narrator who observed and reported everything in an unemotional, matter-of-fact voice. Like the Beat's "Zen Narrator," none of the events that Brautigan's narrator witnessed seemed to have any effect on him and the narrator always moved on to the next observation indifferent, unchanged, and disconnected.

Disconnection seems to have come early in Brautigan's life. It's not definitive, as he refused to discuss his childhood, but what he did tell helps us understand his later years and offers some background for understanding and appreciating his writing.

He was born in Tacoma, Washington, on January 30, 1935, the son of Bernard F. and Mary Lula Brautigan. When he was nine, his mother, according to Brautigan, abandoned him and his younger sister, Barbara, age four, in a hotel room in Great Falls, Montana.

It is unclear how long Brautigan and his sister stayed in Great Falls, but their mother returned later, reclaimed them, and took them back to Tacoma. Later they moved to Eugene, Oregon (Wright 40)."

Brautigan's childhood wasn't a happy one according to Barbara. "I can never remember our Mother giving Richard a hug or telling us that she loved us. We were just there" (Wright 40).

There are hints that Brautigan never knew who his real father was. He apparently made an effort to find Bernard Brautigan, the man named on his birth certificate as his father.

After Brautigan's death the elderly Mr. Brautigan denied that he ever met his son. According to an October 27, 1984, UPI news story,

> "The death of author Richard Brautigan shocked a Tacoma man who learned for the first time he was the 49-year-old writer's father. Bernard Brautigan, 76, a retired laborer, discovered his relationship to the Tacoma-born writer Friday in a telephone call from his ex-sister-in-law, Evelyn Fjetland.
>
> "At first he did not believe the story but he said he called his ex-wife, whom he has not seen in 50 years. Brautigan was formerly married to... Mary Lula Folston... who gave birth to Richard on Jan. 30, 1935.
>
> "Folston...[said] her ex-husband asked 'if Richard was his son, and I said, no. I told him I found Richard in the gutter.'
>
> "Bernard Brautigan said he knew nothing about his famous son...'I never read any of his books,' he said. 'When I was called by Evelyn, she told me about Richard and said she was sorry about his death. I said, 'Who's Richard?' I don't know nothing about him. He's got the same last name, but why would they wait 45 to 50 years to tell me I've got a son?'" (Anonymous).

Brautigan began writing in high school, perhaps as a means of expression, or escape. "He wrote all night," Barbara recalls, "and slept all day. My folks rode him a lot. They never listened to what he was writing. They didn't understand his writing was important to him. I know they asked him to get out of the house several times" (Wright 59).

In 1955, Brautigan showed his writing to a girl he had a crush on. She criticized it and Brautigan was shattered, terrified. He threw a rock through the police station window, was arrested, and spent a week in jail. He was then committed to the Oregon State Hospital and diagnosed as a paranoid schizophrenic (Wright 59).

Barbara says he received shock therapy and after he returned from the hospital he was very quiet and never opened up to her again. A few days later, Brautigan called to say he was going away forever. (Wright 59).

"I guess he hated us," his mother said. "Or maybe he had a disappointed love affair. Whatever. Richard practically abandoned the family when he left here. I haven't the slightest idea why" (Wright 59).

Brautigan always maintained that his formal education consisted only of high school. In later years, Brautigan said that he spent a great deal of time as a young man trying to learn how to write a sentence.

"I love writing poetry but it's taken time, like a difficult courtship that leads to a good marriage, for us to get to know each other. I wrote poetry for seven years to learn how to write a sentence because I really wanted to write novels and I couldn't write a novel until I could write a sentence. I used poetry as a lover but I never made her my old lady.

"One day when I was twenty-five years old, I looked down and realized that I could write a sentence... wrote my first novel Trout Fishing in America and followed it with three other novels.

"I pretty much stopped seeing poetry for the next six years until I was thirty-one or the autumn of 1966. Then I started going out with poetry again, but this time I knew how to write a sentence, so everything was different and poetry became my old lady. God, what a beautiful feeling that was!" [Meltzer 304].

In 1956, Brautigan was 21, and living in San Francisco. It was the heyday of the Beat Generation and San Francisco was full of young writers and poets like Jack Kerouac, Allen Ginsberg, Robert Creeley, Michael McClure, Philip Whalen, Gary Snyder, and others, all hoping to give America a new literary voice.

Brautigan was working at odd jobs and writing poetry but was too shy to read it in any of the North Beach coffeehouses where the Beats hung out. Besides, his more humorous (which they thought queer) and benign view of things was quite out of fashion with Beat sentiments. Brautigan published The Return of the Rivers (a single poem) in 1957, The Galilee Hitch-Hiker (a single poem) in 1958, Lay the Marble Tea (a collection of 24 poems) in 1959, and The Octopus Frontier (22 poems) in 1960, and a novel, A Confederate General from Big Sur in 1964. None were successful.

In 1967, Brautigan at last found success with his novel, Trout Fishing in America. Written in 1961, the manuscript had been rejected by numerous publishers until Four Seasons Foundation of San Francisco decided to take a chance on it. Critics acclaimed Trout Fishing in America as "New Fiction" and welcomed Brautigan to the American literary scene as a fresh new figure, in the tradition of Mark Twain and Ernest Hemingway.

America was looking for a new literary voice then. The Beats were out of favor and the rose-tinted, magical, mystical drug experiences, sexual freedoms, and popular music of the 1960s counter-culture movement were in. Brautigan certainly recognized, among America's youth, a dissatisfaction with the absurdities of the 1960s and a concurrent nostalgic longing for the past and because of media exposure, quickly became the literary guru of this changing young America that identified with his use of imagination and good humor to give zest and humility to life, his unorthodox use of language, and the original, playful, eccentric brilliance of his poetry and fiction which seemed to shatter ordinary notions of experience and then reconstruct them with whimsy and startling metaphors.

With the publication of In Watermelon Sugar in 1968, and a renewed interest in A Confederate General from Big Sur, Brautigan's reputation as a fiction writer seemed secure. These novels, like Trout Fishing in America, were told from the point of view of an "I" narrator who spoke of a new vision for America, suggesting that through imagination one could achieve an escape and a salvation from an increasingly mechanized, urban country.

But while his writing mourned the betrayal of the American Dream and promoted the search for a new American Eden, there was also a darker, more existential philosophy in Brautigan's work.

As in Samuel Beckett's Waiting for Godot, the characters in Brautigan's A Confederate General from Big Sur are waiting for someone who will give meaning to their lives. Brautigan, like Godot, says there is no one ultimate solution or ending but rather multiple endings, infinite endings. He "ends" this novel by saying,

"Then there are more and more endings: the sixth, the 53rd, the 131st, the 9,435th endings, endings going faster and faster, more and more endings, faster and faster until this book is having 186,000 endings per second" [160].

In Watermelon Sugar ends just as it began: in "deeds that were done and done again as my life is done in watermelon sugar." Time does not flow here, it, in the spirit of Kenneth Patchen's Albion Moonlight, "just is." Time is told only by the fact that a different color sun rises every day over the utopian community of... Death.

In this novel Brautigan seems to outline the communal ethics necessary for the success of the new "Aquarian-Agrarian" world that was popularly viewed at the time. In Watermelon Sugar may be considered a "tract"—a guide for survival in the post-apocalyptical world. Brautigan seems to be saying that in order for a utopian community to be successful, a great deal of emotional repression and deprivation is necessary. And, that, like the people of iDeath, one must turn one's back on the surrounding world and shut all emotions and history away, forever, in "The Forgotten Works." In Watermelon Sugar is a Surrealistic aesthetic, an exercise in a world where the I and the not I, the interior and the exterior, the dream and the waking, and even silence and speech are possible forms of equally concurrent reality.

These three novels seemed to capture the spirit of an extraordinary moment in American history which advanced the thought that it was no longer necessary to see things as one had been taught to see them and what one had learned to call reality was only one version, and possibly not the best version, of the surrounding world. These novels seemed to be the first light of the dawning new age. Counter-culture advocates, and indeed, for a short time, the critics, loved them.

Brautigan was suddenly tremendously popular, and in great demand. After years of handing out his poetry on the streets of Haight-Ashbury, he was ensconced as the poet-in-residence at the California Institute of Technology in 1966-1967. He lectured at Harvard, and articles about him appeared in *Time* and *Life* magazine. Brautigan, the untraveled, uneducated, northwest country-bumpkin had arrived.

With the publication of his later novels, critics began to lament that Brautigan was no longer in a shape that was recognizable to them. The Abortion: An Historical Romance, 1966 (published in 1971 and dealing with the extreme narcissism and the implications of being deeply withdrawn into self) brought uneven response, as did All Watched Over by Machines of Loving Grace (collected poetry published in 1967) and The Pill Versus the Springhill Mine Disaster (a collection of most of his previous poetry published in 1968). Critics wondered where the vibrant, exuberant, youthful Brautigan of Trout Fishing in America and In Watermelon Sugar was. They felt these new Brautigan works were unstructured ramblings occasionally sparked by whimsy and wonderful metaphors but wondered if Brautigan could sustain himself.

Brautigan published a collection of short stories entitled Revenge of the Lawn: Stories 1962-1970 in 1971, and it was clear that he was not going to "continue" in the same vein as his earlier work, much less "sustain" it. He experimented with different literary genres: a parody of westerns and gothic horror films in The Hawkline Monster: A Gothic Western (1974), a parody of sadomasochistic books like The Story of O in Willard and His Bowling Trophies: A Perverse Mystery (1975), a study of the alienation and purposelessness of being divided from any world of shared experience in Sombrero Fallout: A Japanese Novel (1976), and a parody of hard-boiled detective fiction in Dreaming of Babylon: A Private Eye Novel 1942 (1977). He also published two more books of poetry, both collections of previous work: Rommel Drives on Deep into Egypt (1970) and Loading Mercury with a Pitchfork (1975).

Because of the timing of his success with Trout Fishing in America, Brautigan was often called "the hippie novelist," a term that puzzled him. "I never thought of myself as a [hippie novelist]," he said in rebuttal, "My writing is just one man's response to life in the 20th Century" [*Bozeman Daily Chronicle* 6].

Brautigan's response to the 20th Century was the casual injection of faintly surrealistic elements into his fiction. There was a quality, suppressed but evident, in his early works which promised much. But he seemed unable to go beyond it, or to develop it [*The Times* 12]. The sincerity and the disconnected, elliptical style of Brautigan's writing that had so charmed critics and readers in the early years, palled. Critics enjoyed his Hemingway style, Twain humor, and unique philosophy, but they generally dismissed Brautigan as a writer who had peaked early and had nothing new to offer.

Terence Malley, in his book Richard Brautigan, summarized the eventual critical consensus when he said,

> "Brautigan's books are for the most part directly autobiographical and curiously elusive. For one thing, it's usually difficult to separate confession from

whimsy.... For another, although he draws heavily on his pre-San Francisco experiences in his writing, those 'old bygone days' are what he describes as 'years and years of a different life to which I can never return nor want to and seems almost to have occurred to another body somehow vaguely in my shape and recognition...'" [18-19].

Richard Brautigan was expelled from the arena of critical literary attention. As Thomas McGuane, noted Western author and Brautigan's friend, succinctly put it: "When the 60s ended, he [Brautigan] was the baby thrown out with the bath water" [*Bozeman Daily Chronicle* 6].

Possibly, because he was disappointed over the lack of positive critical acclaim he received in the United States, Brautigan allegedly refused to give lectures or grant interviews from 1972-1980. He divided his time between California, Montana, and Japan. California was "home," Montana was a solace, a retreat, and Japan was a source of acceptance and acclaim not afforded in America. He had a substantial following in Japan and traveled there often.

He published another book of poetry, June 30th, June 30th in 1978, and another novel, The Tokyo-Montana Express in 1980. Both were about his experiences in Japan and Montana.

With the publication of The Tokyo-Montana Express, Brautigan began granting interviews, giving readings and lectures, and even participating in "writer in residence" programs, teaching creative writing once again.

So the Wind Won't Blow It All Away, Brautigan's last novel, was published in the summer of 1982. When it was not accepted and acclaimed by the critics or the reading public he felt misunderstood and alienated. Accounts from friends say that Brautigan became depressed and drank heavily.

On October 25, 1984, Brautigan's body was discovered in his Bolinas, California home. He apparently had taken his own life some weeks before. He was 49.

Anonymous. "Brautigan." File 260: UPI News—April 1983-May 1987. Dialog Database. Palo Alto, CA: Dialog Information Service, Inc.
    Dateline: Tacoma, WA, October 27, 1984. General news story dealing with Bernard Brautigan, Richard's father.

Brautigan, Richard. A Confederate General from Big Sur. New York: Grove Press, 1964. 160.

Malley, Terence. Richard Brautigan. New York: Warner, 1972.

"Old Lady." The San Francisco Poets. Ed. David Meltzer. New York: Ballantine Books, 1971. 293-97, 304.

Wright, Lawrence. "The Life and Death of Richard Brautigan." *Rolling Stone* Apr. 1985: 29-61.

RICHARD GARY BRAUTIGAN CHRONOLOGY

1935   Born 30 January in Tacoma, Washington, oldest child of Bernard F. Brautigan and Mary Lula Brautigan. Very little is known about his childhood, which he refused to discuss. Some sources say that Brautigan never knew his father, others say that his father never knew of him until Brautigan's death was announced.

1955?   Allegedly committed to Oregon State Hospital after throwing rock through police station window, diagnosed as paranoid schizophrenic and given shock therapy treatments. Left home soon after release from hospital.

1955-1958?   Moved to San Francisco and became involved with the Beat Movement.

1956   "The Second Kingdom," first known poem, published.

1957   Married Virginia Dionne Adler in Reno, NV, 8 June.

1957-1958?   "The Return of the Rivers," a single poem, published.

1958   "The Galilee Hitch-Hiker," a single poem, published.

1959   Lay the Marble Tea published. Twenty-four poems in this first collection.

1960   The Octopus Frontier published.

1960   Daughter Ianthe born, 25 March.

1961   Spent summer camping with wife and child in Idaho's Stanley Basin. Wrote Trout Fishing in America on a portable typewriter alongside the trout streams.

1964   A Confederate General from Big Sur published. Involved with the Diggers and the "hippies" of San Francisco's Haight-Ashbury district. Often gave away copies of his poems on the streets.

1966-1967   Poet-in-residence at California Institute of Technology.

1967   Trout Fishing in America published.

1967   All Watched Over by Machines of Loving Grace published.

1968   Awarded a grant from the National Endowment for the Arts. In Watermelon Sugar and The Pill Versus the Springhill Mine Disaster published. Please Plant This Book also published: eight seed packets, each containing seeds, with poems printed on the sides.

1969   Trout Fishing in America, The Pill Versus the Springhill Mine Disaster, and In Watermelon Sugar published in collection.

1970   Rommel Drives On Deep into Egypt published. Divorced from Virginia, 28 July, in San Francisco.

1970   The Abortion: An Historical Romance 1966 published.

1971   The Revenge of the Lawn published.

1972-1973?	Establishes a residence in Pine Creek, MT, just north of Yellowstone National Park. Allegedly refuses to deliver lectures or grant interviews for the next eight years.
1974	The Hawkline Monster published.
1975	Willard and His Bowling Trophies and Loading Mercury with a Pitchfork published.
1976	Sombrero Fallout published.
1977	Dreaming of Babylon published.
1978	June 30th, June 30th published.
1978	The Abortion, The Pill Versus the Springhill Mine Disaster, Trout Fishing in America, Rommel Drives On Deep into Egypt, and A Confederate General from Big Sur banned in Union Hills High School in northern California. ACLU case decided in favor of Brautigan and his publisher.
1979	At December meeting of Modern Language Association in San Francisco, participated in a panel discussion concerning "Zen and Contemporary Poetry" with Gary Snyder, Philip Whalen, Robert Bly, and Lucien Stryk.
1980	The Tokyo-Montana Express published. Begins lecture/promotion tour.
1982	So the Wind Won't Blow It All Away published.
1983	Commits suicide in house in Bolinas, California. Body discovered 25 October.

KEYS TO ABBREVIATIONS AND SHORT TITLES

OnLine Computer Library Center (OCLC) Acronyms for Libraries

AZS	Arizona State University
BUF	State University of New York at Buffalo
CCH	California State University, Chico
CNO	California State University, Northridge
CDS	San Diego State University
CLE	Cleveland Public Library
CLU	University of California at Los Angeles, Biomedical, Law, Physical Science and Technology
COO	Cornell University
CSH	University of California, Hayward
CSL	University of Southern California
CSF	San Francisco State University
CSP	Stockton-San Joaquin Public Library
CUF	University of San Francisco
CUI	University of California, Irvine
CUS	University of California, San Diego
CUT	University of California, Santa Barbara
CUY	University of California, Berkeley
DLM	University of Delaware
DRB	Dartmouth College

FDM	Fairleigh Dickinson University
FKS	Southern Methodist University, Fikes Hall of Special Collections
FUG	University of Florida
GMA	Mercer University, Atlanta Library
HAY	Hayward Public Library
HLS	Harvard University
IAQ	Parkland College
IAY	University of Illinois at Chicago Circle
IBS	Ball State University
ICU	Texas Christian University
IOD	Drake University
IRU	New Mexico State University
IUL	Indiana University
IXA	University of Texas at Austin
KBC	Bellarmine College
KFH	Fort Hays State University
KSU	Kent State University
KUK	University of Kentucky
LUU	Louisiana State University
QWC	West Chester University
RCE	Rice University
SBM	College of Charleston
SFR	San Francisco Public Library
SJP	San Jose Public Library
TWU	University of the South
UCW	University of Connecticut
UUM	University of Utah
VA@	University of Virginia
WTU	Washington University
YCC	Yuma City-County Library
YQR	Rochester Public Library
YSM	State University of New York at Stony Brook

Short Titles of Books by Brautigan

Return	The Return of the Rivers
Hitch-Hiker	The Galilee Hitch-Hiker
Marble	Lay the Marble Tea
Octopus	The Octopus Frontier

Machines	All Watched Over by Machines of Loving Grace
Plant	Please Plant This Book
Pill	The Pill Versus the Springhill Mine Disaster
Rommel	Rommel Drives On Deep into Egypt
Mercury	Loading Mercury with a Pitchfork
June 30th	June 30th, June 30th
General	A Confederate General from Big Sur
Trout	Trout Fishing in America
Watermelon	In Watermelon Sugar
Abortion	The Abortion: An Historical Romance 1966
Monster	The Hawkline Monster
Willard	Willard and His Bowling Trophies
Sombrero	Sombrero Fallout
Dreaming	Dreaming of Babylon
Express	The Tokyo-Montana Express
Wind	So the Wind Won't Blow It All Away
Revenge	Revenge of the Lawn: Stories 1962-1970

WORKS BY
RICHARD BRAUTIGAN

POETRY
Citations Listed Chronologically

1. "The Second Kingdom." *Epos* 8 (Winter) 1956: 23.

2. "A Young Poet." *Epos* 8 (Summer) 1957: 6.

3. "The Meek Shall Inherit the Earth's Beer Bottles," "The Mortuary Bush," "Twelve Roman Soldiers and an Oatmeal Cookie," and "Gifts." Four New Poets. Ed. Leslie Woolf Hedley. San Francisco: Inferno Press, 1957. 3-9.
   "Richard Brautigan is a young poet who was born January 30, 1935 in Tacoma, Washington. He now lives in San Francisco where he is working on a book of poems, The Horse That Had A Flat Tire." A poem of this title is found in Pill.

4. "The Return of the Rivers." San Francisco: Inferno Press, {1957 or 1958?}
   Out of print. A single poem, two pages, 23 cm, wrappers. Lepper (See 215) indicates 1958 as the publication date, other sources consulted list 1957. OCLC says that the copy located at CNO is "apparently one of the 15 extant copies of the author's first book" and features the author's autograph on

front cover. Wanless and Kolodziej (See 218) say, "Peter Howard at Serendipity Books (1790 Shattuck, Berkeley, CA 94709) notes, in his 'Modern Literature' catalogue, that it is 'a pamphlet poem.'" Reprinted in Pill. Copies held at CNO and CUY.

5. "15 Stories in One Poem." *Hearse* 2 1958: inside back cover.

6. "The Mortuary Bush," "Twelve Roman Soldiers and an Oatmeal Cookie," and "Psalm." *Hearse* 3 1958: 28.

The Galilee Hitch-Hiker

7. San Francisco: White Rabbit Press, 1958.
    Printed by Joe Dunn. Out of print. A single poem. Fifteen pages, 22 cm, illustrated. According to Lepper (See 215), "Wrappers. Only 200 copies printed." According to Wanless and Kolodziej (See 218), "The Serendipity Books catalog calls it 'the first edition of Brautigan's first regularly published book.'" Reprinted in Pill. Copies held at BUF, CNO, FKS, HLS, KFH, and KSU.

Reprinted:
San Francisco: The Cranium Press, 1966.
    Published by David Sandberg. Out of print. A reprint of the First Edition. Wrappers. The last page states: "The first edition of this book was printed by Joe Dunn of the White Rabbit Press in May 1958. This edition is limited to 700 copies, plus 16 numbered and signed copies with a small vaguely amusing drawing of a fish by the author. The cover is by Kenn Davis." The imprint reads: "An or book published by David Sandberg in December 1966[.] Printed at Cranium Press, 642 Shrader Street, San Francisco."

Translated:
8. "Det Amerikanska Hotellet." Lund: Cavefors, 1976.
    Swedish translation by Peter Falk. "The American Hotel" is Part 2 of Hitch-Hiker. Copies held at AZS, BUF, CDS, CSF, CSH, CSL, CUS, FKS, IAY, IRU, LUU, and YCC.

9. "Kingdom Come." *Epos* 9 (Spring) 1958: 20.

10. "Psalm." *San Francisco Review* 1 (Spring) 1959: 63.

Lay the Marble Tea

11. San Francisco: Carp Press, 1959.
    Out of print. Sixteen pages, 22 cm, wrappers. Cover by Kenn Davis. Copies held at BUF, CLU, CNO, CSF, CSL, CUS, FKS, FUG, IBS, and YSM.

    Poem titles in order of appearance. * Reprinted in Pill.
    "Portrait of the Id as Billy the Kid"
    "Sonnet"*
    "The Chinese Checker Players"*
    "Portrait of a Child-Bride on Her Honeymoon"
    "Hansel and Gretel"
    "April Ground"
    "The Ferris Wheel"
    "Night"
    "Cyclops"*
    "The Escape of the Owl"
    "In a Cafe"*
    "Fragment"
    "Herman Melville in Dreams, Moby Dick in Reality"
    "Kafka's Hat"*
    "Yes, the Fish Music"*
    "Cantos Falling"
    "The Castle of the Cormorants"
    "Feel Free to Marry Emily Dickinson"
    "Cat"
    "A Childhood Spent in Tacoma"
    "To England"*
    "A Boat"*
    "Geometry"
    "The Twenty-Eight Cents for My Old Age"

    Published Excerpts:
    "Feel Free to Marry Emily Dickinson." See 31.
    "To England." See 44 and 52.
    "The Chinese Checker Players." See 51 and 58.
    "In a Cafe." See 32 and 66.

The Octopus Frontier

12. San Francisco: Carp Press, 1960. Out of print. Twelve leaves, 17.8 cm, bound in printed paper wrappers. Cover by Gui de Angulo. Copies held at BUF, CLU, CNO, COO, CSH, CUI, CUS, FDM, FKS, KSU, KUK, RCE, SBM, and YSM.

Poem titles in order of appearance. * Reprinted in Pill.
"The Sawmill"*
"1942"*
"The Wheel"*
"The Pumpkin Tide"*
"The Sidney Greenstreet Blues"*
"The Quail"*
"The Symbol"*
"A Postcard from Chinatown"*
"Sit Comma and Creeley Comma"*
"The Rape of Ophelia"*
"The Last Music Is Not Heard"
"The Octopus Frontier"
"The Potato House of Julius Caesar"
"The Fever Monument"*
"The Winos on Potrero Hill"*
"Mike"
"Horse Race"*
"The Old Folk's Home"
"The Postman"*
"Surprise"*
"The Nature Poem"*
"Private Eye Lettuce"*

Previously Published Portions:
The title page states: "Some of these poems appeared in Richard Duerden's magazine *Foot* and Jack Spicer's magazine *j*."

Published Excerpts:
"The Fever Monument," "The Wheel," "Horse Race," and "The Sidney Greenstreet Blues." See 32.
"The Wheel" and "Horse Race." See 39.
"The Winos on Potrero Hill" and "The Quail." See 43.

13. "The American Submarine," "A Postcard from the Bridge," "That Girl," and "The Whorehouse at the Top of Mount Rainer." Beatitude Anthology. San Francisco: City Lights Books, 1960. 34-36.

14. "The Rain." *Hearse* 9 1961:4.

15. "September California." San Francisco: San Francisco Arts Festival Commission, 1964.
    A single poem, printed in broadside by East Wind Printers for the San Francisco Arts Festival Commission. Illustrated by Richard Correll. 300 copies printed; most signed by Brautigan and Correll. Laid in a portfolio (51 cm, 11 sheets) entitled San Francisco Arts Festival: A Poetry Folio: 1964. Copies held at CLU, COO, CSH, CUF, CUY, IBS, IUL, KSU, TWU, and WTU.

16. "Karma Repair Kit: Items 1-4." San Francisco: Communication Company, 1967.
    Broadside (21.5 x 28 cm). Reprinted in Machines and Pill. Copies held BUF and IBS.

17. "All Watched Over by Machines of Loving Grace." San Francisco: Communication Company, 1967.
    Illustrated broadside (21.5 x 28 cm) printed on white paper, illustrated in black. Lepper (See 215) says there are two priorities: 1). "Faint illustration, the most prominent portion of which is the phrase 'Loudspeaker Current'."
    2). "Bold illustration, consisting of hand-drawn small animals and a photograph of a computer bank." Reprinted in Machines and Pill. Copies of first priority held at BUF, IUL, and VA@. A copy of the second priority is held at BUF.

18. "Flowers for Those You Love." San Francisco: The Communication Company, {1967?}
    Broadside. Reprinted in Machines and Pill.

19. "Love Poem." San Francisco: The Communication Company, {1967?}
    Broadside (21.5 x 28 cm), white paper printed in black. Reprinted in Machines and Pill. A copy is held at BUF.

20. "The Beautiful Poem." San Francisco: The Communication Company, 1967.
Broadside (21.5 x 28 cm). Reprinted in <u>Machines</u> and <u>Pill</u>.

21. "It's Raining in Love." *Hollow Orange* {Date? Page number?}

All Watched Over by Machines of Loving Grace

22. San Francisco: Communication Company, 1967.
Out of print. Copies held at CLU, CNO, CSH, CSL, CUS, DLM, GMA, and IXA. These statements appear on the first two pages:
"Permission is granted to reprint any of these poems in magazines, books and newspapers if they are given away free."
"Bill Brock lived with us for a while on Pine Street. He took the photograph in the basement. It was a beautiful day in San Francisco."
"This book is printed in an edition of 1,500 copies by the Communication Company. None of the copies are for sale. They are all free."

Poem titles in order of appearance:
"The Beautiful Poem"
"December 24"
"Milk for the Duck"
"November 3"
"Flowers for Those You Love"
"San Francisco"
"Star Hole"
"Love Poem"
"I Lie Here in a Strange Girl's Apartment"
"It's Raining in Love"
"Hey! This Is What It's All About"
"Our Beautiful West Coast Thing"
"Widow's Lament"
"Lovers"
"December 30"
"A Mid-February Sky Dance"
"Hey, Bacon!"
"After Halloween Slump"

"Hollywood"
"It's Going Down"
"Albion Breakfast"
"Comets"
"The Pomegranate Circus"
"My Nose Is Growing Old"
"At the California Institute of Technology"
"Your Catfish Friend"
"Karma Repair Kit: Items 1-4"
"All Watched over by Machines of Loving Grace"
"A Good-Talking Candle"
"Nine Things"
"A Lady"
"Let's Voyage into the New American House"

All reprinted in Pill where "December 24" appears as "November 24."

Previously Published Portions:
    A statement on the first page says: "Some of these poems first appeared in *Hollow Orange*, *Totem*, *O'er*, and *Beatitude*. Five poems were published as broadsides by the Communication Company." They are:
    "Karma Repair Kit: Items 1-4." See 16.
    "All Watched Over by Machines of Loving Grace." See 17.
    "Flowers for Those You Love." See 18.
    "Love Pocm." See 19.
    "The Beautiful Poem." See 20.
    "It's Raining in Love." See 21.

Published Excerpts:
    "Karma Repair Kit: Items 1-4." See 39.
    "All Watched Over by Machines of Loving Grace." See 30, 50, 51, and 59.
    "The Pomegranate Circus." See 32 and 60.
    "Our Beautiful West Coast Thing." See 32.
    "It's Raining in Love." See 33 and 38.
    "After Halloween Slump," "I Lie Here in a Strange Girl's Apartment," and "Comets." See 60.
    "A Mid-February Sky Dance." See 52, 59, and 60.
    "Let's Voyage into the New American House." See 60 and 62.

"Milk for the Duck," "Star Hole," "Love Poem," "Nine Things," "Hollywood," and "December 24." See 59.

Please Plant This Book

23. San Francisco and/or Santa Barbara: Graham Mackintosh, 1968. Out of print. 16 x 18 cm. Wanless and Kolodziej (See 218) say, "The Serendipity catalogue indicates that the book was published in Santa Barbara, not San Francisco, and that it is made of 'card stock folded to create pockets, with eight seed packets laid in, each containing seeds, with poems printed on the sides'; originally a 'free book'." Copies held at AZS, BUF, CCH, CDS, COO, CSH, CSL, CSP, DRB, FDM, FKS, ICU, IRU, IXA.

Poem titles in order of appearance:
"California Native Flowers"
"Parsley"
"Shasta Daisy"
"Squash"
"Calendula"
"Carrots"
"Lettuce"
"Sweet Alyssum Royal Carpet"

24. "The San Francisco Weather Report." San Francisco: Printed by Graham Mackintosh, 1968.
Broadside (21 x 33 cm). Copies held at BUF and IUL.

Reprinted:
Goleta, CA: Unicorn Books, 1969.
Second printing. Out of print. Broadside (21 x 33 cm). Copies held at AZS, CSH, HLS, IBS, and UCW.

25. "San Francisco Weather Report." *Paris Review* 12 (Winter) 1968: 140.

The Pill Versus the Springhill Mine Disaster

26. San Francisco: Four Seasons Foundation, 1968.
Distributed by City Lights Books, San Francisco. Out of print. Lepper (See 215) says there were "Two issues, no priority: 1).

Hardcover. 50 copies numbered, signed by the author. 2). Wrappers."

First English Edition:
27. London: Jonathan Cape, 1970.

Translated:
28. Die Pille gegen das Grubenunglück von Spring Hill und 104 andere Gedichte. München: Ohnemus, 1980.
German translation by Günter Ohnemus.

29. Die Pille gegen das Grubenunglück von Spring Hill und 104 andere Gedichte. Frankfurt: 'Eichborn Vlg. Ffm., 1987.

Previously Published Portions:
A statement on the copyright page says: "This book was first published by Four Seasons Foundation in its Writing series edited by Donald Allen."
Most of these poems have been previously published in earlier works. Only 37 of these 98 poems did not appear earlier. They are (listed alphabetically):

"A CandleLion Poem"
"Adrenalin Mother "
"Alas, Measured Perfectly"
"Automatic Anthole"
"Boo, Forever"
"Crab Cigar"
"The Day They Busted the Grateful Dead"
"Death Is a Beautiful Car Parked Only"
"Discovery"
"The Double-Bed Dream Gallows"
"Education"
"The First Winter Snow"
"The Garlic Meat Lady from"
"General Custer Versus the Titanic"
"Haiku Ambulance"
"The Harbor"
"The Horse That Had a Flat Tire"
"Horse Child Breakfast"
"I Cannot Answer You Tonight in Small Portions"
"I Live in the Twentieth Century"

"I Feel Horrible. She Doesn't"
"Indirect Popcorn"
"I've Never Had It Done So Gently Before"
"Linear Farewell, Nonlinear Farewell"
"Map Shower"
"Mating Saliva"
"Oranges"
"The Pill Versus the Springhill Mine Disaster"
"Poker Star"
"The Shenevertakesherwatchoff Poem"
"The Silver Stairs of Ketchikan"
"'Star-Spangled' Nails"
"Surprise"
"The Way She Looks at It"
"Xerox Candy Bar"
"Your Necklace Is Leaking"
"Your Departure Versus the Hindenburg"

"November 24" was originally published in <u>Machines</u> as "December 24." "San Francisco Weather Report" was reprinted under a new title. According to Wanless and Kolodziej (See 218), this poem is "Here retitled as 'Gee, You're So Beautiful That It's Starting to Rain'; it is exactly the same poem, except for the spelling of 'harpsicord'." Jones (See 214) agrees about the retitling.

Published Excerpts:

"All Watched Over by Machines of Loving Grace." See 30, 50, 51, and 59.

"The Chinese Checker Players." See 51 and 58.

"General Custer Versus the Titantic," "The Pomegranate Circus," "The Fever Monument," "Our Beautiful West Coast Thing," "The Sidney Greenstreet Blues," "The Wheel," "Fever Monument," and "Horse Race." See 32.

"The Wheel," "Horse Race," and "Karma Repair Kit: Items 1-4," See 39.

"It's Raining in Love." See 33 and 38.

"'Star-Spangled' Nails." See 41.

"The Pill Versus the Springhill Mine Disaster." See 43 and 44.

"The Day They Busted the Grateful Dead." See 44.

"To England." See 44 and 52.

"November 3" and "Mating Saliva." See 52.

"A Mid-February Sky Dance." See 52, 59, and 60.
"The Horse That Had a Flat Tire." See 58.
"Chinese Checker Players." See 51 and 58.
"In a Cafe." See 32 and 66.
"Let's Voyage into the New American House." See 60 and 62.

30. "All Watched Over by Machines of Loving Grace." *TriQuarterly* 11 (Winter) 1968: 194.

31. "Feel Free to Marry Emily Dickinson." Big Venus. Ed. Nick Kimberly. London: Big Venus, 102 Southhampton Row, 1969. 1.

32. "General Custer Versus the Titantic," "The Pomegranate Circus," "The Fever Monument," "The Wheel," "Our Beautiful West Coast Thing," "The Sidney Greenstreet Blues," "Horse Race," and "In a Cafe." A First Reader of Contemporary American Poetry. Ed. Patrick Gleason. Columbus, Ohio: Merrill, 1969. 23-26.

33. "It's Raining in Love." The American Literary Anthology. Second Annual Collection. Eds. George Plimpton and Peter Ardery. New York: Random House, 1969. 56.
Omitted last thirteen lines. See 38.

34. "Wood." *Poetry* Oct. 1969: 30.
Reprinted in Rommel.

35. "Spinning Like a Ghost on the Bottom of a Top" and "I'm Haunted by All the Space That I Will Live Without You."
San Francisco: n.p., {1969?}. Broadside. Lepper (See 215) says the authorship is "anonymous" and this broadside is "one leaf of an unbound anthology in wrappers entitled 'Free City'; it also circulated separately."

Rommel Drives on Deep into Egypt

36. New York: Delacorte Press/Seymour Lawrence, 1970.
Out of print. According to Lepper (See 215) there are "Two issues, no priority: 1). Hardcover, dustwrapper. 'First

Printing' and 2). Wrappers. 'First Delta Printing—April 1970'."

First English Edition:
37. London: Picador-Pan Books, 1973.

Previously Published Portions:
A statement on the copyright page says: "Some of these poems first appeared in *Poetry, Rolling Stone, San Francisco Express Times, The Free You, Heliotrope Catalogue,* and *The San Francisco Public Library: A Publishing House.*"

Published Excerpts:
"Jules Verne Zucchini," "Propelled by Portals Whose Only Shame," "Donner Party," "In Her Sweetness Where She Folds My Wounds" and "The Elbow of a Dead Duck." See 45.
"As the Bruises Fade, the Lightning Aches." See 45, 52.
"Romeo and Juliet." See 52.
"Late Starting Dawn." See 66.

38. "It's Raining in Love." <u>The American Literary Anthology</u>. Third Annual Collection. Eds. George Plimpton and Peter Ardery. New York: Viking, 1970. 384-85.
Corrected version. See 33.

39. "Three Poems." *London Magazine* Nov. 1970: 65.
Poems are: "Horse Race," "The Wheel," and "Karma Repair Kit: Items 1-4."

40. "Fragile, Fading 37/A Poem." *Kaleidoscope-Madison* 17 Sept. 1970: 7.

41. "'Star-Spangled' Nails." {Privately Published: Berkeley, CA, 1970?}
Broadside (31 x 46 cm). Copies held at BUF and IBS.

42. "Five Poems." Berkeley: Serendipity Books, 1971.
Five poems published in broadside (43 x 28 cm.) for the International Antiquarian Book Fair. Poems are: "A Legend of Horses," "Toward the Pleasures of a Reconstituted Crow," "A Moth in Tucson, Arizona," "Death Like a Needle," and

Works by Brautigan—Poetry 37

"Heroine of the Time Machine." Copies held at BUF, CSH, CUS, IBS, IOD, UCW, and UUM.

43. "The Winos on Potrero Hill," "The Quail," "The Pill Versus the Springhill Mine Disaster," "Discovery," and "Adrenalin Mother." *Just What This Country Needs, Another Poetry Anthology.* Eds. James McMichael and Dennis Saleh. Belmont, Calif: Wadsworth, 1971. 22-26.

44. "The Pill Versus the Springhill Mine Disaster," "The Day They Busted the Grateful Dead," and "To England." *Earth, Air, Fire, and Water: A Collection of Over 125 Poems.* Ed. Frances Monson McCullough. New York: Coward, McCann, and Geoghegan, 1971. 27, 130, and 142.

45. "Jules Verne Zucchini," "Propelled by Portals Whose Only Shame," "Donner Party," "In Her Sweetness Where She Folds My Wounds," "The Elbow of a Dead Duck," and "As The Bruises Fade, the Lightning Aches." *The San Francisco Poets.* Ed. David Meltzer. New York: Ballantine Books, 1971. 293-97, 304.

46. "Loading Mercury with a Pitchfork," "It's Time to Train Yourself," "Two Guys Get Out of a Car," and "Punitive Ghosts Like Steam-Driven Tennis Courts." *Another World: A Second Anthology of Works from the St. Marks Poetry Project.* Ed. Anne Waldman. Indianapolis and New York: Bobbs-Merrill, 1971. 345.

47. "On Pure Sudden Days Like Innocence" and "Curiously Young Like a Freshly-Dug Grave." *Mark In Time: Portraits and Poetry / San Francisco.* Ed. Nick Harvey. San Francisco: Glide Publications, 1971.

48. "A Taste of the Taste of Brautigan." *California Living Magazine (San Francisco Sunday Examiner & Chronicle)* 16 May 1971. 7-10.
    Includes "They Are Really Having Fun," "We Meet. We Try. Nothing Happens, but," "Home Again Home Again Like a Turtle to His Balcony," "You Will Have Unreal Recollections of Me," "Finding Is Losing Something Else," "Impasse," and "Homage to Charles Atlas."

49. "Crow Maiden." *Harper's* October 1971: 58.

50. "All Watched Over by Machines of Loving Grace." The Exploited Eden: Literature on the American Environment. Ed. Robert Gangewere. New York: Harper and Row, 1972. 376.

51. "The Chinese Checker Players" and "All Watched Over by Machines of Loving Grace." The Ways of the Poem. Ed. Josephine Miles. Englewood Cliffs, NJ: Prentice Hall, 1972. 376-377.

52. "November 3," "Mating Saliva," "A Mid-February Sky Dance," "To England," "Romeo and Juliet," and "As the Bruises Fade, the Lightning Aches." Shake the Kaleidoscope: A New Anthology of Modern Poetry. Ed. Milton Klonsky. New York: Simon & Schuster, 1973. 274-76.

53. "For Fear You Will Be Alone." *California Living Magazine* (*San Francisco Sunday Examiner & Chronicle*) 18 Nov. 1973: 16.
    Three line poem illustrated by Edmund Shea.

54. "Richard Brautigan." *Mademoiselle* Nov. 1974: 192-93.
    Poem is: "Good Luck, Captain Martin."

55. "Some Montana Poems/1973." City Lights Anthology. Ed. Lawrence Ferlinghetti. San Francisco: City Lights Books, 1974. 95.
    Includes "Night," "Dive-Bombing the Lower Emotions," and "Nine Crows: Two out of Sequence."

Loading Mercury with a Pitchfork

56. New York: Simon and Schuster, 1975.
    Out of print.

    Translated:
57. At Laesse Kviksølv Med en Fork. Københaven: Rosenkilde and Bagger, 1978.
    Danish translation by Tamara Meldsted.

Previously Published Portions:
A statement opposite the copyright page says: "Some of these poems first appeared in *Mademoiselle*, *Harper's Magazine*, *Blue Suede Shoes*, The World, Mark in Time, *California Living*, Five Poems (Serendipity Books), *Esquire*, *Clear Creek*, City Lights Anthology, and *The CoEvolution Quarterly*."

"A Legend of Horses," "Toward the Pleasures of a Reconstituted Crow," "A Moth in Tucson, Arizona," "Death Like a Needle," "Heroine of the Time Machine," See 42.

"Loading Mercury with a Pitchfork," "It's Time to Train Yourself," "Two Guys Get Out of a Car," "Punitive Ghosts Like Steam-Driven Tennis Courts," See 46.

"On Pure Sudden Days Like Innocence" and "Curiously Young Like a Freshly-Dug Grave," See 47.

"They Are Really Having Fun," "We Meet. We Try. Nothing Happens, but," "Home Again Home Again Like a Turtle to His Balcony," "You Will Have Unreal Recollections of Me," "Finding Is Losing Something Else," "Impasse," "Homage to Charles Atlas," See 48.

"Crow Maiden." See 49.
"For Fear You Will Be Alone." See 53.
"Good Luck, Captain Martin." See 54.

"Night," "Dive-Bombing the Lower Emotions," "Nine Crows: Two Out of Sequence," See 55.

Published Excerpts:
"Autobiography (Good-Bye, Ultra Violet)," "We Meet. We Try. Nothing Happens, but," "Impasse," "On Pure Sudden Days Like Innocence," "We Were the Eleven O'Clock News," "Nobody Knows What the Experience Is Worth," See 61.

58. "The Chinese Checker Players" and "The Horse That Had a Flat Tire." Poems Here and Now. Ed. David Kherdian. New York: Greenwillow Books, 1976. 13, 17.

59. "Milk for the Duck," "Star Hole," "Love Poem," "A Mid-February Sky Dance," "Nine Things," "Hollywood," "All

Watched Over by Machines of Loving Grace," and "December 24." The Thunder City Press Broadside Series, No. 5. Birmingham, AL: Thunder City Press, Feb. 1976. "Published in a special edition of 500 February 1976."

60. "After Halloween Slump," "I Lie Here in a Strange Girl's Apartment," "The Pomegranate Circus," "A Mid-February Sky Dance," "Let's Voyage into the American Home," and "Comets." *Aura Literary/Arts Review* Birmingham, AL: Thunder City Press, {1977?}.
An "edition of the Aura Broadside Series." A note says "'Mid-February Sky Dance' appeared previously in Thunder City Press Broadside, Number Five."

61. {"Impasse and Other Poems."} *San Francisco* (19) Aug. 1977: 34-35.
Includes "Autobiography (Good-Bye, Ultra Violet)," "We Meet. We Try. Nothing Happens, but," "Impasse," "On Pure Sudden Days Like Innocence," "We Were the Eleven O'Clock News," and "Nobody Knows What the Experience Is Worth."

62. Dugdale, Anthony. "Romantic Renegades." *Architectural Design* 48(7) 1978: 444-46.
Quotes "Let's Voyage into the New American House."

63. "On the Elevator Going Down." *Quest/77* Nov./Dec. 1977: 108.

June 30th, June 30th

64. New York: Delacorte Press/Seymour Lawrence, 1978.
Out of print.

Previously Published Portions:
A statement on the copyright page says: "One of the poems in this volume first appeared in *Quest/77* magazine."

"On the Elevator Going Down." See 63.

65. "In a Cafe" and "Late Starting Dawn." Postcard Poems. Ed. Paul B. Janeczko. Scarsdale, NY: Bradbury Press, 1979. 46.

66. "Three by Richard Brautigan." *Corona* 2 1981: 12-14.
Poems are: "The Last of What's Left," "Closets," and "The Grasshopper's Mirror."

67. "Rendezvous." Unpublished poem. July 1982.
See Prologue.

68. "The Lost Tree," "Night Flowing River," and "Tokyo and Montana." *Washington Review* 9(5) Feb./Mar. 1984: 9.

69. Shannon, L.R. "The Promise, the Reality and the Hope." *New York Times* 8 Dec. 1987: 27.
Discusses the possibilities of the personal computer from the perspective of the late 1970s saying, "It was a poetic vision, particularly as expressed by Richard Brautigan:

> I like to think/(it has to be!)/of a cybernetic ecology/where we are free of our labors/and joined back to nature,/returned to our mammal/brothers and sisters,/and all watched over/by machines of loving grace."

NOVELS

Citations Listed Chronologically

A Confederate General from Big Sur

70. New York: Grove Press, 1964.
Out of print. According to Lepper (See 215), "Hardcover, dustwrapper. No statement of first edition."

First English edition:
71. Jonathan Cape, 1970.

Translated:
72. Il Generale Immaginario. Milan: Rizzoli, 1967.

73. Generaal in Grijs. Bussum: Agathon, 1973.
Dutch translation by Jos Knipscheer.

74. Biggu sâ no nangun shôgun. Tokyo: Kawade shobô shin-sha, 1976.
Japanese translation by Fujimoto Kazuko.

75. Le Général Sudiste de Big Sur. Paris: C. Bourgois, 1976.
French translation by Michel Doury.

76. En Konføderat General frå Big Sur. Lysaker: Solum, 1976.
Norwegian translation by Morten Austad.

77. Ein Konföderierter General aus Big Sur. München: Ohnemus, 1979.
German translation by Günter and Ilse Ohnemus.

Previously Published Portions:
A statement on the copyright page says: "Three chapters from this book were first published in *TriQuarterly*."

78. "Breaking Bread at Big Sur," "Preparing for Ecclesiastes," and "The Rivets in Ecclesiastes." *TriQuarterly* 1 (Fall) 1964: 62-67.

Trout Fishing in America

79. San Francisco: Four Seasons Foundation, 1967.
According to Lepper (See 215), first released in dustwrappers. Distributed by City Lights Books, San Francisco.

First English Edition:
80. Jonathan Cape, 1970.

Translated:
81. Forellenfischen in Amerika. Munich: Carl Hanser, 1971.
German translation by Celine and Heiner Bastian.

82. Forel Vissen in Amerika. Bussum: De Boer, 1972.
Dutch translation by Helen Knoppen.

83. Sucre de Pasteque et La Pêche a la Truite en Amérique. Paris: C. Bourgois, 1973.
French translation by Michel Doury.

84. La Pêche a la Truite en Amérique. Paris: C. Bourgois, 1973.
French translation by Michel Doury.

85. In Wassermelonen Zucker & Forellenfischen in Amerika: Zwei Romane aus d. Amerika. Berlin: Taschenbuch-Ullstein, 1974.
German translation by Celine and Heiner Bastian.

86. Taimenenkalastus Amerikassa. Helsinki: Otava, 1974.
Finnish translation by Leena Järvi.

87. Ørretfiske i Amerika. Oslo: Gyldendal, 1974.
Norwegian translation by Olav Angell.

88. Amerika no masu Zuri. Tokyo: Shuôbun-sha, 1975.
Japanese translation by Fujimoto Kazuko.

89. La Pêche a la Truite en Amérique. Paris: Union général d'éditions, 1978.
French translation by Michel Doury.

90. Forellenfischen in Amerika. Frankfort: 'Eichborn Vlg. Ffm., 1987.

Previously Published Portions:
A statement on the copyright page says: "Nine chapters of this novel appeared in *Evergreen Review*, three in *City Lights Journal*, and one in The New Writing in the USA."

91. "Trout Fishing in America." *City Lights Journal* (1) 1963: 27-32.
Includes the chapters "Worsewick," "The Salt Creek Coyotes," and "A Half-Sunday Homage to a Whole Leonardo da Vinci."

92. "Trout Fishing in America." *Evergreen Review* 31 Oct./Nov. 1963:12-27.
Includes the chapters "The Hunchback Trout," "Room 208, Hotel Trout Fishing in America," "The Surgeon," and "The Cleveland Wrecking Yard."

93. "Trout Fishing in America." *Evergreen Review* 33 1964: 42-47.
    Includes the chapters "Witness for Trout Fishing in America Peace," "A Note on the Camping Craze That Is Currently Sweeping America," "The Pudding Master of Stanley Basin," "In the California Bush," and "Trout Death by Port Wine."

94. "The Cleveland Wrecking Yard." *The New Writing in the USA*. Eds. Don Allen and Robert Creeley. Harmondsworth, Middlesex: Penguin, 1967. 33-38.

    Published Excerpts:
95. "Hunchback Trout," "Room 208", "The Surgeon," and "The Cleveland Wrecking Yard." *Evergreen Review Reader 1957-1967: A Ten Year Anthology*. Ed. Barney Rosset. New York: Grove, 1968. 586-93.

96. "A Trout Fishing Sampler (from *Trout Fishing in America*)." *The Troubled Vision*. Ed. Jerome Charyn. London: Collier Books, 1970. 497-510.

97. *The Last Whole Earth Catalog: Access to Tools*. Ed. Stewart Brand. Menlo Park, CA: Portola Institute, 1971. 254.
    Excerpts from the novel with mail-order information.

98. "The Cleveland Wrecking Yard" and "The Hunchback Trout." *In Trout Country*. Ed. Peter Corodimas. Boston: Little, Brown and Co., 1971. 10-16, 231-34.
    A "Sports Illustrated Book" of trout fishing stories.

99. "Trout Fishing in America Terrorists." *New Fiction, Non-Fiction*. Eds. John Mahoney and John Schmittroth. Cambridge, MA: Winthrop, 1971. 227-30.

100. "Trout Fishing in America Terrorists." *Story: An Introduction to Prose Fiction*. Second Edition. Eds. Arthur Foff and Daniel Knapp. Belmont, CA: Wadsworth Publishers, 1971. 36-38.

101. "The Cleveland Wrecking Yard." *Three Stances of Modern Fiction: A Critical Anthology of the Short Story*. Eds.

Stephen Minot and Robley Wilson, Jr. Cambridge, MA: Winthrop Publishers, 1972. 113-18.

102. "The Kool-Aid Wino" and "Trout Fishing in America Terrorists." The New Consciousness. Ed. Albert J. La Valley. Cambridge, MA: Winthrop Publishers, 1972. 352-57.

103. "The Cleveland Wrecking Yard." The Short Story. Eds. Wilfred Stone, Nancy Huddleston Packer, and Robert Hoopes. New York: McGraw-Hill, 1976. 3, 4, 17, 572-73.

104. "The Kool-Aid Wino." Faith and Fiction: The Modern Short Story. Eds. Robert Detweiler and Glenn Meeter. Grand Rapids: William B. Eerdmans, 1979. 173-76.

105. Tont, Sargun A. "The Sea: Its Science and Poetry." *Interdisciplinary Science Reviews* 6(1) 1981: 49-56.
Quotes from Trout in this historical, literary perspective of the sea.

In Watermelon Sugar

106. San Francisco: Four Seasons Foundation, 1968.
Edited by Donald Allen for the Writing series. Writing 21. According to Lepper (See 215), there were "Two issues, no priority: 1). Hardcover, 50 copies, numbered, signed by Brautigan, and 2). Wrappers."

First English Edition:
107. London: Jonathan Cape, 1970.

Translated:
108. In Wassermelonen Zucker. Munich: Carl Hanser, 1970.

109. Sucre de Pasteque et La Pêche a la Truite en Amérique. Paris: C. Bourgois, 1973.
French translation by Michel Doury.

110. In Watermeloensuiker. Bussum: Agathon, 1973.
Dutch translation by Helen Knopper.

111. In Wassermelonen Zucker & Forellenfischen in Amerika. Frankfurt: Ullstein, 1974.
     German translation by Celine and Heiner Bastian.

112. Melonin Mehu. Helsinki: Otava, 1975.
     Norwegian translation by Olav Angell.

113. Suika-tô no hibi. Tokyo: Kawade Shobô shinsha, 1975.
     Japanese translation by Fujimoto Kazuko.

114. Arbuusisuhkrus. Tallin: Periodika, 1977.
     Estonian translation by Enn Soosaar.

Published Excerpts:
115. "The Tigers Again," "Arithmetic," and "She Was." The New Consciousness. Ed. Albert J. La Valley. Cambridge, MA: Winthrop Publishing, 1972. 357-60.

The Abortion: An Historical Romance 1966

116. New York: Simon and Schuster, 1971. Copyright 1970.
     According to Lepper (See 215), there were "Two issues, no priority: 1). Hardcover, dustwrapper and 2). Wrappers. 'First Printing' [was indicated and] uncorrected proofs in printed wrappers preceded publication."

First English Edition:
117. London: Jonathan Cape, 1973.

Translated:
118. Avortement. Paris: Editions du Seuil, 1973.
     French translation by Georges Renard.

119. L'Aborto. Milano: Rizzoli, 1976.
     Italian translation by Pier Francesco Paolini.

120. Goyohan apeum. Seoul: Gyeweon Publishers, 1978.
     Korean translation by Lee Gyeong Sig.

121. Die Abtreibung. München: Ohnemus, 1978.
     German translation by Günter and Ilse Ohnemus.

122. Die Abtreibung. Eine amerikanische Romanze 1966. Frankfort: 'Eichborn Vlg. Ffm., 1985.

   Previously Published Portions:
   A statement on the copyright page says: "A portion of this book appeared originally in *The Dutton Review*, Volume 1."

123. "The Library." *The Dutton Review* (1) 1970:167-82.
   Includes "The Library," "The Automobile Accident," "The 23," and "Buffalo Gals, Won't You Come Out Tonight?"

   Published Excerpts:
124. "Vida." Bussum: De Boer, 1971.
   Dutch translation by Helen Knoppen.

The Hawkline Monster

125. New York: Simon and Schuster, 1974.
   According to Lepper (See 215), there were "Two issues, priority as listed: 1). Hardcover, dustwrapper and 2). Wrappers, '1 2 3 4 5 6 7 8 9 10' on copyright page, and uncorrected proofs in printed wrappers preceded publication."

   First English Edition:
126. London: Jonathan Cape, 1975.

   Translated:
127. Hawkline-ke no Kaibutsu. Tokyo: Shôbun-sha, 1975.
   Japanese translation by Fujimoto Kazuko.

128. Det Kolde Hu i Ørken. København: Gyldendal, 1976.
   Danish translation by Finn Holten Hansen.

129. Det Kolde Hu i Ørken. København: Samlerens Bogklub, 1976.
   Danish translation by Finn Holten Hansen.

130. Hawkline Monstret. Stockholm: Wahlström & Widstrand, 1976.
   Swedish translation by Caj Lundgren.

131. Hawkline-uhyret. Oslo: Gyldendal, 1977.
   Norwegian translation by Olav Angell.

132. Kartanon peto: Kauhuromanttinen lännenromaani. Helsinki: Otava, 1977.
Finnish translation by Jarkko Laine.

133. Het Monster in de Kelder. Bussum: Agathon, 1977.
Dutch translation by Jos Knipscheer.

134. Le Mostre des Hawkline. Paris: C. Bourgois, 1977.
French translation by Michel Doury and Lorraine de La Valdene.

135. El Monstruo de Hawkline: Un Western Gotico. Barcelona: Anagrama, {1979?}.
Spanish translation.

136. Das Hawkline Monster. Ein seltsamer Western mit 2 Killern, 2 schonen Frauen und 1 Monster. Frankfort: 'Eichborn Vlg. Ffm., 1986.

Willard and His Bowling Trophies

137. New York: Simon and Schuster, 1975.
Out of print.

First English Edition:
138. London: Jonathan Cape, 1976.

Translated:
139. Willard et ses Trophées de Bowling. Paris: C. Bourgois, 1978.
French translation by Robert Pépin.

140. Tori no shinden. Tokyo: Shôbun-sha, 1978.
Japanese translation by Fujimoto Kazuko.

141. Willard y sus Tofeos de Bolos. Barcelona: Anagrama, 1980.
Spanish translation by José Manuel Alvarez Florel and Anglea Pérez.

142. Willard und seine Bowlingtrophäen: Ein perverser Kriminalromon. München: Ohnemus, 1980.
German translation by Günter and Ilse Ohnemus.

Sombrero Fallout

143. New York: Simon and Schuster, 1976.
Out of print.

    First English Editon:
144. London: Jonathan Cape, 1977.

    Translated:
145. Sonburero rakka su. Tokyo: Shôbun-sha, 1976.
Japanese translation by Fujimoto Kazuko.

146. Retombées de Sombrero. Paris: C. Bourgois, 1980.
French translation by Robert Pépin.

Dreaming of Babylon

147. New York: Delacorte Press/Seymour Lawrence, 1977.

    First English Edition:
148. London: Jonathan Cape, 1978.

    Translated:
149. Babylon o yume mite. Tokyo: Shinchô-sha, 1978.
Japanese translation by Fujimoto Kazuko.

150. Träume von Babylon. Ein Detektivromam 1942. München: Ohnemus, 1981.
German translation by Günter and Ilse Ohnemus.

151. Un privé a Babylon. Paris: C. Bourgois, 1981.
French translation by Marc Chéntier.

152. Detective en Babilonia: Novela Negra. Barcelona: Anagrama, {1985?}
Spanish translation.

153. Träume von Babylon. Ein Detektivromam 1942. Frankfort: 'Eichborn Vlg. Ffm., 1986.

The Tokyo-Montana Express

154. New York: Delacorte Press/Seymour Lawrence, 1980.
Out of print.

First English Editon:
155. London: Jonathan Cape, 1981.

Other Editions:
156. Japanese edition published by *Playboy*.

Translated:
157. Express. Paris: C. Bourgois, 1981.
French translation by Robert Pépin.

158. Der Tokyo-Montana-Express. Frankfort: 'Eichborn Vlg. Ffm., 1987.

Previously Published Portions:
Statements on the copyright page say: "Portions of this work first appeared in *Mademoiselle, Esquire, Outside, California Living, Earth, Evergreen, TriQuarterly, New Ingenue, The CoEvolution Quarterly, New Orleans Review, San Francisco Stories,* and *The Overland Journey of Joseph Francl* published by William P. Wreden."
"A limited edition of *The Tokyo-Montana Express* was published in different form by Targ Editions."
"The author thanks them and *Playboy* (Japanese edition) for publishing his work."

159. "The Overland Journey of Joseph Francl and the Eternal Sleep of His Wife Antonia in Crete, Nebraska." The Overland Journey of Joseph Francl: The First Bohemian to Cross the Plains to the California Gold Fields. San Francisco: W.P. Wreden, 1968.
This chapter of Express was originally published as the introduction to a limited edition (540 copies) of this book.

160. "Dogs on the Roof." *Outside* Sept. 1977: 7.

So the Wind Won't Blow It All Away

161. New York: Delacorte Press/Seymour Lawrence, 1982. Out of print.

    First English Edition:
162. London: Arena-Arrow Books, 1986.

SHORT STORIES
Citations Listed Chronologically

163. "The Post Offices of Eastern Oregon." *Kulchur* (13) 1964: 51-55.

164. "A Study in California Flowers." *Coyote's Journal* (5/6) 1966: 81.

165. "Revenge of the Lawn" and "A Short History of Religion in California." *TriQuarterly* 5 (Winter) 1966: 55-59.

166. "1/3,1/3,1/3." *Ramparts* Dec. 1967: 43-45.

167. "A Study in California Flowers." *Grossteste Review* 1 (Winter) 1968: 3.

168. "The Weather in San Francisco." *Vogue* Oct. 1969: 126.

169. "Complicated Banking Problems." *Evergreen Review* (84) Nov. 1970: 41.

170. "Little Memoirs: Three Tales by Richard Brautigan." *Playboy* Dec. 1970: 164-65.
    Includes "Corporal," "The Literary Life in California, 1964," and "Halloween in Denver."

171. "Talk Show." *Kaleidoscope-Milwaukee* (3) Oct. 1970: 1.

172. "The Auction." *Vogue* Jan. 1970: 179.

173. "The Betrayed Kingdom." *Evergreen Review* (76) Mar. 1970: 51.

174. "The Lost Chapters of *Trout Fishing in America*." *Esquire* Oct. 1970: 152-53.

175. "Winter Rug." *Vogue* Aug. 1970: 98.

176. "Three Stories by Richard Brautigan." *Mademoiselle* July 1970: 104-05.
Includes "1692 Cotton Mather Newsreel," "Sand Castles," and "Pacific Radio Fire."

177. "Homage to the San Francisco YMCA." *Vogue* July 1971: 96-97.

178. "The Old Bus." *Vogue* Feb. 1971: 192.

179. "The World War I Los Angeles Airplane." *New American Review* #12. Ed. Theodore Solotaroff. New York: Simon and Schuster-Touchstone Books, 1971: 123-26.

Revenge of the Lawn

180. New York: Simon and Schuster, 1971.

First English Edition:
181. London: Jonathan Cape, {1972?}.

Translated:
182. *Shibafu no fukushû*. Tokyo: Shôbun-sha, 1976.
Japanese translation by Fujimoto Kuzuko.

183. *Die Rache des Rasens. Geschichen 1962-1970*. München: Ohnemus, 1978.
German translation by Günter Ohnemus. Epilogue by Patrick Anderson.

Previously Published Portions:
A statement on copyright page says: "Some of these stories first appeared in *Rolling Stone, Playboy, Ramparts, New American Review, Vogue, Coyote's Journal, Mademoiselle, Nice, TriQuarterly, Esquire, Evergreen Review, Kulchur, Now Now, Sum, Jeopardy, R.C. Lion, Parallel*, and *Change*."

"The Post Offices of Eastern Oregon." See 163.
"A Study in California Flowers." See 164 and 167.
"Revenge of the Lawn" and "A Short History of Religion in California." See 165.
"1/3, 1/3, 1/3." See 166.
"The Weather in San Francisco." See 168.
"Complicated Banking Problems." See 169.
"Corporal," "The Literary Life in California, 1964," and "Halloween in Denver." See 170.
"Talk Show." See 171.
"The Auction." See 172.
"The Betrayed Kingdom." See 173.
"The Lost Chapters of Trout Fishing in America." See 174.
"Winter Rug." See 175.
"1692 Cotton Mather Newsreel," "Sand Castles," and "Pacific Radio Fire." See 176.
"Homage to the San Francisco YMCA." See 177.
"The Old Bus." See 178.
"The World War I Los Angeles Airplane." See 179.

Published Excerpts:
184. "The World War I Los Angeles Airplane." The Best American Short Stories 1972. Ed. Martha Foley. Boston: Houghton Mifflin Co., 1972. 16-20.

185. "A Short History of Religion in California." The Stone Wall Book of Short Fictions. Eds. Robert Coover and Kent Dixon. Iowa City, IA: The Stone Wall Press, 1973. 29-31.

186. "The Lost Chapters of Trout Fishing in America: 'Rembrandt Creek' and 'Carthage Sink'." The Secret of Our Times: New Fiction from Esquire. Ed. Gordon Lish. Garden City, NY: Doubleday, 1973. 349-54.

187. "An Eye for Good Produce." *Mademoiselle* Nov. 1974: 192.

188. "A Gun for Big Fish." *Esquire* Mar. 1975: 70, 134.

189. "Football." *TriQuarterly* 35 (Winter) 1976: 89.

190. Hulesberg, Richard A. "Homage to the San Francisco YMCA." Instructor's Manual for "The Art of Fiction, 3rd Ed." Eds.

Richard F. Dietrich and Roger H. Sundel. New York: Holt, Rinehart & Winston, 1978. 1-4.

191. "Homage to the San Francisco YMCA." Fantastic Worlds: Myths, Tales, and Stories. Ed. Eric S. Rabkin. New York: Oxford University Press, 1979. 453-55.

192. "Great Golden Telescope." *Redbook* Aug. 1979: 57.

193. "The Post Offices of Eastern Oregon," "A Long Time Ago People Decided to Live in America," and "The World War I Los Angeles Airplane." Updike and Brautigan. Ed. H. Makino and M. Takahashi. Tokyo: Wako-Shuppan, 1980. {Page?}
    English language text book for Japanese readers.

194. "Revenge of the Lawn" and "A Short History of Religion in California." The Best of TriQuarterly. Ed. Jonathan Brent. New York: Washington Square Press, 1982. 5-11.

195. "Revenge of the Lawn" and "A Short History of Religion in California." Story: Fictions Past and Present. Eds. Boyd Litinger and Joyce Carol Oates. Lexington, MA: D.C. Heath and Co., 1985. 880-85.

COLLECTION

Trout Fishing in America, The Pill Versus the Springhill Mine Disaster, and In Watermelon Sugar

196. New York: Delacorte Press/Seymour Lawrence, 1969. New York: Houghton Mifflin, 1989.

    Previously Published Portions:
    See these titles for information on where portions have appeared prior to their collection.

ESSAYS AND ARTICLES
Citations Listed Chronologically

197. "The Menu." *Evergreen Review* (42) Aug. 1966: 30-32, 86.
Brautigan discusses the menu served to San Quentin Death Row prisoners saying, "It's so stark, so real... it's like a poem. This menu alone condemns our society. To feed somebody this kind of food who is already effectively dead represents all the incongruity of the whole damn thing. It's senseless."

198. "Old Lady." The San Francisco Poets. Ed. David Meltzer. New York: Ballantine Books, 1971. 293-97, 304.
Introduction to six poems from Rommel in which Brautigan discusses writing poetry.

> "I love writing poetry but it's taken time, like a difficult courtship that leads to a good marriage, for us to get to know each other. I wrote poetry for seven years to learn how to write a sentence because I really wanted to write novels and I figured that I couldn't write a novel until I could write a sentence. I used poetry as a lover but I never made her my old lady.
> "One day when I was twenty-five years old, I looked down and realized that I could write a sentence...wrote my first novel Trout and followed it with three other novels.
> "I pretty much stopped seeing poetry for the next six years until I was thirty-one or the autumn of 1966. Then I started going out with poetry again, but this time I knew how to write a sentence, so everything was different and poetry became my old lady. God, what a beautiful feeling that was!
> "I tried to write poetry that would get at some of the hard things in my life that needed talking about but those things you can only tell your old lady." See 45.

199. "The Silence of Flooded Houses." The Beatles' Lyrics. New York: Dell, 1975.
Introduction by Richard Brautigan.

LETTERS/PAPERS

The Richard Papers, 1948-1984
Held in the Bancroft Library, University of California, Berkeley. The collection contains correspondence to and from Brautigan regarding business and personal matters; miscellaneous personal papers, works by other authors; reviews of Brautigan's work; miscellaneous printed material; financial and travel records; copies of Brautigan's published works including original typescripts, corrections, and galley proofs; individual prose works; individual poems; notebooks; and fragments.

200. "Letter to John Barber."
Letter received Mar. 1984 from Brautigan who was at the time in Tokyo, Japan. Held by John Barber.

201. "Letter to Tom Clark."
Letter to Tom Clark, English poetry editor of the *Paris Review*. Held at Spencer Library, University of Kansas.

202. "Letter to James Koller."
Letter to James Koller. Held at the Homer Babbidge Library, Special Collections, University of Connecticut, Storrs.

202a. Richard Brautigan Papers, 1948-1984
Xxxxx
Xxxx

RECORDINGS

203. Listening to Richard Brautigan Produced by Miles Associates and Richard Brautigan, 1970. Distributed by Harvest Records, 1750 N. Vine Street, Hollywood, California 90028. Stereo phonodisc, 33 1/3 rpm, 54:45 minutes, order #St-424.
Brautigan reads some of his work to a background of environmental sounds.

GENERAL COMMENTARY ABOUT BRAUTIGAN

BOOK-LENGTH STUDIES
Citations Listed Alphabetically

204. Abbott, Keith. Downstream from "Trout Fishing in America." Capra Press, 1989.
    A memoir of experiences shared with Brautigan from 1966-1984. Concludes with commentary on Brautigan's writing and his place in American literature. "[Brautigan's] writing has been relegated to the shadowland of popular flashes, the peculiar American graveyard of overnight sensations. When a writer dies, appreciation of his work seldom reverses field, but continues in the direction that it was headed at the moment of death, and this has been true for Brautigan. Even during Brautigan's bestseller years in the United States, critical studies of his work were few. Those there were never exerted a strong influence on the chiefs of the American critical establishment."

205. Boyer, Jay. Richard Brautigan. Boise: Boise State University, 1987.
    Criticism and interpretation of Brautigan's novels. Boyer says that as either a Western writer or a post-modern writer, Brautigan's contribution seems slight. "But Brautigan's work may give us cause to rethink assumptions about the disparity

between the two sensibilities. Looking toward who we are and who we might like once again to become, Brautigan's novels suggest cultural myths and personal realities that can inform one another, if they're given a chance. America is often 'only a place in the mind' he wrote in Trout Fishing in America, and that expresses about as well as anyone might the key to the connection between post-modern and traditional Western views. For what Brautigan's novels do is to bring the territorial impulse of the Western, with all that suggests, to the experiential dilemmas of twentieth-century life.... Brautigan's greatest contribution to American letters may lie neither in post-modernism nor in Westernism, in other words, but rather in pointing us toward a juncture where the two might yet meet."

206. Chénetier, Marc. Richard Brautigan. London: Methuen, 1983.

Argues that Brautigan's dismissal by American critics has less to do with the quality of writing than with the nature of the scholarship applied to it. Says Brautigan's work falls outside the scope of traditional American scholarship and that it seeks to liberate fiction from the premises on which traditional mythology is based. "Brautigan has been identified as a 'minor' writer.... An apparent thematic thinness has alienated philosophically inclined critics, while his very popularity has repelled many serious critical analysts. More classical critics have been disturbed by the gradual disappearance from his work both of predictable content and traditionally dominant features of the novel (plot, character, setting); while his lack of explicit theoretical assertion has not won him the interest of those concerned with innovative developments in American fiction. [He is] oddly placed, then, on the margins of 'metafiction' and 'postmodernism'.... For me, Brautigan, if a 'minor' writer, is a far more important miner than many recognized writers.... Mapping out a territory is as important as settling it, and one may prefer census-taking to sense-making: the actual weighing of the nuggets will be left to others."

207. Foster, Edward Halsey. Richard Brautigan. Boston: Twayne, 1983.

Says that Brautigan's writing offers a bridge between the Beats and the next generation of American writers. "It may be... helpful to see [Brautigan] specifically as a writer of the

Beat generation, sharing their techniques and literary theories, as it is to see him in relation to the literature of the Northwest, Eastern mysticism, and the nineteenth-century American tradition represented by [Ralph Waldo] Emerson, [Walt] Whitman, and [Henry David] Thoreau."

207a. Grossman, Claudia. Richard Brautigan: Pounding at the Gates of American Literature. (Untersuchungen zu Seiner Lyric und Prose). Heidelberg: C. Winter, 1986.

208. Malley, Terence. Richard Brautigan. New York: Warner, 1972. Devotes a chapter each to Pill, Rommel, Revenge, Abortion, General, Watermelon, and Trout.

BIBLIOGRAPHIES

209. American Authors and Books. Third Revised Edition. Eds. William Jeremiah Burke and Will David Howe. New York: Crown Publishers, Inc., 1962. 75.

210. "Brautigan, Richard." The Encyclopedia of Science Fiction and Fantasy Through 1968. 3 vols. Comp. Donald H. Tuck. Chicago: Advent Publishers, 1974. Vol. 3, 628.
    Cites the paperback publication of Watermelon by Dell in 1968.

211. Contemporary Poets of the English Language. Eds. Rosalie Murphy and James Vinson. New York: St. Martin's Press, 1970. 131.
    Lists bibliographical information for poetry through Pill and novels through Trout.

212. Cumulative Book Index. New York: H.W. Wilson Company. 1970-1988. Vol. 1, 1965-1966, 406; 1969, 262; 1970, 243; 1971, 240; 1972, 280; 1973, 209; 1974, 244; 1974, 286; 1976, 259; 1977, 280; 1978, 297; 1979, 306; 1980, 316; 1981, 312; 1984, 346.

Publication information.
213. Davis, Lloyd and Robert Irwin. Contemporary American Poetry: A Checklist. Metuchen, NJ: Scarecrow Press, 1975. 14.
Publication information regarding Return, Hitch-Hiker, Marble, Octopus, Pill, and Rommel.

214. Jones, Stephen R. "Richard Brautigan: A Bibliography." *Bulletin of Bibliography* 33(1) Jan. 1976: 53-59.

215. Lepper, Gary M. A Bibliographical Introduction to Seventy-Five Modern American Authors. Berkeley: Serendipity Books, 1976. 81-85.

216. Science Fiction and Fantasy Literature. 2 vols. Comp. R. Reginald. Detroit: Gale Research Co., 1979. Vol. 1, 68.
Lists publication information regarding Monster, Watermelon, and collection of Trout, Pill, and Watermelon.

217. Science Fiction Book Review Index, 1974-1979. Ed. H.W. Hall. Detroit: Gale Research Company, 1981. 39.
Publication information for Monster, Watermelon, and Trout.

218. Wanless, James and Christine Kolodziej. "Richard Brautigan: A Working Checklist." *Critique* 16(1) 1974: 41-52.

THESES AND DISSERTATIONS

219. Barber, John F. "Richard Brautigan: An Annotated Bibliography." Master's Thesis, 1988. University of Alabama at Birmingham.

220. Butts, Leonard Culver. "Nature in the Selected Works of Four Contemporary American Novelists." *Dissertation Abstracts International* 40 (1980): 6277A. The University of Tennessee.
Concerns James Dickey, John Gardner, Richard Brautigan, and John Updike.

221. Chaffin, Terrell. "Seven Pieces for Violin and Piano," "I Lie Here in a Strange Girl's Apartment (Oh Marcia)," and "Erotica II." Unpublished Master's Thesis, 1983. University of California, San Diego.
Work includes violin and piano music, songs for the harp, electronic, and computer music.

222. Graddy, Julia Colomitz. "Richard Brautigan and the Pastoral Romance." *Masters Abstracts* 16 (1978): 232. Florida Atlantic University.

223. Hearron, William Thomas. "New Approaches in the Post-Modern American Novel: Joseph Heller, Kurt Vonnegut, & Richard Brautigan." *Dissertation Abstracts International* 34/06A (1973): 3398A-99A. State University of New York at Buffalo.
"For Brautigan, the only reality is that which is created through the power of language. To him the imagination is a magical faculty, empowered with the ability to transform, through the medium of language, the reality which contemporary man encounters. And since this reality is dominated by a vast, sprawling urban civilization which has virtually destroyed the actual wilderness in which literary predecessors as [James Fenimore] Cooper and [Mark] Twain could find refuge, such a transformation is not only desirable, but also essential for survival in our age."

224. Horvath, Brooke Kenton. "Dropping Out: Spiritual Crisis and Countercultural Attitudes in Four American Novelists of the 1960s." *Dissertation Abstracts International* 47/06A (1986): 2157A-58A. Purdue University.
Deals with John Updike, Walker Percy, Thomas Pynchon, and Richard Brautigan. Chapter Five discusses several works by Brautigan and the various ploys they use to gain imaginative control over death.

225. Robbins, Gwen A. "A Magic Box and Richard Brautigan." *Dissertation Abstracts International* 40/08A (1980): 4592A. Oklahoma State University.
"This dissertation examines Richard Brautigan's novels in reaction to a magic box metaphor, that is, an implied comparison to a fictional technique that portrays through multiple modes of perception the various layers of reality....

Brautigan sees reality as a construct that can be exemplified in multilevel dimensions. To Brautigan, reality is based on the personal perception of one's own multifaceted construct in which concrete experience is only the beginning departure."

226. Schroeder, Michael Leroy. "Rhetoric in New Fiction." *Dissertation Abstracts International* 4709A (1986): 3430A. Kent State University.
Deals with Kurt Vonnegut, Donald Barthelme, Robert Coover, and Richard Brautigan. "Richard Brautigan uses naive narrators to create ambiguity and irony through the conflict between their innocent tone and the frequently unpleasant and death-filled worlds they depict. Brautigan's outrageous similes and metaphors and his fantastic content illustrate his recurrent theme about the importance of the healthy imagination."

227. Sweatt, Suzanne Mitchell. "Postmodernism in the Fiction of Richard Brautigan." *Dissertation Abstracts International* 46/09A (1985): 2690A. Middle Tennessee State University.
Identifies postmodernist elements in Brautigan's fiction, establishes Brautigan as an early initiator of postmodernism, and evaluates his place in contemporary literature.

228. Wheeler, Elizabeth Patricia. "The Frontier Sensibility in Novels of Jack Kerouac, Richard Brautigan and Tom Robbins." *Dissertation Abstracts International* 46/04A Oct. 1985: 985A. State University of New York at Stony Brook.
"In Richard Brautigan's Trout the frontier only exists in the imagination, but in the novel, creations of imagination are the equal of objective reality."

PARODIES

229. Keillor, Garrison. "Ten Stories for Mr. Brautigan, and Other Stories." *New Yorker* 18 Mar. 1972: 37.
Keillor parodies Brautigan's style and effects. "Ten stories for Mr. Brautigan are nothing. He never eats lunch until he's thought up 110."

230. -----. "Ten Stories for Mr. Brautigan." Happy to Be Here. New York: Antheneum Publishers, 1981: 189-92.

General Commentary—Censorship Litigation

231. -----. "Ten Stories for Mr. Brautigan." Happy to Be Here. Harmondsworth, Middlesex, England: Penguin Books, Ltd., 1983. 245-248.

232. Percy, Walker. "The Mercy Killing." *The New York Times Book Review* 6 June 1971: 7.
Parodies Brautigan's writing style in a short story like those in Revenge.

CENSORSHIP LITIGATION

233. Anonymous. "Book Censorship Increasing in Schools." *The New York Times* 2 Jan. 1979, Sec. 3: 12.
"Among the books involved in 300 reported incidents of censorship [this year] were... the works of Richard Brautigan including his well-known Trout."

234. Cheatham, Bertha M. "School Board Socked with ACLU Suit in Brautigan Book-Banning Incident." *School Library Journal* Dec. 1978: 8.
"In a suit filed in Superior Court by the San Francisco American Civil Liberties Union on October 5, the banning of five books written by Richard Brautigan from Anderson Union High School in Northern California was challenged by two teachers, three students and Brautigan's hard cover publisher, Seymour Lawrence, Inc. According to Margaret Crosby, one of the two ACLU attorneys representing the plaintiffs, Anderson principal, J.D. Leitaker confiscated the books Abortion and Pill because the titles suggested that the books might contain obscenities and objectionable sexual references. The books had been used (without complaint) for several years in a developmental reading class, an elective for students who want to expand their reading interests and backgrounds. Subsequently, all Brautigan titles were banned from the student's optional reading lists, including Trout (on the ALA's 1975 Young Adult Notable Books list), Rommel, and General.... The suit marks the first time that a publisher has become involved in a book banning case of this type, said Crosby, who believes that the publisher's constitutional rights are being infringed.... Crosby and Ann Brick, an ACLU cooperative lawyer, expect the case will set a precedent for

future book-banning occurrences in California, which has no law specifying the limitations on school boards' authority in restricting reading materials."

235. Holt, Patricia. "Seymour Lawrence and ACLU Fight Ban on Brautigan Books." *Publishers Weekly* 16 Oct. 1978: 32.
   American Civil Liberties lawyer Margaret Crosby "noted that 'the issue is neither the way in which books are selected for school use nor the literary quality of the Brautigan novels, as the books are widely used in California schools and have been highly acclaimed. The issue is whether a school board can suddenly and arbitrarily ban certain books that have been in use for some time because of the board member's own moral, social or political views'."

236. -----. "Judge Advances Fight against Brautigan Book Ban." *Publishers Weekly* 9 Apr. 1979: 19-20.
   Brautigan's books became the center of a book-banning controversy in a northern California high school. The American Civil Liberties Union and Brautigan's hard cover publisher, Seymour Lawrence joined students and teachers in a suit against the Shasta County school board after several of Brautigan's works were removed from the classroom. The case was decided in Brautigan's favor.

TEACHING EXPERIENCES

237. Anonymous. "Brautigan Discusses His Writing, Teaching." *Montana State University Staff Bulletin* 25 June 1982: 3.
   Brautigan says that teaching a creative writing course at MSU was a "rare opportunity to go to college.... I told my class the first day that it's impossible to teach creative writing. I told them that what I could provide was a creative atmosphere and the experience of 30 years of writing.... I've been extremely pleased by the high quality of writing I've seen... from extreme realism to extreme imagination." Brautigan says good writers must be "courageous." He mentions writing another book whose working title is An Unfortunate Woman [never published]. He said "it will be as sad as it sounds."

238. Miller, Ellen K. "Distinguished Writer Joins MSU English Staff." *Exponent* 4 June 1982: 28.
"Richard Brautigan... came to MSU this quarter to teach creative writing. Although Brautigan was a poet in residence at MSU and had lectured at several colleges, such as Harvard, Duke, and Stanford, he had never taught a class before. 'I don't think it's possible to teach creative writing,' Brautigan said, but he wanted to provide a creative atmosphere and make his experience available.... 'I hope that after the end of this class, the students can enjoy writing and realize the possibilities are endless'."

239. Schmidt, Carol. "Writer Sights In on Bozeman Life." *Bozeman Chronicle* 26 Apr. 1982: 1-2.
Brautigan talks about his childhood, his self-taught writing abilities, his early publication struggles, his unexpected popularity, his residency in Japan and Montana, the controversial banning of five of his books, his sensitivity to the concerns of children, his concern over criticism against his work, and his future saying, "I don't know where or what I'll be working on, but I do know why I'll be writing. Because I like it."

240. Young, Barbara. "Author Goes to College—as a Teacher." *Great Falls Tribune* 14 June 1982: 9A.
"Brautigan, who did not attend college and considers himself self-taught, instructed a creative writing course in MSU's English Department this spring.... 'I think education provides the tools for a person to understand and enjoy life on this planet.' he says. 'The more you know, the more you can enjoy during our brief stay here. You can't get too much education. It should be a lifelong process'."

CRITICISM OF BRAUTIGAN

GENERAL CRITICISM
Citations Listed Alphabetically

241. Adams, Robert. "Brautigan Was Here." *The New York Review of Books* Apr. 1971: 24-26.
    Discusses General, the collection of Trout, Pill, and Watermelon, and Abortion. Says one cannot "call them novels or even fictions—they may well go down in literary history as Brautigan's."

242. The Annual Obituary Index 1984. Ed. Margot Levy. Chicago: St. James Press, 1985. 462-64.
    Biographical information, critical overview, and bibliography. "Surreal and comical in their mixture of the minute details of daily life with fantastic, impossible events, Brautigan's novels, short stories and poems were published in 12 languages, and he was revered especially in the US as a leader of the counter-culture.... The appeal of his work was, first of all, its specifically American, and more particularly its Californian character."

243. Anonymous. "Bloomsbury Comes to Big Sky, and the New Rocky Mountains." *People* 3 Nov. 1980: 26-31.
    Discusses the phenomenon of "Hollywood on the Yellow-

stone" noting that a movie director, a cinematographer, a painter, and several actors and writers, including Richard Brautigan, have settled in Montana's Paradise Valley.

244. Anonymous. "Brautigan, Richard." Academic American Encyclopedia. 21 vols. Danbury, CT: 1988. Vol. 3. 458.
"Poet and novelist Richard Brautigan, b. Tacoma, Wash., Jan. 30, 1935, d. an apparent suicide, October 1984, is identified with the U.S. counterculture movement of the 1960s. From his first successful novel, Trout (1967), most of his work features eccentric plots related by gentle, self-deprecating narrators. Brautigan never shed his hippie persona, and his later writings attracted a younger audience than his contemporaries, who had once been his most ardent readers."

245. Anthony, Gene. The Summer of Love. Berkeley: Celestial Arts, 1980. 27, 28, 29, 34, 143.
Photographs of Brautigan involved with the Diggers in the Haight-Ashbury neighborhood of San Francisco. Says "The Communication Company was the work of several writers including Richard Brautigan, Michael McClure, Lenore Kandel, Emmett Grogan, Peter Berg, and others. Communications were mimeographed on 8" x 11" sheets alerting hippies to events and free services."

246. Barth, John. "The Literature of Exhaustion." *Atlantic* Aug. 1967: 29-34.
Barth argues that contemporary literature has exhausted its traditionally recognized potentials. But Brautigan's work suggests, by its very uniqueness, that literature still offers yet unexploited possibilities.

247. The Best American Short Stories 1972. Ed. Martha Foley. Boston: Houghton Mifflin Co., 1972. 393.
"Richard Brautigan was born in the Pacific Northwest in 1935. He is the author of Trout, Pill, and Watermelon published in one volume by Delacorte Press/Seymour Lawrence. The books were first published by Four Seasons Foundation in San Francisco. His verse includes Hitch-Hiker, Marble, Octopus, Machines, and Plant."

Criticism—General Criticism 69

248. Biography Almanac. Third Edition. Vol. I. Ed. Susan L. Stetler. Detroit: Gale Research Co., 1987. 230.
"American, Author, Poet. Became campus hero, 1960s with whimsical novel Trout. b. Jan. 30, 1935 in Tacoma, Washington. d. Oct. 25, 1984 in Bolinas, California."

249. Bloodworth, W. "Literary Extensions of the Formula Western." *Western American Literature* 14(4) Winter 1980: 287-96.
"This paper proposes to define the relationship between the so-called Formula or Popular Western and a still-emerging tradition of American writers which draws upon the Formula Western for setting and characters but which does not sit easily under the rubric of popular culture... Somewhere within the tradition I am trying to describe there may even be a place for such idiosyncratic works as Richard Brautigan's Monster...."

250. Blue Book: Leaders of the English Speaking World. 1976 Edition. New York: St. Martin's Press, 1976. 192.
Lists novels through Willard, poetry through Rommel, and Revenge. Gives address as: "c/o Simon and Schuster Inc., 630 Fifth Ave., New York, NY 10020, USA."

251. Bokinsky, Caroline G. "Richard Brautigan." Dictionary of Literary Biography Vol. 5. American Poets Since World War II. Ed. Donald J. Greiner. Detroit: Gale Research Company, 1980. 96-99.
Critical comments on Return, Hitch-Hiker, Marble, Octopus, Machines, Pill, Rommel, Mercury, and June 30th and some biographical and bibliographical information. See these titles.

252. Bryan, Scott, Paul Graham, and John Somer. "Speed Kills: Richard Brautigan and the American Metaphor." *Oyez Review* 8(2) 1974: 64-72.

252a. Cambridge Handbook of American Literature. Ed. Jack Salzman. Cambridge, England: Cambridge University Press, 1986. {Page?}.

253. Cariage, Daniel. "Introspection d'un Tubiste." *Los Angeles Times* 18 Mar. 1984, Sec. C: 47.
Concert review concerning the Modular Theater in Valencia, CA, mentions Brautigan.

254. Celebrity Register. Third Edition. Ed. Earl Blackwell. New York: Simon and Schuster, 1973. 61.
"Brautigan's is the slightly wistful voice of 'the Woodstock generation,' longing for a time that never was in a place that might have been. He is the J.D. Salinger of the 1970s."

255. Chappel, Steve. "Brautigan in Montana." *San Francisco Examiner Review* 2 Nov. 1980: 4-5.
Brautigan says, "whimsy is not a word used in reviews of my books in Japan. My books are often seen as fragmented and pointless in America, not in Japan. They appreciate the structure of my novels there."

256. Clockwork Worlds. Eds. Richard D. Erlich and Thomas P. Dunn. Westport, CT: Greenwood Press, 1983. 184.
Mentions Brautigan as a writer who, in Machines, has visions of 'cybernetic ecology' in the future in which man, animals, plants, and machines will all live together in harmony and grace...."

257. Contemporary Authors Vols. 53-56. Ed. Clare D. Kinsman. Detroit: Gale Research Company, 1975. 63-64.
Biographical and bibliographical information.

258. Contemporary Literary Criticism. Vol. 1. Ed. Carolyn Riley. Detroit: Gale Research Company, 1973. 44-45.
Excerpts from 416, 500, 501, 782, and 801.

259. Contemporary Literary Criticism. Vol. 3. Ed. Carolyn Riley. Detroit: Gale Research Company, 1975. 86-90.
Excerpts from 208, 277, 333, 409, 423, 530, and 560.

260. Contemporary Literary Criticism. Vol. 5. Ed. Carolyn Riley. Detroit: Gale Research Company, 1976. 67-72.
Excerpts from 477, 492, 506, 516, 517, 567, 577, 595, and 605.

261. Contemporary Literary Criticism. Vol. 9. Ed. Dedria Bryfonski. Detroit: Gale Research Company, 1978. 123-25.
Excerpts from 332, 614, 652, 679, 680, 684, and 694.

262. Contemporary Literary Criticism. Vol. 12. Ed. Dedria Bryfonski. Detroit: Gale Research Company, 1980. 57-74.
Excerpts from 241, 271, 273, 296, 310, 325, 347, 395, 410, 420, 442, 444, 461, 468, 481, 491, 499, 504, 534, 549, 561, 584, 598, 627, 638, 657, 689, 788, 800, and 803.

263. Contemporary Literary Criticism. Vol. 42. Eds. Daniel G. Marowski and Roger Matuz. Detroit: Gale Research Company, 1980. 48-66.
Excerpts from 206, 207, 266, 313, 503, 542, 603, 687, 703, 711, 715, 733, 755, 758, and 759.

264. Contemporary Literary Criticism Yearbook 1984. Vol. 34. Ed. Sharon K. Hall. Detroit: Gale Research Company, 1985. 314-19.
Excerpts from 356, 834, 846, and 851.

265. Cook, Bruce. The Beat Generation. New York: Charles Scribner's Sons, 1971. 205-08, 212.
Speculations on Brautigan's place in the Beat movement. "[Brautigan's] poems are charming, often witty, sometimes successful-but rather slight. He gets his best effects from those brief, spontaneous bits of word play in which a single idea is twisted into the shape of a poem, almost in the manner of a haiku.... There [is] no writer around quite like him—no contemporary, at any rate. The one who is closest is Mark Twain. The two have in common an approach to humor that is founded on the old frontier tradition of the tall story. In Brautigan's work, however, events are given an extra twist so that they come out in respectable literary shape, looking like surrealism."

266. Cooley, John. "The Garden in the Machine: Three Postmodern Pastorals." *Michigan Academician* 13(4) Spring 1981: 405-20.
Says Brautigan provides "the cool and therapeutic tonic of his imaginative fictions. Thus Brautigan invokes not so much

the power of nature but of the imagination, under the influence of nature, to heal and transform."

267. A Dictionary of Literature in the English Language from 1940 to 1970. Comp. and Ed. Robin Myers. Oxford, England: Pergamon Press, 1978. 41.

268. A Directory of American Poets. 1975 Edition. New York: Poets & Writers, Inc., 1974. 4.
Lists Brautigan's address as: 2546 Geary Street, San Francisco, CA.

269. A Directory of American Poets and Fiction Writers. 1983-84 Edition. New York: Poets & Writers, Inc., 1983. 115.
Lists Brautigan's address as c/o Helen Brann, 14 Sutton Place South, New York, NY.

270. A Directory of American Writers. 1975 Edition. New York: Poets & Writers, Inc., 1974. 3.
Lists Brautigan's address as: 2546 Geary Street, San Francisco, CA.

271. Ditsky, John. "The Man on the Quaker Oats Box: Characteristics of Recent Experimental Fiction." *Georgia Review* 26 (Fall) 1972: 297-313.
"Richard Brautigan's fiction shares many of the qualities of his poetry—charm, brevity, whimsy, and in many cases a total inability to leave a residue in the consciousness."

272. Earth, Air, Fire, & Water. Ed. Frances Monson McCullough. New York: Coward, McCann, & Geoghegan, 1971. 27, 130, 142, and 173.
"Richard Brautigan was born in 1935 in the Pacific Northwest and has lived there for a long time. He has published three novels and has just recently emerged publicly after acquiring a strong underground reputation."

273. Feld, Michael. "A Double with Christina." *London Magazine* Aug./Sept. 1971: 150-52.
A patronizing review of General, Trout, and Watermelon. Says Brautigan's writing is "california [sic] prose poetry, an eminently greasy brand of verbal psychedelicatessen."

274. Gillespie, B. {Title?} *Science Fiction Commentary.* (40) May 1974: 52-54.
{Deals with Trout and Watermelon?}

275. Greenman, Myron. "Understanding New Fiction." *Modern Fiction Studies* 20(3) Autumn 1974: 307-16.
Discusses theories related to the "mimetic impulse" in light of several writers representing "new fiction." Says "the plain fact remains, though it seems to be seldom acknowledged, that it is still the concrete detail in new fiction that makes it readable, however devalued, incongruous, or apparently—though only apparently—abandoned." Using Abortion as an example, Greenman says, "we are not able to enjoy the book very much, because its slight narrative substance is not compensated by any noteworthy aesthetic, stylistic, psychological, or commentarial innovations or values; but to a slight degree we do find pleasure in it, and despite all of Brautigan's cuteness, we are indebted to his believable presentation of setting, story, and character."

276. Hamilton, David Mike. "Richard Brautigan." Critical Survey of Long Fiction, English Language Series. 8 vols. Ed. Frank N. Magill. Englewood Cliffs, NJ: Salem Press, 1983. Vol. 1, 290-95.
Comments on principal long fiction, other literary forms, achievements, biography, analysis, major publications other than long fiction, and bibliography.

277. Hansen, Allen J. "The Celebration of Solipsism: A New Trend in American Fiction." *Modern Fiction Studies* 19 (Spring) 1973: 5-15.
Believes that, in Brautigan's fiction, mankind shapes its world rather than being shaped by it.

278. Hart, James David. A Companion to California. New York: Oxford University Press, 1978. 50.
[Brautigan is an] "author associated with the San Francisco Beat movement, whose whimsical, amusing, and atmospheric sketches have been collected in short books called 'novels' including General (1964), Trout (1967), and Abortion (1970). He has also gathered brief poems in Pill (1968), Rommel (1970), and other works."

279. Hassan, Ihab. Contemporary American Literature, 1945-1972. New York: Ungar Publishing Co., 1973. 122, 171.
"Lucid, precise, whimsical, idyllic, Brautigan develops a unique fragmentary style.... Yet beneath the surface of happy love and naive humor, the reader feels the lurking presence of loss, madness, death...."

280. Hendin, Josephine. Vulnerable People. A View of American Fiction Since 1945. New York: Oxford University Press, 1978. 20, 44-50, 217, 224.
Discusses the social and political implications of acting in the manner of typical Brautigan characters: gentle, withdrawn, and emotionally distant.

281. -----. "Experimental Fiction." Harvard Guide to Contemporary American Writing. Ed. Daniel Hoffman. Cambridge: Harvard University Press, 1979. 260, 268.
"Brautigan is a spokesman for the disenchanted, seeking to allay anxiety by blurring the distinctions of status, wealth, and ambition which exist in the real world."

282. Hewitt, Geof. "Brautigan, Richard." Contemporary Poets. Second Edition. Ed. James Vinson. New York: St. Martin's Press, 1975. 167-169.
Criticism of Pill and Rommel and some biographical and bibliographical information.

283. -----. "Brautigan, Richard." Contemporary Poets. Third Edition. Ed. James Vinson. New York: St. Martin's Press, 1980. 163-164.
Criticism of Pill and Rommel and some biographical and bibliographical information.

284. Hicks, Jack. In the Singer's Temple: Prose Fictions of Barthelme, Gaines, Brautigan, Piercy, Kesey, and Kosinski. Chapel Hill, NC: University of North Carolina Press, 1981. 12, 140, 151-61.
Chapter 4 discusses Brautigan as a counterculture writer and draws examples from his work, especially Revenge.

285. Holden, J. "Poems Versus Jokes." *New England Review* 4(3) Spring 1982: 469-77.
   Contends that poems summon desirable feelings and glorify them. Jokes tend to condense experiences and offer them as substitute metaphors—especially when they deal with sex. Says, "all of Richard Brautigan's erotic pieces are on the borderline between poems and jokes. [When read on the page they are taken as poems, but] uttered before a live audience, they lose their character of being meditations on the task of love; they become instead thinly veiled boasts, verbal seductions."

286. Horvath, Brooke Kenton. "Richard Brautigan's Search for Control Over Death." *American Literature* 57(3) Oct. 1985: 434-55.
   Says that central to Brautigan's fiction is "death and the anxiety an awareness of death engenders.... Death-obsessed, Brautigan's characters find they must dissociate themselves from a culture that both throws death constantly in their paths and fails to give it meaning. These characters typically retreat into private life-enhancing religions, but habitually this ploy does not... engage life-and-death fears head on and fruitfully; rather, it intensifies that hopelessness and numbness that makes death so fearsome within the establishment.... [Brautigan's] work... continues to forward an especially severe critique of American society, one that moves beyond politics into prophecy, implicitly sounding a call for repentance, for a turning from death toward life."

287. -----. "Wrapped in a Winter Rug: Richard Brautigan Looks at Common Responses to Death." *Notes On Modern American Literature* 8(3) Winter 1984: Item 14.

288. Hunt, Robert. "Science Fiction for the Age of Inflation: Reading Atlas Shrugged in the 1980s." Coordinates. Eds. George E. Slusser, Eric S. Rabkin, and Robert Scholes. Carbondale: Southern Illinois University Press, 1983. 80.
   "In many high schools and colleges, one had to read [Ayn] Rand (as one later had to read [William] Golding, [Kurt] Vonnegut, or Brautigan) in order to stay intellectually au courant."

289. International Authors and Writers Who's Who. Seventh Edition. Ed. Ernest Kay. Cambridge, England: Melrose Press, 1976. 69.
Notes that Brautigan was the "Recipient, Grant, National Endowment For The Arts, 1968."

290. International Who's Who in Poetry. Fifth Edition. Ed. Ernest Kay. Cambridge, England: International Biographical Centre, 1977. 66.
Lists Brautigan's birthdate (30 Jan. 1935), published works (through Pill in poetry and Trout in novels), and address (San Francisco).

291. International Who's Who in Poetry. Fourth Edition. Ed. Ernest Kay. Cambridge, England: Melrose Press, 1974. 62.
Lists published works through Trout and gives address as San Francisco.

292. Jeffrey, David L. "Literature in an Apocalyptic Age, or, How to End a Romance." *Dalhousie Review* 61(3) Autumn 1981: 426-46.
"Most of us, perhaps will have reflected on contemporary literature which, uncertain of the question of meaning in history, develops its own problematique concerning the business of ending." [In footnote] "Richard Brautigan's famous 'Mayonnaise' chapter in Trout is another example, as is the 186,000 possible endings per second he allows in General - to indicate his abandonment of any temporal form for conclusion at all."

293. Justus, James H. "Fiction: The 1930s to the Present." American Literary Scholarship: An Annual 1972. Ed. Albert Robbins. Durham, NC: Duke University Press, 1974. 269, 307-08.
Reviews 355, 459, and 500.

294. -----. "Fiction: The 1930s to the Present." American Literary Scholarship: An Annual 1973. Ed. James Woodress. Durham, NC: Duke University Press, 1975. 259, 265, 299.
Reviews 205, 276, 278, 333, and 336.

295. Karl, Frederick R. American Fictions 1940-1980. New York: Harper & Row, 1983. xii, 27, 42, 64, 70-71, 384, and [394 sic].
Brautigan is discussed in the context of other American fiction writers. Criticism of Trout on pages 70-71. Mentioned as a minimalist on 384. Reference to page 394 should be 393.

296. Kern, Robert. "Williams, Brautigan, and the Poetics of Primitivism." *Chicago Review* 27(1) 1975: 47-57.
Compares Brautigan's poetry to William Carlos Williams' in terms of their shared "primitivist poetics."

297. Kerouac, Jan. Trainsong. New York: Henry Holt and Company, 1988. 154-57.
Discusses meeting Brautigan in Amsterdam in October 1983 saying, "He was tall, yet somehow unfinished in his build, like a giant adolescent, with a pot belly under a bright red T-shirt that advertised Montana.... blond, mustachioed, deeply disturbed.... This was Richard Brautigan.... Like me, he was here for the poetry festival.... In the three days before the reading he must have drunk six quarts of whiskey.... By the time he was scheduled to read, he had drunk himself stone sober, and I think he was terrified.... He went on with the same attitude I'd seen in the breakfast room the morning of his arrival: hangdog, terminally sad. He belatedly began to tell a story. It was all about an ant.... [After five minutes, without warning, he stopped. The crowd was] outraged and wanted more. Brautigan meekly apologized... then he left. That was the first and last time I saw Richard Brautigan.... strange, sweet fellow with so much unseen trauma inside. One year later he was found dead in his cabin in Livingston, Montana, having shot himself." [Brautigan was actually found in his house in Bolinas, California.]

298. Kline, Betsy. "A Cult Figure in the 1960s, Brautigan Has Successfully Moved into a New Era." *Kansas City Star* 21 Dec. 1980: 1, 12D.
Brautigan says "my work is one man's opinion of life and death and the 20th Century."

299. Klinkowitz, Jerome. The American 1960s. Ames: Iowa State University Press, 1980. vii, 34, 41-46, 49, 55, 58.
   Mentions General, Watermelon, "The Post Offices of Eastern Oregon," and Trout. Says Brautigan draws "the larger aesthetic of his poetry from [San Francisco's] most vital artistic period, just as the Beat movement turned into the Haight-Ashbury 'hippie' culture of the 1960s" [and before the national media exploited it and diluted its substance as a native community phenomenon] and that "conservativism of theme and form in fifties fiction [gave way] to the success of topically radical and structurally innovative books by Kurt Vonnegut, Richard Brautigan, and Donald Barthelme...."

300. -----. "Avant-Garde and After." *Sub-Stance* 27 1980: 125-38.
   This article taken from the chapter entitled "Epilogue, Avant-Garde and After" of 303.

301. -----. "Brautigan, Richard." Academic American Encyclopedia. 21 vols. Danbury, CT: 1981. Vol. 3, 458.
   "Poet and novelist Richard Brautigan, b. Tacoma, Wash., Jan. 30, 1935, is identified with the counterculture movement in San Francisco during the 1960s. His Trout (1967) and Pill (1968) feature witty dislocations of common perceptions related by a genuine, unassuming, offbeat narrator. In 1974 he began publishing satirical novels, including a western, a detective story, and a mystery."

302. -----. Literary Disruptions. Urbana: University of Chicago Press, 1975. 2, 7, 20-22, 51, 61, 98, 169, 187.
   Brautigan mentioned in association with Kurt Vonnegut, Jr. Trout mentioned on pages 20-22.

303. -----. The Practice of Fiction in America: Writers from Hawthorne to the Present. Ames: Iowa State University Press, 1980. 8, 85, 117.
   "There are several strategies by which the writer can fix his or her action (and hence the reader's attention) on the page, making the words hold fast to their created image. A favorite technique is the comically overwrought metaphor, which in the very distance between its tenor and vehicle creates a mimetically unbridgeable gap, closeable only by the

reader's imagination which appreciates how ridiculous the implied comparison is. In the 1960s Richard Brautigan was the master of this technique. His Trout tosses such metaphors at the reader like one-line jokes.... Because of their exotic and self-consciously fantastical nature, these phrases can only be accepted as metaphors, as artifacts designed by the writer not for referential value... but as objects in themselves, items crafted by the author for our imaginative delight."

304. -----. The Self-Apparent Word. Carbondale: Southern Illinois University Press, 1984. 32-33, 64-65.
Says Brautigan is a master of "stretching metaphors to incredible lengths between tenor and vehicle... [so that the] original object from the world is lost, to be replaced by something made of its author's language...."

305. -----. Vonnegut in America. New York: Delacorte Press/Seymour Lawrence, 1977. 63.
Brautigan mentioned with other modern writers in terms of the difficulty they encounter with the "critical community."

306. Le Vot, André. "Distinctive and Conjunctive Modes in Contemporary American Fiction." *Forum* 14(1) Spring 1976: 44-55.
Places Brautigan in a generation of "disjunctive" writers whose works represent "a flat, bi-dimensional world where objects and characters seem to be cut out from their background, projected into the foreground, allowed a few motions and spirited away.... Another vignette follows, as sketchy and impersonal.... [E]verything seems to happen on the same plane, and each detail, magnified as it were, forms an autonomous unit which occupies the whole field of vision." Narration is "framed" into "practically autonomous units" which are isolated, distant, and dehumanized. Disjunctive diction, with its emphasis on loose juxtaposition of words to form sentences "without constituting an organic whole" is "the third aspect of the disjunctive mode" where "the obsessive concern for the fragment finds its most efficient field of application."

307. Lhamon, W.T. "Break and Enter to Breakaway, Scotching Modernism in the Social Novel of the American Sixties." *Boundry 2* 3(2) Winter 1975: 289-306.
Contends that "much of the very best American fiction of the sixties is social and political.... [Much of it has] a sense of the obscene presence of American institutions. Most often their authors do not put this presence directly, as they might have in the thirties, but rather indirectly, metaphorically, hysterically... costumes and quick changes are important for Brautigan.... Novels like Trout and Portnoy's Complaint, since they assume the currency of a repressive fact, render the result of that fact: the pain and the bizarre alternative. These novels, even the life of the whole decade, might be criticized for not answering that which is necessary to know. Meaning: we don't have the categories to recognize the society in these novels. The society is undifferentiated, with no attention to class. But that is only befitting the kind of perception that is instead very real here: that the official culture, not the middle-class per se, is the totalizing force.... In fact, one might read [Trout] as a test case, for it would be hard to name another novel of the sixties that seems more ruthlessly to hide its social involvement.... Brautigan demonstrates how to be free with his language, disconnections, metaphors.... But this availability of freedom causes the problem that anyone can pretend to be free.... The conclusions... then, are that though freedom from society is possible, the very accessibility of the freedom pollutes it. Further, even for those who genuinely want to escape the routines of city life (or just routines), the process of expurgation is virtually impossible."

308. *Literary and Library Prizes*. Eighth Edition. Eds. Jeanne J. Henderson and Brenda G. Piggins. New York: R. R. Bowker Company, 1973. 146.
Cites the award of a National Endowment for the Arts grant to Brautigan in 1968-1969.

309. Lodge, David. "Modernism, Antimodernism and Postmodernism." *New Review* May 1977: 39-44.
Some postmodernist writers have deliberately taken metaphoric or metonymic strategies to excess, tested them, as it were, to destruction, parodied and burlesqued them in the process of using them, and thus sought to escape from their

tyranny. Richard Brautigan's <u>Trout</u>, for example, is notable for its bizarre similes, which frequently threaten to detach themselves from the narrative and develop into little self-contained stories—not quite like the heroic simile, because they never return to their original context."

310. Loewinsohn, Ron. "After the (Mimeograph) Revolution." *TriQuarterly* 18 Spring 1970: 221-36.
Within the context of discussing the success of various small presses, this article mentions the collection of <u>Trout</u>, <u>Pill</u>, and <u>Watermelon</u>. Says <u>Trout</u> is "one of the funniest books you will ever read," <u>Pill</u> "collects most of the poems Brautigan has written and published over the past ten years," and that <u>Watermelon</u> is a peculiar book because "the surface of the novel is gentle, even banal, but under that surface lurk predictability and repression [and] self-repression." Also discusses Brautigan's style of poetry saying his "poems are either very clever or very sentimental." Brautigan "does not seem to have much sense of the possibilities the line proposes, so that poems often seem like one-liner jokes chopped up into verse." Defines Brautigan's poetry as a "closing off." Says "what Brautigan leaves outside the door of classification is any acknowledgement of the on-going-ness of things, and of himself. You finish one poem and go on to the next because the poems don't resonate beyond the final (and final-sounding) line."

311. Lynch, Dennis. "Brautigan, Richard." <u>Contemporary Poets</u>. Fourth Edition. Eds. James Vinson and D. L. Kirkpatrick. New York: St. Martin's Press, 1985. 85-86.
[In his poetry,] "Brautigan cuts through the intellectual and emotional noise to touch us all." Lists published works and bibliographical and critical studies.

312. McCall, Cheryl. "A Happy But Footsore Writer Celebrates His Driver's Block." *People* 8 June 1981: 113, 116, 120.
Brautigan discusses not driving and not owning a car. "Not driving is a personal decision, not a protest in a socially active way.... My lack of appreciation of the automobile doesn't extend to other forms of technology.... I don't have a love affair with the car.... My favorite form of transportation is walking anywhere with someone I love."

313. McIlroy, Gary. "Pilgrim at Tinker Creek and the Burden of Science." *American Literature* (59) March 1987: 71-84.
 Footnote reference to Cooley's (See 266) mention of Trout saying "the hopefulness of these stories... resides only in the 'green language' of their telling. [Annie] Dillard, on the other hand, and nature writers like her, celebrate nature, even if it is only the vibrant nature of a diminished wilderness."

314. Manso, Peter, and Michael McClure. "Brautigan's Wake." *Vanity Fair* May 1985: 62-68, 112-16.
 A re-evaluation of Brautigan, after his death, by his peers: Manso (writer), McClure (poet), Ron Loewinsohn (poet), Don Carpenter (novelist), Lawrence Ferlinghetti (poet and publisher, City Lights Books), Don Allen (editor and publisher), Helen Brann (literary agent), Richard Hodge (confidant and California Superior Court judge), Bobbie Louise Hawkins (poet and performer), David Fechheimer (private investigator and friend), Ianthe Brautigan (daughter), Peter Berg (founder, with Emmett Grogan and Peter Coyote, of the Diggers), Tom McGuane (novelist), Dennis Hopper (actor), Siew-Hwa Beh (girlfriend), Peter Fonda (actor), John Doss (doctor and friend), Margot Patterson Doss (writer and columnist), Joanne Kyger (poet), Tony Dingman (friend), Ken Holmes (assistant coroner, Marin County), and Anthony Russo (detective sargeant, Marin County Sheriff's Office).

315. Mellard, James M. "Brautigan's 'Trout Fishing in America'." The Exploded Form: The Modernist Novel in America. Urbana: University of Illinois Press, 1980. 16, 21, 155-68, 173.
 Trout as exemplar of sophisticated phase of modernist novel, 155-68; Trout as center of later modernist fiction, 155; Brautigan and Wallace Stevens, 168; Brautigan mentioned, 16, 21, and 173. "Trout is not naively naive, not a simple pastoral fiction; it is a subtle poetic novel by a lyrical poet, built upon the popular conventions of a widely shared tradition.... Trout seems most easily read through the conventions of the pastoral element of the oral/colloquial tradition."

316. Modern American Literature. Fourth Edition. Vol. 4 Supplement to Fourth Edition. Eds. and Comps. Dorothy Nyren Curley, Maurice Kramer, and Elaine Fialka Kramer. New York: Ungar Publishing Co., 1976. Vol. 4, 64-69.
Excerpts from 265, 279, 325, 457, 464, 473, 481, 501, 512, 566, 595, 773, and 782.

317. Morton, Brian. "How Hippies Got Hooked on Trout Fishing in America." *The Times Higher Education Supplement* 16 Nov. 1984: 12.
Discusses Express, Watermelon, Wind, and Trout, saying "Brautigan's best novel is almost certainly his second, Trout...." Says that "Brautigan's 'zen' prose did much to endear him... to the hippie generation of the late 1960s and early 1970s" and that "Brautigan had always been a highly literary author but his interest in genre soon lapsed into a kind of formula writing.... He relied more and more on pastiche. As with many popular writers, his success became a barrier to understanding. Only Tony Tanner (See 504) in England and Marc Chénetier (See 206) in France gave him extended attention. The majority of critics mistook his economy of means and minimal style for slightness, his humour and playfulness for irresponsibility. In reality, his books are particularly sombre, centering on decay, disfigurement and violence...."

318. Mottram, Eric. "Brautigan, Richard." *The Penguin Companion to American Literature*. Eds. Malcolm Bradbury, Eric Mottram, and Jean Franco. New York: McGraw-Hill Co., 1971. 41.
"He is above all a writer of the place in which he lives: the landscape and cities of the Pacific coast. His novels and stories are funny, quirkily original, and resist any categorization, just as his heroes are those whose freedom is anarchistic."

319. Mug Shots: Who's Who in the New Earth. Comp. and Ed. Jay Acton. New York: Meridian Book-World, 1972. 26.
"Moved to San Francisco, 1954. No college. Poet-in-Residence, California Institute of Technology. Brautigan writes with soft, blurred images, intermingling fantasy with reality so deftly that the reader moves from dimension to

dimension as easily as one moves from the present to rememberance of the past.... A commune, a free school, and an underground newspaper have all taken their names from Trout."

320. Mullen, Michael P. "Richard Brautigan." Dictionary of Literary Biography Yearbook 1984. Ed. Jean W. Ross, Detroit: Gale Research Company, 1985. 166-69.
Overview of Brautigan's works by Mullen and tributes by Helen Brann and Kurt Vonnegut. Mullen says: "The playfulness of Brautigan's work attracted readers; his books could be read for pleasure. At the same time, however, his books had substance, which satisfied the critics.... The critical attention Brautigan's books received during his lifetime indicates that he was more than a voice for a generation, forgotten as that generation gave way to the one that followed, and the attention given Brautigan after his death should highlight even more the lasting qualities of his work." Brann says, "Richard Brautigan was a writer I was honored to represent as his literary agent from 1968 on. I think Richard was an American genius, a pure artist, an original voice out of the West from which he came. I believe Richard's work will last, not only because of his brilliant style so individual, spare, and alternately sharp and gentle, but because... he explored the funny, phony, violent, romantic America he loved enough to see with open-eyed vision." Vonnegut says, "I never knew Richard Brautigan, except through his writings.... At this great distance from the man himself, I will guess that he, like so many other good writers, was finally done in by the chemical imbalance we call depression, which does its deadly work regardless of what may really be going on in the sufferer's love life or his adventures, for good or ill, in the heartless marketplace."

321. The New Consciousness. Ed. Albert J. La Valley. Cambridge, MA: Winthrop Publishers, 1972. 329-31.
"His novels are poetic novels, filled with vivid and often chance metaphors, and rich images. They celebrate, in the spirit of [William Carlos] Williams, the Beat poets, and [Allen] Ginsberg, innocence, romance, and ceremony in the most commonplace and often mundane acts.... Nevertheless, on balance, fantasy... predominates over reality... [it is] the

wedding of fantasy and reality, the growing accommodation to a complex world.... But there are disturbing implications which another novelist might have followed up psychologically.... Brautigan need not follow through psychologically, but he should not let his problems lapse and settle for mere wonder. In much of his later work he does just that, keeping his world far removed from this one. [His writing seems to suggest] life as sugar coating, a vision more worthy of Rod McKuen than of Richard Brautigan."

322. Novak, Robert. "Richard Gary Brautigan." Dictionary of Literary Biography Vol. 2. American Novelists Since World War II. Ed. Jeffrey Helterman. Detroit: Gale Research Company, 1978. 65-70.
Deals with General, Trout, Watermelon, Abortion, Revenge, Monster, Willard, Sombrero, and Dreaming. Also provides some biographical and bibliographical information.

323. -----. "The Poetry of Richard Brautigan." Windless Orchard (14) 1973: 17, 48-50.

324. Novels and Novelists. Ed. Martin Seymour-Smith. New York: St. Martin's Press, 1980. 105.
"His novels are offbeat, deliberately zany, completely different. People either love him or can't read him. The critical consensus might be summed up thus: he has more wit than wisdom."

325. O'Hara, J. D. "Happier (but Not Holier) than Thou." Chicago Tribune Book World 11 Jan. 1970: 3.
"Brautigan... is funny, but seldom satiric, sometimes bored but hardly ever angry, frequently happier than you but never holier than thou...."

326. The Oxford Companion to American Literature. Fifth Edition. Ed. James D. Hart. New York: Oxford University Press, 1983. 96.
"San Francisco author [who writes]... short 'novels' composed of comic, whimsical, and surrealistic sketches of gently anarchic, unselfish, and Beat ways of life...."

327. Poems Here and Now. Ed. David Kherdian. New York: Greenwillow Books, 1976. 59.
"Richard Brautigan (b. 1935) was proclaimed as the first hippie poet, but he is perhaps better known for his novels and short stories. Among them are: General (1964) and Trout (1967). Pill (1968) is his major book of poems."

328. Postmodern Fiction. A Bio-Bibliographical Guide. Ed. Larry McCaffery. New York: Greenwood Press, 1986. 165, 286-88, 430.
Ron Silliman ("New Prose, New Prose Poem," 165) says, Brautigan represents "the laidback side of the San Francisco Renaissance" when one considers the "gamut of possibilities" within New American poetry. Craig Thompson ("Brautigan, Richard," 286-88) provides a critical review of Brautigan's works. Lynn McKean ("Klinkowitz, Jerome," 430) says that Klinkowitz collaborated with "such newly mainstream fictionists as Kurt Vonnegut, Richard Brautigan, and Donald Barthelme."

329. Rabkin, Eric S. The Fantastic in Literature. Princeton: Princeton University Press, 1976. 152-53.
"Richard Brautigan has already absorbed the world in which.... nature is now metaphorized by technology."

330. Ritter, Jess. "Teaching Vonnegut on the Firing Line." The Vonnegut Statement. Eds. Jerome Klinkowitz and John Somer. New York: Delacorte Press/Seymour Lawrence,1973. 33.
Cites Brautigan as an author that young people read.

331. Roberts, Peter. "Brautigan, Richard." The Science Fiction Encyclopedia. Ed. Peter Nicholls. Garden City: Doubleday and Co., 1979. 87.
"American writer and poet, known primarily for his work outside the SF field. Most of his fiction is whimsical and on the borderline of fantasy. Monster (1974), described as a 'Gothic Western,' is SF, however, and plays with the Frankenstein theme, while Watermelon (1968), a fantasy in an indeterminate setting echoes the post-holocaust novels of conventional SF."

332. Russell, Charles. "The Vault of Language: Self-Reflective Artifice in Contemporary American Fiction." *Modern Fiction Studies* 20(3) Autumn 1974: 349-57.
"....Brautigan creates some of the most particularly ungainly metaphors... [that] call attention not only to the radical newness of the analogy, thus freeing it from a closed system of received meanings, but they also insure, by their very ungainliness, their transitory existence. At most, they may sustain themselves long enough to give birth to another metaphor or variation on themselves.... [Thus] his stories are in a constant flux of emerging and receding.... It is an abortive fiction. His metaphors lead toward little more than themselves. The experiences he describes are evoked for their own worth, and for the value of allowing the mind to play with the possibilities of imagination. But that imagination is never sustained in absence of the original experience which is forever fleeing from consciousness."

333. Schmitz, Neil. "Richard Brautigan and the Modern Pastoral." *Modern Fiction Studies* 19 (Spring) 1973: 109-25.
Examines the pastoral myth as portrayed in Brautigan's work.

334. Science Fiction Source Book. Ed. David Wingrove. New York: Van Nostrand Reinhold Co., 1984. 109.
American offbeat novelist whose works occasionally touch upon the concerns of SF and fantasy. Watermelon is vaguely an Utopian fantasy, whilst Monster (1974) toys with the Frankenstein theme. Hard SF fans might find him far too trivial."

335. Steele, Judy. "Brautigan: Success Has Drawbacks." *Idaho Statesman* 16 Nov. 1980, Sec. D: 1.
Discusses Brautigan's thoughts about his writing, and his advice to writers: "Don't look back. The most exciting novel is the next one."

336. Stevick, Phillip. "Naive Narration: Classic to Post-Modern." *Modern Fiction Studies* 23(4) 1977-78: 531-42.
Says Brautigan practices "naive narration"—a simple and immature perspective without the intrusion of a matured, distanced, authorial voice. The appeal of this naive narration

may lie in its recognition of vulnerability and openness. "Anything by Brautigan suggests further possibilities for naive narration, as well as further risks, an openness and tenderness to experience rare in prose fiction, the risks being an arch, precious, cloying quality."

337. -----. "Scheherazade Runs Out of Plots, Goes on Talking; The King, Puzzled, Listens: An Essay on New Fiction." *TriQuarterly* 26 (Winter) 1973: 332-63.

Discusses Richard Brautigan, Robert Coover, and Donald Barthelme calling them writers of "new fiction" because "recent fiction no longer orients itself according to its own relations to the modernist masters and... this sense of discontinuity with the dominant figures of modernism is one of the few qualities that unites new fiction."

338. Stickney, John. "Gentle Poet of the Young." *Life* 14 Aug. 1970: 49-52, 54.

Biographical information, several photographs, and some of Brautigan's thoughts on his work. Of Brautigan's writing, Stickney says, "Thoughtful hedonism, it might be called: celebrate the pleasures of life and love on the midway, he advises, because tragedy lurks just outside the gates."

339. Streitfeld, David. "Hippie Poet Laureate." *Washington Post Book World* 9 Apr. 1989: 15.

Discusses Keith Abbott's Downstream From "Trout Fishing in America" (See 204) and mentions the reprint of Trout, Watermelon, and Pill by Houghton Mifflin (See 196). Concludes by saying, "The best of Brautigan will survive, even if the man himself doesn't seem like one you'd care to bring home with you. Or find waiting for you. Once, he was waiting in a friend's house for the guy to return, and started drinking with a third friend. To pass the time, Abbott recounts, 'Richard and his partner emptied the friend's refrigerator and painted the kitchen wall with mustard, mayonnaise and jam'."

340. The Supplement. Winter 1976. New York: Poets & Writers, Inc. 1976. 3.

Lists Brautigan's address as 314 Union Street, San Francisco, CA.

341. The Supplement. Summer 1976. New York: Poets & Writers, Inc. 1976. 3.
Lists Brautigan's address as c/o Helen Brann, Literary Agent, 14 Sutton Place South, New York, NY.

342. Thomson, George H. "Objective Reporting as a Technique in the Experimental Novel: A Note on Brautigan and Robbe-Grillet." *Notes On Contemporary Literature* 8(4) 1978: 2.
"Objective reporting as a narrative style is associated with a certain kind of realism in which ostensibly reality speaks for itself while the implied author concentrated on his fingernails.... The first person narrator [in Brautigan's Watermelon], who appears detached, fails to mention what motives or causes might explain the events of the story.... Brautigan puts his detached style of narration in the foreground only to undercut and then displace its effect by his reliance on fantasy-like subject matter. On the other hand, Robbe-Grillet puts his realistic style of narration in the foreground and then undercuts but does not displace its effect by his use of confusing, obsessional, and bizarre subject matter. Though the approaches differ, the technique in each case is designed to allow the author under the guise of order and detachment to introduce discontinuity and improbability: literal fantasy in Brautigan, psychological fantasy in Robbe-Grillet.... The result is deliberately to subvert the kind of realism originally aspired to by the fictional practitioners of reportorial objectivity."

343. The Traveler's Reading Guide. Ed. Maggy Simony. Revised, Expanded Edition. New York, Freelance Publications, 1987. 577, 584, 685, 747.
Includes Abortion, Dreaming, Express, and Monster in "ready-made reading lists for the armchair traveler."

344. Vogler, Thomas A. "Brautigan, Richard." Contemporary Novelists. Ed. James Vinson. Third Edition. New York: St. Martin's Press, 1982. 99-100.
Critical comments on Trout and Watermelon and biographical and bibliographical information.

345. -----. "Brautigan, Richard." Contemporary Novelists. Ed. James Vinson. Second Edition. New York: St. Martin's Press, 1976. 179-80.

346. -----. "Brautigan, Richard." Contemporary Novelists. Ed. James Vinson. New York: St. Martin's Press, 1972. 172-74.
    Deals with Brautigan's theme of rebirth of the American Dream and the metamorphosis of language and attitude in Brautigan's work.

347. Walker, Cheryl. "Richard Brautigan: Youth Fishing in America." *Modern Occasions* 2(2) 1972: 308-13.
    "His appeal consists primarily in an irrepressible optimism.... A style flashing with artifice, and a total disregard for effete university culture."

348. Who Was Who in America. Vol. VIII 1982-1985. Chicago: Marquis Who's Who, Inc., 1985. 50.
    Lists works through Express.

349. Who's Who in America. 38th Edition. 1974-1975. Vol. 1. Chicago: Marquis Who's Who, Inc., 1974. 357.
    Lists works through Revenge and gives address as c/o Sterling Lord Agency, 660 Madison Ave., New York, NY

350. Who's Who in America. 39th Edition. 1976-1977. Vol. 1. Chicago: Marquis Who's Who, Inc., 1976. 372.
    Lists works through Monster and gives address as c/o Sterling Lord Agency.

351. Who's Who in America. 40th Edition. 1978-1979. Vol. 1. Chicago: Marquis Who's Who, Inc., 1977. 387.
    Lists works through Willard and gives address as c/o Simon and Schuster, Inc., 630 Fifth Ave., New York, NY

352. Who's Who in America. 41st Edition. 1980-1981. Vol. 1. Chicago: Marquis Who's Who, Inc., 1980. 402.
    Lists works through June 30th and gives address as c/o Brann-Hartnett Agency, 14 Sutton Place South, New York, NY

353. Who's Who in America. 42nd Edition. 1982-1983. Vol. 1. Chicago: Marquis Who's Who, Inc., 1982. 373.
Lists works through June 30th.

354. Who's Who in America. 43rd Edition. 1984-1985. Vol. 1. Chicago: Marquis Who's Who, Inc., 1984. 376.
Lists works through Express and gives address as c/o Simon and Schuster, Inc.

355. Wickes, George. "From Breton to Barthelme: Westward the Course of Surrealism." *Proceedings: PNW Conference on Foreign Languages* (22) 1971: 208-14.

356. World Authors, 1970-1975. Ed. John Wakeman. New York: H.W. Wilson Co., 1980. 115-18.
Remarks on General, Trout, Watermelon, Abortion, Monster, Willard, Sombrero, and Revenge. Says "Brautigan has become as great a campus idol as [Hermann] Hesse, [J.R.R.] Tolkein, [Kurt] Vonnegut.... How seriously he should be taken as a literary phenomenon is a matter of opinion." Lists published works and cites some sources of articles about Brautigan.

357. Wright, Lawrence. "The Life and Death of Richard Brautigan." *Rolling Stone* Apr. 1985: 29-61.
Incorporates comments and remembrances from friends.

358. The Writers Directory 1976-78. New York: St. Martin's Press, 1976. 121.
Lists works through Willard and gives address as c/o Simon and Schuster, Inc., 630 Fourth Ave., New York, NY.

359. The Writers Directory 1980-1982. New York: St. Martin's Press, 1979. 143.
Lists works through Willard and gives address as c/o Simon and Schuster, Inc.

360. The Writers Directory 1980-1982. Detroit: Gale Research Company, 1981. 109.
Lists bibliographical information for works through June 30th and gives address as c/o Simon and Schuster, Inc.

361. The Writers Directory 1984-1986. Chicago: St. James Press, 1983. 113.
   Lists works through Express and gives address as c/o Helen Brann, 14 Sutton Place South, New York, NY.

GENERAL INTERNATIONAL CRITICISM

362. Auwera, Fernand. "Lucky Punch." *Dietsche Warande en Belfort: Tijdschrifit vour Letterkunde, Kunst en Geestesleven* (122) 1977: 783-85.
   Criticism of Kurt Vonnegut and Richard Brautigan from a German perspective.

363. Baronian, Jean-Baptiste. "Loufoque Brautigan?" *Magazine Littéraire* May 1983: 52-53.
   Criticism from a French perspective. Says time is a central for Brautigan's work but that it is annihilated by the style of writing. Ends with an interview with Brautigan in which he discusses his writing.

364. Benoit, Claude. "El Regresso del Detective Privado [The Return of the Private Detective]." *Cuadernos del Norte* 4(19) 1983: 46-59.
   Criticism of the private detective genre novel. Says "Richard Brantigan" [sic] is a writer who does not specialize in police novels, that his intention is parody, and that Dreaming is a false police novel.

365. Blake, Harry. "American Post-Modernism." *Tel Quel 71 /73* (Autumn) 1977: 171-82.
   Criticism from a French perspective. Brautigan is compared to other "post-modern" American writers John Barth, Donald Barthelme, Robert Coover, William Gass, and Jerzy Kosinski. Says "Brautignan" [sic] is a "dreck arranger" who utilizes scenes representing the unedited flow of the mind which follow one another and neutralize one another without logic.

366. Chénetier, Marc. "Harmonics on Literary Irreverence: Boris Vian and Richard Brautigan." *Stanford French Review* 1(2) Fall 1977: 243-59.
Criticism from a French perspective.

367. -----. "Richard Brautigan, écriveur: Notes d'un Ouvre-Boîtes Critique." *Caliban* 12 1975: 16-31.
Criticism from a French perspective. Says that for Brautigan, life, rather than a continuum, is a succession of transient and ephemeral states, and that identity is constantly destroyed and renewed. Says this is called "iDEATH" (the death of the ego) and that it is the foe of "inBOIL" (interior turbulence).

368. -----. "'Bits and Pieces': La Rhétorique du Pararéel Dans l'Oeuvre de Richard Brautigan." *Trema* 1 1975: 95-131.
Criticism from a French perspective.

369. Clancey, Laurie, Murray Bramwell, and Dennis Altman. "Notes on the Counter Culture." *Southern Review* [Adelaide, South Australia] 6(3) Sept. 1973: 239-51.
Presented at the 5th Conference of the Australian and New Zealand American Studies Association, 1972. Bramwell says that in the works of Richard Brautigan, Allen Ginsberg, and Gary Snyder and in song lyrics, the counter culture shows "a fascination with words in themselves, with the cryptic and surreal... paradox and whimsy... and less concern... with education than with pleasure."

370. Gallego, Candido Perez. "Ultima narrative norteamericana." [Ultimate North-American Narratives.] *Cuadernos Hispanoamericanos* 411 Sept. 1984: 137-47.
Says Brautigan develops subjects in Trout and Watermelon that he expounds upon in later novels.

371. -----. "Heroe y Estile en la Novela Norteamericana Actual." [Heroes and Style in the Contemporary American Novel.] *Insula* [*Revista de Letres y Ciencias Humans*] 39(449) April 1984: 1, 12.
Criticism from a Spanish perspective. Says that the terror of confronting nature and not having anything to say to it, is a theme that Brautigan repeats in Trout.

372. Hoffmann, Gerhard "Social Criticism and the Deformation of Man, Satire, the Grotesque and Comic Nihilism in the Modern and Postmodern American Novel." *Amerikastudien* (American Studies) 28(2) {Date?} 1983: 141-203.

373. Inoue, Kenji. "Dream or Nightmare: The Image of America as Reflected in the Works of Some Contemporary American Writers." Proceedings of the Conference on the Comparative Study of Chinese Ideal and the American Dream. 6-8 Oct. 1978. Taipei: Institute of American Culture, Academia Sinica. 205-13.
    Comments on Brautigan from a Taiwanese perspective.

374. Kraft, Werner. "Zweimal [Twice] Richard Brautigan: I. Ein Gedicht-scheinbar einfach [A Poem—Apparently Simple]." *Merkur* (288) 26 Apr. 1972: 395-96.
    Criticism from a German perspective. Says that a close reading of Brautigan's poem "April 7, 1969" [from Rommel] refutes contentions that corruptions exerted by advertising and politics on language lead to a certain distrust of the expressive and definitory capacity of language. Kraft finds this poem artistically effective.

375. Le Vot, André. "La nouvelle fiction contre le consensus." *Quinzaine* (330) 15 Aug. 1980: 27-28.
    Survey of American fiction since 1949 that seems to run counter to the consensus. Mentions publication of Trout in 1967 and General in 1964 citing it as a "premier publication and a significant work."

376. Lewis, Paul. "Faces of Fiction." *Stand* 19(4) 1978: 66-71.
    Criticism from a British perspective. "It is easier to understand why Richard Brautigan became a cult figure than why he has remained one. The novelty, charm and wit of his early work were refreshing, especially in the context of American fiction, since here was an innovative writer with a distinctive offbeat imagination who was not trying to compete with [Saul] Bellow, [John] Barth, [Joseph] Heller or [Thomas] Pynchon, not trying to write the Great Serious Comic Epic in Prose of some other typically American leviathan.... Yet very enjoyable as some of Brautigan's novels are, can he bear the strain of the heavy scholarship being erected on his slight

oeuvre?.... Like most cult figures, Brautigan has been the victim of his admirers, with the result that even his feeblest books have received rave reviews. Only totally misplaced devotion could have led to the critical praise for.... Monster, a trite fable on the Frankenstein theme couched in a mainly unfunny Gothic burlesque and replete with cheap, instant surrealism.... [In Willard] Brautigan is presumably trying to make serious points about American society... but his amoral flippancy and detachment trivialise the themes. In Sombrero... Brautigan's fantasy, while bringing out the logic of lunacy, is essentially anodyne.... Brautigan's transformation of the private-eye novel [Dreaming] into burlesque terms is, perhaps, as much nostalgic as subversive, but it does have the effect of belittling the social comment of more serious writers of the genre like [Raymond] Chandler, and puts nothing in its place but easy laughs.... To describe [Brautigan] as an entertainer or lightweight is, of course, heretical, considering his prestige in academe, but he now seems to be writing his own kind of pop-art pot-boiler, nihilistic at heart. His popular success seems to have stunted the development of his not inconsiderable talent."

377. Manske, Eva. "Individual and Society in Contemporary American Fiction." *Zeitschrift für Anglistik und Amerikanistik* 28(4) 1980: 320-28.
   Criticism from a German perspective. Says that recent American fiction shows the increasing powerlessness and loss of identity felt by the individual. This is accompanied by only the vaguest sense of the possibility of social change as the crisis of capitalism deepens. In comparing American writers, Manske says that novels by Brautigan show a reaction against a "swinging life style" promoted in Ken Kesey's work.

378. Nemoianu, Anca. "Richard Brautigan." *Secolul* 20(2) {Date?} 1973: 161-63.

379. Pétillon, Pierre-Yves. "Des Fjords Pluvieux.... Du Nordouest...." *Critique: Revue Générale des Publications Français et Etrangères.* 31(338) {Date?} 1975: 688-95.
   Criticism from a French perspective.

380. -----. "Lieux Américains: Richard Brautigan." *Critique: Revue Générale des Publications Français et Etrangéres.* Dec. 1972: 1054-73.
Criticism from a French perspective.

381. Puetz, Manfred. The Story of Identity: American Fiction of the Sixties. Stuttgart: J.B. Metzlersche Verlagsbuchhandlung, 1979.
Examines, from a German perspective, Brautigan's concern with the place of the individual in America and points out parallels with the Transcendentalists.

382. -----. "Transcendentalism Revived: The Fiction of Richard Brautigan." *Occident* (8) Spring 1974: 39-47.
"Though concealed by blithe indifference, carelessness, and ostentatious flippancy, a secularized and diluted version of Transcendentalism is discernible in the works of Richard Brautigan.... Yet, in spite of all resemblances Brautigan fails in his imitation of Transcendentalist attitudes and in his dual effort at dissociation and retreat.... Brautigan's failure to transform nineteenth-century attitudes into a meaningful answer to twentieth-century problems can hardly surprise, if one considers what is probably the most crucial distinction between him and his predecessors. Transcendentalism was a predominantly religious movement. Behind the detachment from all-absorbing society and the retreat to nature a distinctly religious motivation was at work. This orientation gave the Transcendentalists' flight its direction and it made nature and the simple life intermediary symbols of a universal truth and a higher order of the divine." With Brautigan, "the concrete aim of the Transcendentalist step beyond has vanished, and with its exit nature and divine primitivism have lost their symbolic qualities.... Brautigan seems to be conscious of this failure from time to time; consequently a sense of futility, waste, of being too late, and an imminent threat of being corrupted and finally taken over by the enemy taint his picture of nature. It is for this reason that the energy of repulsion carries him only a short distance in the direction of his dream."

383. Rabate, Jean-Michel. "The End-of-the-Novel and the Endings of Novels." *Etudes Anglaises* 36(2-3) Apr.-Sept. 1983: 197-212.
Mentions Brautigan's multiple endings in General.

384. Riedel, Cornelia. ["America, More Often Than Not, Is Only a Place in the Mind."] *Zur Dichotomischen Amerikakonzeption bei Richard Brautigan*. Frankfurt am Main: P. Lang, 1985.
Criticism from a German perspective.

385. Rosselli, Aldo. "Richard Brautigan piccolo eroe della controcultura." *Nuovi Argomenti* 23/24 1971: 46-50.
Criticism from an Italian perspective.

385a. Schonfelder, Karl-Heinz. "Richard Brautigan: Forellenfischen in Amerika." Weimer Beitrage: *Zeitschrift für literaturwissenschaft Asthetik und Kulturtheorie*, 34(3) 1988: 461-470.

386. Sugiura, Ginsaku. "Sonzai no Jokon kara Sonzai Jitai e: Richard Brautigan ni tsuite." [From Condition of Existence to Existence Itself.] *Eigo Seinon* [The Rising Generation] 120 1975: 450-52.
Criticism from a Japanese perspective.

387. Taylor, L. Loring. "Forma Si Substanta Umorului la Richard Brautigan." *Steaua* 24(17) 1974: 27-28.
Criticism from a Romanian perspective.

388. Tsurumi, Seiji. "Gendai Shosetsu No Ending: Pynchon, Barth, Brautigan." *Oberon: Magazine For The Study of English and American Literature*. (45) 1982: 80-93.
Compares, from a Japanese perspective, the use of narrative endings by Thomas Pynchon, John Barth, and Richard Brautigan.

389. Villar, Raso. M. "El Mito Como Consumo: Richard Brautigan." *Camp de L'Arpa: Revista de Literatura* 19 1975: 23, 25.
Criticism from a Spanish perspective.

390. Wiegensten, Roland H. "Zweimal [Twice] Richard Brautigan: II. Allerlei Geschichten—scheinbar verrückt [All Sorts of Poems—Apparently Mad]." *Merkur* (288) 26 Apr. 1972: 396-97.
Criticism from a German perspective. Says that *Trout* is for the disaffected youth at the end of the 1960s what [John]

Steinbeck's Cannery Row was for those of the 1940s and [Jack] Kerouac's On the Road was for those of the 1950s. It is Brautigan's literary version of a non-coercive pastoral counter-mythology to the demands and realities of life in technological America. The short, casual prose vignettes contain the escapist set-scenes needed for the romantic elation of his readers but they abound in snickering self-ridicule and ironic detachment that add to the intellectual pleasure by putting things into perspective.

391. Willis, David. "Icarus in Timbuktu." *Australian Journal of French Studies* 19(3) Sept.-Dec. 1982: 295-308.

A paper about the relation of metaphoric and metonymic operation. "It is no longer the critic's concern whether Timbuktu is a mirage or a reality, whether an incident in a novel or poem is a reflection of an incident in the author's life, or subconscious, or whatever; if that is no longer relevant then the pure gratuity or poetic expression returns with a vengeance. Like Richard Brautigan's poem 'Haiku Ambulance' [from Pill]: 'A piece of green pepper fell off the wooden salad bowl, so what?'"

REVIEWS OF WORKS BY BRAUTIGAN

POETRY
Titles Listed Chronologically, Citations Listed Alphabetically

The Return of the Rivers

392. Bokinsky, Caroline J. "Richard Brautigan." Dictionary of Literary Biography Vol. 5. American Poets Since World War II. Ed. Donald J. Greiner. Detroit: Gale Research Company, 1980. 96-99.
"An observation of the external world as a surreal, romanticized setting in which the cycle of life is exemplified in the river, sea, rain, and ocean."

The Galilee Hitch-Hiker

393. Bokinsky, Caroline J. "Richard Brautigan." Dictionary of Literary Biography Vol. 5. American Poets Since World War II. Ed. Donald J. Greiner. Detroit: Gale Research Company, 1980. 96-99.
"The book consists of nine separate poems in which the speaker describes his encounters with [Charles] Baudelaire, who appears in a different pose in each section."

394. Contemporary Literary Criticism. Vol. 12. Ed. Dedria Bryfonski. Detroit: Gale Research Company, 1980. 57-74.
Excerpts from 395.

395. Sorrentino, Gilbert. "Ten Pamphlets." *Poetry* April 1968: 56-61.
Comments on the "comic genius" and "camp" style of Brautigan's work.

Lay the Marble Tea

396. Bokinsky, Caroline J. "Richard Brautigan." Dictionary of Literary Biography Vol. 5. American Poets Since World War II. Ed. Donald J. Greiner. Detroit: Gale Research Company, 1980. 96-99.
"Brautigan's exploration of language extends to similes and metaphors with humorous twists...."

397. Frumkin, Gene. "A Step toward Perception." *Coastlines* 13 (Autumn) 1959: 45.
"This first book is good ore. What is needed now is to dig hard for the subject that goes with the method. What is Brautigan's bit of world? His method will ripen, I think, as that bit is finally discovered and explored."

The Octopus Frontier

398. Bokinsky, Caroline J. "Richard Brautigan." Dictionary of Literary Biography Vol. 5. American Poets Since World War II. Ed. Donald J. Greiner. Detroit: Gale Research Company, 1980. 96-99.
"Continues Brautigan's creation of order and meaning from objects in the literal world by using them to construct a fantasy world within his own imagination."

All Watched Over by Machines of Loving Grace

399. "All Watched Over by Machines of Loving Grace." The Exploited Eden: Literature on the American Environment. Ed.

Robert J. Gangewere. New York: Harper and Row, 1972. 376.
"American poets seldom portray the happy marriage of technology and the natural world. Thus the optimism of [this] poem is somewhat unique—unless the reader detects irony, in which case the poem joins the mainstream of antitechnological American verse."

400. Bokinsky, Caroline J. "Richard Brautigan." Dictionary of Literary Biography Vol. 5. American Poets Since World War II. Ed. Donald J. Greiner. Detroit: Gale Research Company, 1980. 96-99.
[This book] "provides a transition to... his most popular [collection Pill] and [establishes] his position as a poet.... Recalling the romanticism of Return while looking forward to the humor that characterizes Pill, [this] long poem... presents a vision of an ideal world where man and nature exist in harmony, 'where mammals and computers/live together mutually/programming harmony,' and where the perfect world is 'all watched over/by machines of loving grace.'"

The Pill Versus the Springhill Mine Disaster

401. Anonymous. "Books." *Time* 24 Jan. 1969: 72-76.
"In this book of selected poems Brautigan is Harlequin on a tightwire, poised between Earth and Heaven, simultaneously mocking the passions of the populace below and his own frail fumblings toward the stars.... Occasionally Brautigan fails, tumbling from his poetic perch, but the dare is worth every one of the falls."

402. Bokinsky, Caroline J. "Richard Brautigan." Dictionary of Literary Biography Vol. 5. American Poets Since World War II. Ed. Donald J. Greiner. Detroit: Gale Research Company, 1980. 96-99.
"... [I]ncludes most of the poems that appeared in previous volumes and new poems that confirm his magical powers of transforming an image into something else."

403. Brownjohn, Alan. "Absorbing Chaos." *New Statesman* 4 Dec. 1970: 772-73.
"Richard Brautigan's novels are highly praised. His poems are minor adjuncts to his prose: more coherent and funny than [Ted] Berrigan's [In The Early Morning Rain also reviewed] but with the dreadful, characteristic soft-centredness...."

404. Contemporary Literary Criticism. Vol. 3. Ed. Carolyn Riley. Detroit: Gale Research Company, 1975. 86-90.
Excerpts from 409.

405. Malley, Terence. Richard Brautigan. New York: Warner, 1972.
Chapter One deals with Pill and Rommel.

406. Nilsen, Don L.F., and Allen Pace Nilsen. "An Exploration and Defense of the Humor in Young Adult Literature." *Journal of Reading* 26 Oct. 1982: 64.
Recommends Pill, General, and Watermelon as humorous books and Richard Brautigan as a humorous author. See also 465 and 520.

407. Porter, Peter. "Dazzling Landscapes." *The Observer* 3 Jan. 1971: 30.
"I didn't enjoy Richard Brautigan. Liberated jokes and instant mysticism—his poems turn everything to favour and prettiness."

408. *The Seattle Times.*
"They are pretty special poems, for if Brautigan never writes another one, he will have left a great amount of poetry in our literature." Quoted on the first page of the Laurel Edition (1978).

409. Warsh, Lewis. "Out of Sight." *Poetry* Mar. 1970: 440-46.
Deals with Pill and Watermelon. "Brautigan writes whenever an interesting thought or phrase strikes him, or when something occurs that he feels needs to be celebrated or described. His poems are easy to read, which is a pleasure in itself, and there is very little literary feedback—that is, you're startled by what's being set down, or by a single twist either in content or in image, or by the honesty with which the poet

is expressing himself, and then you continue, turning the page, without having to look back...." See also 524.

410. Williams, Hugo. "Strolling across the Bridge." *London Magazine* (10) Feb. 1971: 81-84.
"... [S]ugary, predigested and schoolgirlish, his naiveté is actually cynical it is so accurately researched to touch the dewy and vulgar adolescent heart.... With his own heart safely given over to justified lines he has been able without a qualm to write down as low as needs be to reach that smiling majority who are always waiting.... He deserves a sucky medal with a picture of himself on it for his own personal sweetness."

Rommel Drives On Deep into Egypt

411. *Athens* (Ohio) *Messenger*.
"Publication of a Richard Brautigan book is cause for celebration.... There's not a more exciting, more challenging writer working in America today.... Finishing a Richard Brautigan book is difficult, because you don't want it to end." Quoted on the first page of the Laurel Edition (1978).

412. Bokinsky, Caroline J. "Richard Brautigan." Dictionary of Literary Biography Vol. 5. American Poets Since World War II. Ed. Donald J. Greiner. Detroit: Gale Research Company, 1980. 96-99.
"Brautigan continues his experiments with similes and metaphors... but... also begins to move into social commentary."

413. Contemporary Literary Criticism. Vol. 1. Ed. Carolyn Riley. Detroit: Gale Research Company, 1973. 44-45.
Excerpts from 416.

414. Contemporary Literary Criticism. Vol. 3. Ed. Carolyn Riley. Detroit: Gale Research Company, 1975. 86-90.
Excerpts from 423.

415. Contemporary Literary Criticism. Vol. 12. Ed. Dedria Bryfonski. Detroit: Gale Research Company, 1980. 57-74.
Excerpts from 420.

416. Horwitz, Carey A. *Virginia Quarterly* 46 (Autumn) 1970: R134.
Reprint of 417.

417. -----. "Brautigan, Richard." *Library Journal Book Review 1970*. Ed. Judith Serebnick. New York and London: Bowker Company, 1970. 442.
". . . [T]his is, not poetry for the ages, but a set of communications with this age, providing emotional correlatives that will be felt and identified with by those who can."

418. Malley, Terence. Richard Brautigan. New York: Warner, 1972.
Chapter One deals with Rommel and Pill.

419. Pritchard, William H. "Shags and Poets." *Hudson Review* 23(3) Autumn 1970: 563-77.
"Brautigan has already attained mythical status so must be something more than what used to called a wiseguy, but he's at least that and a clever one."

420. Rose, Kate. "The Grand Penny Tour: Brautigan's 'Rommel Drives on Deep into Egypt'." *Minnesota Review* 10(3-4) 1970: 115-16.
"Sometimes I just can't see his images...."

421. Spector, Robert D. "Betwixt Tradition and Innovation." *Saturday Review* 26 Dec. 1970: 25.
"Sometimes witty, always fashionable anti-Establishment, Richard Brautigan's Rommel comes off as a game children play."

422. *Syracuse News Times* .
"... [O]ne of the most original American authors alive and writing today." Quoted on the first page of the Laurel Editon (1978).

423. Williams, Jonathan. "'Anyway, All I Ever Wanted to be was a Poet.' Said Leon Uris, with a Smile, as We Strode Together

into the Vomitorium...." *Parnassus* 1 (Fall/Winter) 1972: 94-105.
"There is less here than meets the eye.... [Brautigan] writes for kids who eat macrobiotic food.... You'd starve to death on these no-cal poems."

Loading Mercury with a Pitchfork

424. Anonymous. "Brautigan, Richard." *Kirkus Review* 15 Mar. 1976: 355.
"Brautigan-the-poet is at it again... and this fey little volume, with its modest startles, immortalized yawns, and affected yet likable artlessness, should reopen the languid debate over whether what he's writing is American haiku or surrealist Rod McKuen."

425. Anonymous. "Brautigan, Richard." *The Booklist* 15 May 1976: 1329.
"Typical Brautigan whimsy, whether insightful or seemingly meaningless, in short poems with appeal mainly for the writer's following."

426. Anonymous. "Brautigan, Richard." *Choice* Sept. 1976: 815.
"The best of his works are coy little presences that won't go away, cute little poem-pooches, while the worst are harmless neighbors of the first."

427. Bokinsky, Caroline J. "Richard Brautigan." Dictionary of Literary Biography Vol. 5. American Poets Since World War II. Ed. Donald J. Greiner. Detroit: Gale Research Company, 1980. 96-99.
"Brautigan's terse messages and witty similes are overshadowed by a blacker humor and a darker, more pensive mood... filled with foreboding and pessimism."

428. Creeley, Robert.
"Weirdly delicious bullets of ineffable wisdom. Pop a few!" Quoted on the back cover of the Touchstone Edition (1976).

429. Daum, Timothy. "Brautigan, Richard." The Library Journal Book Review 1976. Ed. Janet Fletcher. New York: R.R. Bowker Company, 1977. 344.
Reprint of 430.

430. -----. "Brautigan, Richard." *Library Journal* 1 Sept. 1976: 1780.
"Brautigan's poetic style, previously centered around eclectic insights into how everyday events are transformed into art, is here reduced to quick simulacra of bitter thoughts and cynical visions—his verse abounds with misplaced love, lonely nights, and jealous stabs at previous lovers... [F]ew poetry collections can afford to be without this work."

431. Fletcher, Connie. "Brautigan, Richard." *The Booklist* 15 May 1976: 1317.
"The latest volume of poetry by a controversial novelist contains his counterculture pronouncements in several long poems fragmented into terse statements. Their quality varies from insightful and charming to puerile, posed, and maddeningly meaningless. Brautigan cultists will lead the applause."

432. Gannon, Edward. "Brautigan, Richard." *Best Sellers* 36(1) Oct. 1976: 226-27.
"It took a little under thirty minutes to read the whole book twice. I was not detained to savor. I was not puzzled or startled. Nothing obscure exploded when I'd got to the point of it. How to describe it all? Well, I suppose it's a collection of jottings. A trifle."

433. Hirschman, Jack. "Five Poets." *Poetry* July 1968: 274-75.
"... Brautigan writes simply, awkwardly like the words stumbling out of the corner of his mouth [sic].... The craft harks back to [Kenneth] Patchen, which is to say: Hello, I'm expressing myself, and that's IT."

434. McLellan, Joseph. "Paperbacks." *Washington Post BookWorld* 13 June 1976: M4.
"Brautigan's first collection of poems six years shows no growth, a lot of cuteness and just enough substance to keep you reading."

June 30th, June 30th

435. Anonymous. "Brautigan, Richard." *Kirkus Review* 1 July 1978: 743.
". . . [T]here is every once in a while a testament to the variety and flexibility of poetry that's very refreshing."

436. Anonymous. "Brautigan, Richard." *Choice* Dec. 1978: 1364-65.
Notes the desperate quality of the poems and suggests that this is "an often good book," that will be "served well by the winnowing process that will eventually take place."

437. Anonymous. "New in Paperbacks." *Washington Post BookWorld* 1 Oct. 1978: E2.
"On June 30th, 1976 the poet left Japan with this collection of limpid, haiku-like poems."

438. Bokinsky, Caroline J. "Richard Brautigan." Dictionary of Literary Biography Vol. 5. American Poets Since World War II. Ed. Donald J. Greiner. Detroit: Gale Research Company, 1980. 96-99.
"[This is] the most unified of Brautigan's volumes... because the speaker of all the poems is Brautigan himself examining his reactions to his experience."

439. Contemporary Literary Criticism. Vol. 12. Ed. Dedria Bryfonski. Detroit: Gale Research Company, 180. 57-74. Excerpts from 442 and 444.

440. Harrison, Jim.
"What can I say? It is your work that has touched me the most deeply, the least mannered and most exact in its insistent nakedness. It is not a succession of lyrics but finally ONE BOOK. A long poem that offers us its bounty in fragments. It is saturated with the 'otherness' we know to be our most honest state and the true state of poetry. It offers itself in perhaps the unconscious but ancient fabled form of the voyage. It is about the stately courage and loneliness of this voyage into a strange land which is both Japan and the true self of the poet, where there are no barriers to admitting and singing all. It is about love and exhaustion and permanent

transition, so fatal that it is beyond the poet's comprehension. I love the book because it is a true song, owning no auspices other than its own; owning the purity we think we aim at on this bloody journey." Quoted on the back cover of the Delta Editon (1978).

441. Knowles, Carrie J. "Brautigan, Richard." *The Booklist* 15 Sept. 1978: 147.
"Clearly a case of terminal poetic pretentiousness.... For devoted readers only."

442. Petticoffer, Dennis. "Brautigan, Richard." The Library Journal Book Review 1978. Ed. Janet Fletcher. New York: R.R. Bowker Company, 1979. 314.
Reprint of 443.

443. -----. "Brautigan, Richard." *Library Journal* 15 Feb. 1978: 465.
"Taken individually, many of these poems do not hold up well. Brautigan himself concedes that the collection is 'uneven.'... It may prove less enticing than Brautigan's earlier works."

444. Schuster, Arian. "Brautigan, Richard." *Young Adult Cooperative Book Review Group of Massachusetts* Dec. 1978: 18.
"A collection of eight poems, several just fragments—written... on a visit Brautigan made to Japan.... Like so many literary journeys, it becomes a point of departure for an exploration of the self in relation to the world of the nonself. The Brautigan wit is fleetingly present, but there is a haunting feeling of loneliness in the poetry—a sense of a stranger in a strange land—that ultimately makes Japan seem like a metaphor for alienation. Brautigan fans may like this; but he has moved away from the concerns of the young adult, and if one already has Brautigan books, skip this one."

445. Stuttaford, Genevieve. "Brautigan, Richard." *Publishers Weekly* 23 Jan. 1978: 371.
"Meant to be an intimate record, the book is merely haphazard. Brautigan devotees... will wince and wonder at this decline in Brautigan's talent."

446. Taylor, David M. Dictionary of Literary Biography. Yearbook: 1980. Eds. Karen L. Rood, Jean W. Ross, and Richard Ziegfeld. Detroit: Gale Research Co., 1981. 18-21.
"[This] collection of poetry in diary form, records Brautigan's first visit to Japan in the spring of 1976. The title is based on the date of departure for the United States after his seven-week sojourn, the date repeated because the day is recaptured as the airplane crosses the international date line. The tone of the... poems shifts at fairly identifiable junctures in correspondence with the author's changes in mood."

NOVELS
Titles Listed Chronologically, Citations Listed Alphabetically

A Confederate General from Big Sur

447. An Annotated Bibliography of California Fiction, 1664-1970. Eds. Newton D. Baird and Robert Greenwood. Georgetown, California: Talisman Literary Research, 1971. 55.
"Story of a 'beat character' who, together with a few like-minded friends, wander around San Francisco and Big Sur, collectively believing in, among other things, an apparently mythical ancestor and marijuana."

448. Anonymous. "Brautigan, Richard." *Choice* May 1965: 156.
"This work exists primarily within the pastoral-primitive tradition of the American novel... [and] does not pretend to high seriousness. It is well wrought and suitable for undergraduates beyond the freshman level."

449. Anonymous. "A Confederate General from Big Sur." *Playboy* Mar. 1965: 22.
"... [A] surrealist synopsis of everything that was worth missing in the now-fading literary scene."

450. Bienen, Leigh B. "New American Fiction." *Transition* 5(20) 1965: 46-51.
Says General resembles "discursive essays on search for self.... The vague and aimless observer who describes the events in General seems to bounce unfeelingly back from a series of odd and sometimes amusing encounters with fellow

eccentrics... without finding either himself or much else of any interest."

451. Brown, F. J. "Richard Brautigan." *Books & Bookmen* Apr. 1971: 46-47.
"This is a surrealist novel kept going by the exuberance of the author's invention. Until almost the end it capers satisfyingly enough... on the edge of reality. Curiously enough, it collapses into something like flatness when he ends up describing a 'trip' on hallucinatory drugs.

452. Cadogan, Lucy. "New from Africa." *New Statesman* 29 Jan. 1971: 155.
"I liked the book."

453. Ciardi, John.
"Brautigan manages effects the English novel has never produced before." Quoted on the back cover of the Evergreen Black Cat edition (1970).

454. Coleman, John. "Irishman at Large." *The Observer* 31 Jan. 1971: 23.
"Richard Brautigan is an acquired taste and his... General will be too slack and sugary for many.... Typically, Mr. Brautigan supplies five or six alternative endings."

455. Contemporary Literary Criticism. Vol. 12. Ed. Dedria Bryfonski. Detroit: Gale Research Company, 1980. 57-74.
Excerpts from 461 and 468.

456. Gilroy, Harry. "End Papers." *The New York Times* 24 Feb. 1965: 39.
Mr. Brautigan is a writer. Somewhat funny, somewhat coarse, somewhat pointless—but let it be said again, funny—he has transmuted Big Sur into surrealism."

457. Gold, Arthur. "Fun in Section Eight." *Book Week* 14 Feb. 1965: 18.
"The best thing about Richard Brautigan's first published novel is the language, which is consistently more inventive and delicate than you might expect from one of the so-called 'Beats'.... His metaphors alone make... good whimsical

reading. Perhaps however, General might have been more than merely whimsical if there had been more tension between the imagined society and the one we all live in, or between the writer's fancy and his reason."

458. Hogan, William. "Rebels in the War with Life." *Saturday Review* 13 Feb. 1965: 49-50.
"A comic valentine from the subterraneans that rattles on like a tattoo on a bongo drum. [William] Saroyan, [Jack] Kerouac, and the ghost of Sherwood Anderson may have been looking over Brautigan's shoulder as he shaped his prose."

459. Killinger, J.R. "Some Novels for the Pastor's Study." *Theology Today* July 1979: 251-57.
"Among numerous other fine novels claiming the minister's attention [is] Richard Brautigan's General (a hilarious 'American' novel in the tradition of Mark Twain, Stephen Crane, and Ernest Hemingway)."

460. Levin, Martin. "A Reader's Report." *The New York Times Book Review* 24 Jan. 1965: 42.
"Richard Brautigan... has put into General some essential beatificnick ingredients.... Mr. Brautigan throws in some surrealist (sorry) whimsy... a touch here and there of artiness—and a selection of five possible endings. I don't like any of them."

461. Locklin, Gerald and Charles Stetler. "Some Observations on A Confederate General from Big Sur." *Critique* 13(2) 1971: 72-82.
Compares the similiar uses of symbolism in General, The Sun Also Rises, and The Great Gatsby and points out the contradictions in General, primarily in the tension between characterization and apparent themes.

462. *Los Angeles Herald Examiner* .
"An amazing story.... You'll feel better about the whole world after reading this." Quoted on the back cover of the Evergreen Black Cat edition (1970).

463. Malley, Terence. Richard Brautigan. New York: Warner, 1972.
Chapter Five deals with General.

464. Muggeridge, Malcom. "Books." *Esquire* Apr. 1965: 58-60.
    "... General provides as good an account as has come my way of Beat life and humor.... Poor Beats! Mr. Brautigan has convinced me that we are better off without them."

465. Nilsen, Don L.F., and Allen Pace Nilsen. "An Exploration and Defense of the Humor in Young Adult Literature." *Journal of Reading* 26 Oct. 1982: 64.
    Recommends General, Watermelon, and Pill as humorous books and Brautigan as a humorous author. See also 520 and 406.

466. Nye, Robert. "A Confederate General from Big Sur." *The Times* (London) 28 Jan. 1971: F11.
    "Very whimsical, very fantastical, very American-agrarian by the author of Trout. And oh it flows."

467. Parkinson, Thomas. *San Francisco Chronicle*.
    "An absorbing, irritating, and terribly amusing book... that brings to American humor a new and disturbing voice." Quoted on the back cover of the Evergreen Black Cat edition (1970).

468. Rahv, Phillip. "New American Fiction." *The New York Review of Books* 8 Apr. 1965: 8-10.
    "... [S]trikes me as very crude indeed.... There is little to say of Richard Brautigan's General except that it is only a series of improvised scenes in the manner of Jack Kerouac. It is pop-writing of the worst kind, full of vapid jokes and equally vapid sex-scenes which are also a joke, though scarcely in the sense intended by the author."

469. Randall, Dudley. [The Confederate general...] *Negro Digest* Aug. 1965: 92.
    [Brautigan] "seems to write whatever comes first to the top of his head, and what comes out is sometimes meaningless, sometimes inane and sometimes a nice simile or metaphor. The characters are zany like those in comic strips. The book is froth, and like the fiction of ladies' magazines, is to be read in a summer hammock or in bed when you can't go to sleep, and then be forgotten."

470. Rollyson, Carl E., Jr. "The Confederate General from Big Sur." Masterplots II. American Fiction Series. 4 vols. Ed. Frank N. Magill. Englewood Cliffs, NJ: Salem Press, 1986. Vol. 1, 325-29.

"As Edward Halsey Foster (See 358) puts it, 'the feeling that an individual should not be understood primarily as a function of time and place, as a psychological compromise between public and private needs, but rather as a self potentially and ideally independent of history underlies Brautigan's best work.' That human beings are only 'potentially and ideally independent of history' is what accounts for the melancholy strain and truncated achievement of much of the author's work."

471. Tannenbaum, Earl. "Brautigan, Richard." *Library Journal* 15 Mar. 1965: 1345.

"Less than a novel, this series of impressionistic sketches manages to catch the 'beat' character without the usual false seriousness so common to the genre... whimsy there is aplenty."

472. Van Vactor, Anita. "Hip Elect." *The Listener* 28 Jan. 1971: 121.

"Brautigan seems to imply, a temporary community of the hip elect, free of ego hang-ups and cohering, in its own improbable way, by delicate spiritual affinities, by 'touching the same ether.'... What troubles me about this book is that you can't read it without joining it. It practices a special form of elitism: on the face of things, its manner is open and amiable, it 'hangs loose,' and yet its fun seems deliberately calculated to provoke defensive responses, and if you do respond defensively, if you don't dig, you're out—there's no other provision made for you."

473. Waugh, Auberon. "The Rest of the Iceberg." *Spectator* 27 Feb. 1971: 287-88.

"Mr. Brautigan writes five thousand times better than [Jack] Kerouac ever did, and could easily produce some modern equivalent of W.H. Davie's Autobiography of a Super-Tramp with a little more effort, a little more discipline and a little less of the semi-articulate exhibitionism which is what people apparently mean nowadays when they talk of 'creative writing'."

474. Wordsworth, Christopher. "Bleak Choice." *Guardian Weekly* 20 Feb. 1971: 18.
"As usual Brautigan is celebrating the American dream at a point where the stallions of hope have long since turned to dead meat on the prairie, or into clotheshorses, or any of the absurd turns that dreams can take, in a tumbleweed style that can shift through rapture, mock-rapture, to nonsense, with matching inconsequentiality."

Trout Fishing in America

475. Allen, Trevor. "Richard Brautigan." *Books & Bookmen* June 1973: 138.
"This wayout pop writer angles for more than trout in river of life, gets some magical catches."

476. Anonymous. "Polluted Eden." *The Times Literary Supplement* 14 Aug. 1970: 893.
Review and comparison of Trout and Watermelon. Says "Watermelon has the charm of the fairy story it almost is. But it has neither the emotional complexity, nor the imaginative ingenuity, nor the implicit historical and cultural awareness, nor the acute and tough critical-mindedness of Trout."

477. Bales, Kent. "Fishing the Ambivalence, or, a Reading of 'Trout Fishing in America'." *Western Humanities Review* 29 (Winter) 1975: 29-42.
Says that Trout discloses the relationship of the individual ambivalence to its social forms in creating and deriving the social myths we live by. Brautigan's literary art, suggest[s] the better way of recapturing the simple while remaining aware of the complex.

478. Brand, Stewart. "Trout Fishing in America." The Last Whole Earth Catalog: Access to Tools. Ed. Stewart Brand. Menlo Park, CA: Portola Institute, 1971. 254.
"If it's fish you're after, go to p. 280. For headfishing, stick around."

479. Busani, Marina. "Altre Seduzioni: Trout Fishing in America di Richard Brautigan." *Il Lettore di Provincia* (60) 16 Mar. 1985: 50-59.
    Criticism from an Italian perspective.

480. Ciardi, John.
    "The man's a writer and the writing takes over in its own way, which is what writing should do. Brautigan manages effects the English novel has never produced before." Quoted on the back cover of the Delta edition (1969).

481. Clayton, John. "Richard Brautigan: The Politics of Woodstock." New American Review, #11. Ed. Theodore Solotaroff. New York: Simon and Schuster, 1971. 56-68.
    Deals with Trout and Brautigan's "sense of life and... politics." Clayton says the novel reflects the nostalgia "for a simpler, more human, pre-industrial America.... Brautigan's value is in giving us a pastoral vision which can water our spirits as we struggle." But there is a downside, the danger that both Brautigan and the youth culture "will forget the struggle," because of tendencies to escape into a nostalgia "which cannot be a viable social future."

482. Cleary, Michael. "Richard Brautigan's Gold Nib: Artistic Independence in 'Trout Fishing in America'." *English Record* 35 [Second Quarter] 1984: 18-20.
    "... Trout can be read... as an insistence that every artist must free himself from all literary shackles and discover his unique artistic consciousness, one most compatible with his vision.... Ultimately, Brautigan's understanding of artistic autonomy satisfies only himself.... It is significant that the last Trout Fishing metaphor is "The Trout Fishing in America Nib," the narrator's gold-tipped fountain pen which clearly represents his coming to terms with his artistic purpose."

483. Coleman, John. "Finny Peculiar." *The Observer* 26 July 1970: 25.
    Reviews both Trout and Watermelon. "Trout is a pleasant surprise, though probably not so for aspiring anglers. It's a little as if Hemingway had stopped worrying about his masculinity, being a simple anecdotal ramble around memories and rural America." See also 510.

484. Contemporary Literary Criticism. Vol. 42. Eds. Daniel G. Marowski and Roger Matuz. Detroit: Gale Research Company, 1980. 48-66.
Excerpts from 230, 277, and 503.

485. Contemporary Literary Criticism. Vol. 12. Ed. Dedria Bryfonski. Detroit: Gale Research Company, 1980. 57-74.
Excerpts from 311, 481, 491, and 499.

486. Contemporary Literary Criticism. Vol. 5. Ed. Carolyn Riley. Detroit: Gale Research Company, 1976. 67-72.
Excerpts from 477, 492, and 506.

487. Downing, Pamela. "On the Creation and Use of English Compound Nouns." *Language* Dec. 1977: 810-42.
Collects and analyzes "non-lexicalized compounds" (noun+noun combinations) in Trout and Monster. See also 585.

488. Farrell, J.G. "Hair Brained." *Spectator* 8 Aug. 1970: 133.
Review of Trout and Watermelon. Says "the best of Trout is very good indeed." Concludes by saying that Brautigan's writing, "when he has his imagination under control, however, is frequently splendid and his imagery so supple as to make more conventional writers look hopelessly musclebound." See also 514.

489. Fiene, Donald M. "Trout Fishing in America." Masterplots II. American Fiction Series. 4 vols. Ed. Frank N. Magill. Englewood Cliffs, NJ: Salem Press, 1986. Vol. 4, 1702-06.
"Some of [his] earlier novels received respectful critical attention, especially by young academic critics, but most... were dismissed by established critics as trivial, embarrassing, crazy, or simply too cute. Measured against all of Brautigan's writings, one sees that Trout is the author's best work—an inspired first novel. Even the critics who do not admire his later works would allow that Trout was and will be the true and abiding voice of the flower children who bloomed for a few short years and then disappeared."

Reviews—Novels

490. Furbank, P.N. "Pacific Nursery." *The Listener* 6 Aug. 1970: 186.
     General discussion of Trout and Watermelon. Says "... it is best to think of them as children's books."

491. Hayden, Brad. "Echoes of 'Walden' in 'Trout Fishing in America'." *Thoreau Journal Quarterly* Jul. 1976: 21-26.
     "... [S]imilarities between [Henry David] Thoreau's Walden and Brautigan's novel [Trout] are very striking both in the form their arguments take, as well as the arguments themselves."

492. Hearron, Thomas. "Escape through Imagination in 'Trout Fishing in America'." *Critique* 16(1) 1974: 25-31.
     "The novel's theme, much like that of [William] Wordsworth's 'The Prelude,' is the development of the power of the imagination... [through which] one can still achieve an escape to the wilderness and a salvation from the anxieties of the city—even a mechanized, urban America from which literal escape and salvation have become increasingly harder to attain.

493. *Kansas City Star.*
     "My thanks to Mr. Brautigan for an enjoyable evening's reading." Quoted on the back cover of the Delta edition (1969).

494. Kolin, Phillip C. "Food for Thought in Richard Brautigan's Trout Fishing in America." *Studies in Contemporary Satire: A Creative and Critical Journal* 8 (Spring) 1981: 9-20.
     Says Brautigan uses literal and metaphorical images of food to "praise America's lost virtues or satirize its present vices. From the first chapter where the poor are deceived with a spinach leaf sandwich to the last word of the novel ('mayonnaise') food is a symbolic staple in Brautigan's satiric inventory of American values."

495. {Lottman, Eileen?}. "Trout Fishing in America." *Publishers Weekly* 3 Jan. 1972: 66.
     "... [T]his book is like a carelessly-strung chain of beads—some plastic, chipped and broken, some perfect

diamonds... the whole is an almost beautiful puzzle with pieces missing."

496. Malley, Terence. **Richard Brautigan**. New York: Warner, 1972.
Chapter Six deals with Trout.

497. Martins, Heitor. "Pescando Trutas na América com Richard Brautigan." *Minas Gerais, Suplemento Literário* 30 Aug. 1975: 6.
Criticism from a Brazilian perspective.

498. Parkinson, Thomas. *San Francisco Chronicle*.
"In a world where people seriously think about the unthinkable, this book accepts the unacceptable, believes the incredible, and describes the indescribable. The result is an absorbing, irritating, and terrible amusing book." Quoted on the back cover of the Delta edition (1969).

499. Ritterman, Pamela. "Trout Fishing in America." *Commonweal* 26 Sept. 1969: 601.
"Trout is a funny, delightful book that draws freely on American mythic attitudes, the tones and rhythms of drifting, searching out trout streams, thinking slow thoughts in wide country."

500. Scheneck, Stephen. "Trout Fishing in America." *Ramparts* Dec. 1967: 80-87.
A glowing review lauding Brautigan's style and his disposition to see the bright side of American life. Ends by saying something good is "cooking on the American hot plate. Thank you Mr. Brautigan, for a change it isn't naked lunch."

501. Seib, Kenneth. "Trout Fishing in America: Brautigan's Funky Fishing Yarn." *Critique* 13(2) 1971: 63-71.
"Trout is a solid achievement in structure, significance, and narrative technique. For all its surface pecularity, moreover, the book is centrally located within a major tradition of the American novel—the romance—and is conditioned by Brautigan's concern with the bankrupt ideals of the American past.... Lying just below the comic exuberance of the book, furthermore, is the myth of the American Adam, the ideal of

the New World Eden that haunts American fiction from [James Fenimore] Cooper to the present. The narrator is... modern man longing for the restoration of the agrarian simplicity of pioneer America."

502. Siegel, Mark. "Trout Fishing in America." <u>Survey of Modern Fantasy Literature</u>. 5 vols. Ed. Frank N. Magill. Englewood Cliffs, NJ: Salem Press, 1983. Vol. 4, 1979.

"<u>Trout</u> is a collage of excerpts and images bound together by the presence of an anonymous narrator, peculiar references to trout fishing, and a unique, hypnotic literary voice... America desperately needs to cope with its present, unsettled reality. Imagination [as portrayed metaphorically by the character Trout Fishing in America] is a potent form, but it must be used to construct rather than merely to escape."

503. Stull, William L. "Richard Brautigan's <u>Trout Fishing in America</u>: Notes of a Native Son." *American Literature* Mar. 1984: 68-80.

"Dark, deep, and teeming with remembrances of things past, Brautigan's 'trout stream of consciousness' branches off the mainstream of American literature."

504. Tanner, Tony. <u>City of Words: American Fiction 1950-1970</u>. New York: Harper & Row, 1971 and London: Jonathan Cape, 1971. 393, 406-15.

Examines Brautigan's use of language and the place of <u>Trout</u> in American literature calling it "refreshingly new, unhysterical, unegotistical, often magical... a minor classic.... Each chapter is a separate fragment, unpredictable because unrelated in any of the usual ways. Each one engages us for a moment with its humour, or strangeness, or unusual evocation, and then fades away.... It is one of Brautigan's distinctive achievements that his magically delicate verbal ephemera seem to accomplish their own vanishings."

505. -----. "The Dream and the Pen." *The Times* (London) 25 July 1970: 5.

"...[O]ne of the most original and attractive novels to have come out of America during the last decade.... In <u>Trout</u>, Richard Brautigan has already added a minor classic to American literature."

506. Vanderwerken, David L. "Trout Fishing in America and the American Tradition." *Critique* 16(1) 1974: 32-40.
"In choosing to write the kind of fiction that he does—symbolic, parabolic, fantastic—Brautigan clearly aligns himself with the tradition of American romancers, as opposed to that of the realists. The 'actual and imaginary' collide on every page of Trout. In his conviction that the imaginative ideal America is the only true America, Brautigan joins the tradition of [Henry David] Thoreau, who says: 'Time is but the stream I go a-fishing in. I drink at it; but while I drink I see the sandy bottom and detect how shallow it is. Its thin current slides away, but eternity remains.'... As with Thoreau, all ultimates are absorbed into and transcended by the imagination in an effort to create a universe that 'answers to our conceptions'."

507. The Viking Press.
"Mr. Brautigan submitted a book to us in 1962 called Trout. I gather from the reports that it was not about trout." Quoted on the back cover of the Delta edition (1969).

In Watermelon Sugar

508. Allen, Trevor. "Richard Brautigan." *Books & Bookmen* Apr. 1973: 141.
"Still more fantasy about people who've rejected hate, violence of old gang, lead gentle lives in watermelon sugar. An allegory not to everyone's taste but individual; a cult among US young."

509. Anonymous. "Polluted Eden." *The Times Literary Supplement* 14 Aug. 1970: 893.
Review and comparison of Trout and Watermelon. "Watermelon has the charm of the fairy story it almost is. But it has neither the emotional complexity, nor the imaginative ingenuity, nor the implicit historical and cultural awareness, nor the acute and tough critical-mindedness of Trout."

510. Coleman, John. "Finny Peculiar." *The Observer* 26 July 1970: 25.
Reviews Trout and Watermelon. Says, concerning Watermelon, "There may be an idea lurking and Mr. Brautigan has a genuine gift for imposing the unexpected, a loner's vision. But this myth, slackly sustained, dismisseth me." See also 483.

511. Contemporary Literary Criticism. Vol. 3. Ed. Carolyn Riley. Detroit: Gale Research Company, 1975. 86-90.
Excerpts from 524.

512. Contemporary Literary Criticism. Vol. 5. Ed. Carolyn Riley. Detroit: Gale Research Company, 1976. 67-72.
Excerpts from 516 and 517.

513. Contemporary Literary Criticism. Vol. 9. Ed. Dedria Bryfonski. Detroit: Gale Research Company, 1978. 123-25.
Excerpts from 296.

514. Farrell, J.G. "Hair Brained." *Spectator* 8 Aug. 1970: 133.
Review of Watermelon and Trout. Calls Watermelon "a fairy story." Says, "when [Brautigan] has his imagination under control, however, is frequently splendid and his imagery so supple as to make more conventional writers look hopelessly musclebound." See also 488.

515. Furbank, P.N. "Pacific Nursery." *The Listener* 6 Aug. 1970: 186.
General discussion of Trout and Watermelon. Says "... it is best to think of them as children's books."

516. Hernlund, Patricia. "Author's Intent: In Watermelon Sugar." *Critique* 16(1) 1974: 5-17.
Discusses the emotional repression and the deprivation that is necessary for "the gentle life" in Watermelon to succeed. "Brautigan judges his utopian commune and finds it wanting, and 'the curious lack of emotion' is the very reason for the negative judgement. Brautigan reminds us that a worse thing than violence and death could be a life without pity or joy."

517. Leavitt, Harvey. "The Regained Paradise of Brautigan's In Watermelon Sugar." *Critique* 16(1) 1974: 18-24.
"By any standard, most utopian novels are not exciting reading, and yet an emotional appeal that demands every man to speculate on a future good exerts a pulling force on the reader. Brautigan takes us a step beyond because he bends the language, he shapes a universe of half-inch rivers and grand old trout, statues of grass and a waste land that even the birds avoid. The poet is inseparable from the novelist, so utopia gains a new dimension.... The novel finally becomes the new Genesis, the bible for a new world, with new assumptions, that is carried in the hearts of the young. Such moral stricture according to Brautigan is naturally rather than divinely inspired."

518. Malley, Terence. Richard Brautigan. New York: Warner, 1972.
Chapter Three deals with Watermelon.

519. *Newsweek*.
"Watermelon... is Brautigan at his best." Quoted on the back cover of the Laurel Edition (1981). Excerpted from 803.

520. Nilsen, Don L.F., and Allen Pace Nilsen. "An Exploration and Defense of the Humor in Young Adult Literature." *Journal of Reading* 26 Oct. 1982: 64.
Recommends Watermelon, General, and Pill, as humorous books and Brautigan as a humorous author. See also 406 and 465.

521. Rohrberger, Mary. "In Watermelon Sugar." Masterplots II. American Fiction Series. 4 vols. Ed. Frank N. Magill. Englewood Cliffs, NJ: Salem Press, 1986. Vol. 2, 787-91.
"... [I]t is certain that Watermelon will be numbered among the lasting works of the 1960s—a book which captures as few others do the spirit of that extraordinary moment in American history."

522. Rohrberger, Mary and Peggy C. Gardner. "Multicolored Loin Cloths, Glass, Trinkets of Words: Surrealism in In

<u>Watermelon Sugar</u>." *Ball State University Forum* 23(1) Winter 1982: 61-67.
"<u>Watermelon</u> is the Surrealist aesthetic. It is an exercise in language, a magical incantation in which words link in syncretic fashion—the I and the not I, the interior and the exterior, the dream and reality, even silence and speech."

523. Tanner, Tony. "The Dream and the Pen." *The Times* (London) 25 July 1970: 5G.
Deals mostly with <u>Trout</u> but Tanner says <u>Watermelon</u> is a "charming and original work; perhaps a little too obvious in its parabolic form—though the parable itself is extremely relevant."

524. Warsh, Lewis. "Out of Sight." *Poetry* Mar. 1970: 440-46.
Deals with <u>Watermelon</u> and <u>Pill</u>. "In... [Watermelon] the pace... is incredibly slow, almost listless: most of the activity seems the cause of something happening outside the persons involved.... Like Brautigan's other novels, this one is written in very short sections, so that a single consecutive activity... often takes several sections; and this is where the possibilities of transition or pacing take control of the book, for it's just as much how you read—how fast or slow—as what has actually been written that is important, how you let the weight of that simplicity stay in your head." See also 409.

The Abortion: An Historical Romance 1966

525. Adams, Phoebe-Lou. "The Abortion." *Atlantic* Apr. 1971: 104.
"Mr. Brautigan's prose is spirited and ingenious, and he defies sentimental convention by depicting a clean, sane, and efficient illegal abortionist."

526. Anonymous. "Brautigan, Richard." *Kirkus Review* 1 Jan. 1971: 16.
"You can't really persuade yourself into thinking this is important, but you can easily be charmed by its gentle, funny, offbeat state of innocence which is its most appealing assumption and best protection."

527. Anonymous. "Brautigan, Richard." *The Booklist* 1 July 1971: 894.
"On one level the novel is a portrayal of contemporary California hedonism, on another it is a profile of a society that takes deposits from life but gives back no issue to mankind."

528. Anonymous. "Brautigan, Richard." *Choice* Oct. 1971: 1010.
"Brautigan's world is one-third wish-fulfillment, one-third escape, and one-third gentle longing for a simplicity and detachment that modern America repudiates. Hence, his fans' continuing appetite for his ingratiating books. This one will not disappoint them."

529. Anonymous. "Paperbacks." *Best Sellers* 32(1) Apr. 1972: 24.
Classifies this book as suitable only for adults because of advanced content. "Richard Brautigan's 'The Abortion' is about footless fumblers and libraries and abortion...."

530. Anonymous. "Precious Little: Richard Brautigan; The Abortion: An Historical Romance 1966." *The Times Literary Supplement* 2 Feb. 1973: 113.
"There is possibly a minor talent flitting round somewhere in Mr. Brautigan's books. He will continue to write and be read; but it is too late for him ever to begin to try."

531. Baker, Roger. "Fiction." *The Times* (London) 1 Feb. 1973: 12.
"A gentle little book, wittingly written and nicely structured."

532. Bannon, Barbara A. "The Abortion." *Publishers Weekly* 25 Jan. 1971: 258.
"Brautigan is... the most authentic spokesman the Age of Aquarius has yet produced.... A gentle and loving book with a curiously innocent approach to life."

533. Blakeston, Oswell. "Richard Brautigan." *Books & Bookmen* Mar. 1973: 76.
"... [W]hat happened suddenly to Mr. B's originality? Yet however much one grieves for the collapse of invention, I think the book is still worth your attention for the lovely whacky wayout library operation."

534. Butwin, Joseph. "The Abortion: An Historical Romance 1966." *Saturday Review* 12 June 1971: 52, 67.
Brautigan's work reflects current questions, trends, and problems in American culture. The manner in which Brautigan deals with these makes him simultaneously a mythmaker and a myth. "That a cult should grow around Brautigan is no accident.... Everything he writes reinforces the modern sense that literary style might also be a life-style. His writing is as brief and immediate as a telegram or a message left on a door for a friend."

535. Cabibbo, Paola. "The Abortion: An Historical Romance 1966 di Richard Brautigan, Ovuero l'Aborto dell'Eroe." in Sigfrido nel Nuovo Mondo: Studi sulla Narrativa D'iniziazione. Ed. Paola Cabibbo. Rome: Goliardica 1983. 206-16.
Review from an Italian perspective.

536. Clark, William Bedford. "Abortion and the Missing Moral Center: Two Case Histories from the Post-Modern Novel." *Xavier Review* 4(1-2) 1984: 70-75.
"Since the Supreme Court's 1973 decision... virtually all legal restraints on abortion have been lifted by judicial fiat: In a secular society, what is legal is assumed to be moral. The attitudes behind the Court's decision, and those in turn nurtured by it, are now finding fictional expression, and I believe that... Richard Brautigan's Abortion... is useful if we are to grasp the literary consequences of this radical shift in values.... While Brautigan presents his characters in a sympathetic enough light... his own attitude toward their actions remains tentative and ambiguous. This ambiguity, a vital one in my estimation, stems from the fact that the novel lacks a definable moral center. The author is unwilling to condemn abortion outright, but neither is he willing to avoid its reality—life is destroyed in the process.... Instead, he wrestles, however inconclusively, with the painful dilemmas arising from a clash of old and new moralities. He is wiser than his characters, perhaps wiser than he knows, and as a result his novel has a measure of moral complexity that repays the efforts of the reader, Christian or otherwise, who is willing to approach it seriously."

537. Coats, Reed. "Brautigan, Richard." *Library Journal* July 1971: 2375.
"... [P]lot, even a crazy one is essentially unessential... as one enjoys Brautigan, if at all, for style rather than structure. For uninitiated freaks (and mature YAs [young adults]) a treat is in store; for his fans this is once again satisfying fare."

538. *College Review Service*.
"His new novel... is about 'the romantic possibilities of a public library in California.' There are, as one would expect, many delicious moments in the book such as the first time the Librarian and Vida make love.... A gentle, funny, beautiful, serious book, and old Brautigan fans will not be disappointed." Quoted on the first page of the Pocket Books Edition (1971).

539. Contemporary Literary Criticism. Vol. 3. Ed. Carolyn Riley. Detroit: Gale Research Company, 1975. 86-90.
Excerpts from 530 and 560.

540. Contemporary Literary Criticism. Vol. 12. Ed. Dedria Bryfonski. Detroit: Gale Research Company, 1980. 57-74.
Excerpts from 533, 549, and 561.

541. Contemporary Literary Criticism. Vol. 42. Eds. Daniel G. Marowski and Roger Matuz. Detroit: Gale Research Company, 1980. 48-66.
Excerpts from 542.

542. Hackenberry, Charles. "Romance and Parody in Brautigan's 'The Abortion'." *Critique* 23(2) 1981-1982: 24-36.
"The greatest strength of [Abortion] is that it is not just parody. The work is also a testimony to the enduring truth of literary forms, however incomplete and imperfect—their power to shape human behavior and render psychological reality in dream-like sketches."

543. Hill, Susan. "Americas." *The Listener* 25 Jan. 1973: 124.
"... [A] third-year Creative Writing student turning in Abortion as an exercise would do well to rate C minus.... A total absence of good writing, perceptive description or insights into human purpose, though there's plenty of non-philosophy. A charismatic name dosen't make up for a lack of

literary quality. Being a cult-hero hasn't done Mr. Brautigan's work much good."

544. Hughes, Catherine. "The Abortion." *America* 12 June 1971: 616-17
"... Brautigan writes with such style and insouciance that it all winds up surprisingly disarming, even engaging. Off the edges somewhere there's a nice little allegory, but it never gets in the way of Abortion being an almost pleasant little book."

545. Keele, A. F. "Ethics in Embryo-Abortion and the Problem of Morality in Post-War German Literature." *Germanic Review* 51(3) 1976: 229-41.

546. Kroll, Stephen. "Very natural and no childbirth." *Washington Post Book World* 28 Mar. 1971: 3.
"The patterns of our lives and the way things just happen to happen. The search for self. Gentle laughter. The likelihood of unlikely romance. The absurdities of human beings. All these are a part of Abortion.... Bizarre putdowns... acute comic observations.... Who but Brautigan could divide a seduction into four parts and get away with it?... A whimsical delight."

547. Lahr, Anthea. "Bed and Books." *National Observer* 31 May 1971: 18-19.
"The simple story is told with just enough wit and irony to keep the reader interested, but the writing too often veers toward pretentiousness... . Like its central act, this book is fast and competent, with nothing left afterwards."

548. Langlois, Jim. "Brautigan, Richard." *Library Journal* 15 May 1971: 1726.
Says Brautigan is "carving out new syntax, his own geography of the imagination."

549. Lask, Thomas. "Move Over, Mr. Tolstoy." *The New York Times* 30 Mar. 1971: 33.
Says "the substance of Abortion is thin to the point of invisibility."

550. *Look.*
"Richard Brautigan is slowly joining [Hermann] Hesse, [William] Golding, [J. D.] Salinger and [Kurt] Vonnegut as a literary magus to the literate young." Quoted on the first page of the Pocket Books Edition (1972).

551. Major, Clarence. "Open Letters." *American Poetry Review* 4(1) Jan.-Feb. 1975: 29.
Reviews Abortion and Monster in the form of a letter to a friend. "The way I see it, this book [Abortion] is making fun of the conventional novel, laughing out one side of its mouth at the routines expected of novels. It seems to be a story about innner solitude and outward needs." See also 592.

552. Malley, Terence. Richard Brautigan. New York: Warner, 1972.
Chapter Five deals with Abortion.

553. Mount, Douglas. "A Counterculture 'Love Story'." *Life* 26 Mar. 1971: 14.
"Literary critics and particularly friends of Richard Brautigan should stop taking him so seriously.... [He is] a pleasing lightweight, writing harmless and often smile-provoking fantasies about a kind of super-cool, hassle-free, semi-stoned life that a lot of the young in this country have been trying awfully hard to live."

554. Peterson, Clarence. "More than Meets the Eye." *Chicago Tribune Book World* 30 May 1971: 9.
"There is not much to... Abortion, but what there is is a whimsical delight which appears to have been written in no more time than it takes to read it."

555. Phillips, Al. "Brautigan, Richard." *Best Sellers* 15 May 1971: 78-79.
"A far-out library for far-out folks with a side trip to Tiajuana to receive an abortion. That is the way to review 'The Abortion' in capsule form.... May I suggest that before reading 'The Abortion' you go out and buy a string of beads, a buckskin jacket, open-toed sandals and refrain from bathing for at least a week. You will then be ready to read 'The Abortion.' No pain, no worry, and above all, relax."

556. Pritchard, William H. "Stranger than Truth." *Hudson Review* 24(2) Summer 1971: 355-68.
"I was also pleased by the throwaway quality of many lines in Richard Brautigan's latest historical romance.... [I] had no fear of being bludgeoned to death by overactive prose."

557. *Rutgers Daily Telegram*.
"Abortion is not very different from Brautigan's other novels. There is the same delicate and erotic exploration of the world, with Brautigan making love to every word that he uses to describe it. There is also that same strange and beautiful talent for saying simply the things that we all know but find difficult to say out loud.... Brautigan has written another very ecstatic novel celebrating life." Quoted on the back cover of the Pocket Books Edition (1972).

558. Sampson, Sally. "Hang-Ups." *New Statesman* 2 Feb. 1973: 169.
"Amusing as they are, I confess to finding Brautigan's parables a bit cloying; certainly a little of his faux-naif style goes a long way, and it can degenerate into self-parody...."

559. *San Francisco Examiner & Chronicle*.
"But there is nothing like Richard Brautigan anywhere. Perhaps, when we are very old, people will write 'Brautigans,' just as we now write novels. Just a genre, a whole new shot, a thing needed, delightful, and right. At the same time, and this is very important, Brautigan's style, strange as it is, is as easy to read as the plainest prose of say, science fiction or detective stories. You start in, and within three pages you are trapped until the book ends." Quoted on the first page of the Laurel Edition (1981).

560. Skow, John. "Cookie Baking in America." *Time* 5 Apr. 1971: 94-95.
"Brautigan... floats through his books on pure talent. If he does not seem to work very hard at his writing, well, they repealed the Protestant work ethic after all and insouciance is one of his major attractions."

561. Smith, Mason. "Pink and Fading, in Watermelon Ink." *The New York Times Book Review* 28 Mar. 1971, Sec. 7: 4, 16.

"The... book is written almost entirely with sugar-water sprezzatura... watermelon ink which one imagines to be vaguely pink and fading while one reads.... Abortion is short, swift and formally neat, and though it contains some very offbeat experimental writing, this experiment along the limits of the watermelon thinness of Brautigan's ink is cheeky enough, and there are enough indelible sketches where the watermelon ink rinses out some India...."

562. Sprug, Joseph W. "Professionally Speaking." *Catholic Library World* Apr. 1972: 474-77.

"I... found this frothy fiction to be a waste of time to read, a waste of money to pay for, and a waste of space on the library shelf."

563. Thwaite, Anthony. "Girl Who Stayed Behind." *Observer* 4 Feb. 1973: 36.

"... Abortion begins to pall quite quickly.... I still can't fathom why Richard Brautigan has become a part of the cult-pantheon of American youth. He seems harmless but soft."

564. Waugh, Auberon. "Unwanted Books—in Fiction and Fact." *Spectator* 27 Jan. 1973: 108-09.

An unenthusiastic response from the British point of view.

565. Wiggen, Maurice. "Aspects of Americans." *The Sunday Times* (London) 28 Jan. 1973: 39.

"Mr. Brautigan, for lack of discipline, either self-imposed or otherwise, is falling away even farther from his early promise."

566. Yardley, Jonathon. "Still Loving." *New Republic* 20 Mar. 1971: 24.

Says Brautigan "is the Love Generation's answer to Charlie Schulz.... Brautigan is so warm it's impossible to say anything very nasty about him... that the young should have taken so passionately to Brautigan is not surprising. He is the literary embodiment of Woodstock, his little novels and poems being right in the let's-get-back-to-nature-and-get-it all together groove.... The book is modestly funny, can be read in a matter of an hour or so, and will not hurt a soul."

The Hawkline Monster

567. Ackroyd, Peter. "Grotesquerie." *Spectator* 5 Apr. 1975: 411.
"Fortunately, the novel is arranged as a series of brief chapters, and the print is very large, so the tedium of its self-indulgent whimsy is camouflaged for quite long periods."

568. Adams, Phoebe-Lou. "The Hawkline Monster." *Atlantic* Oct. 1974: 119-20.
"[Brautigan] calls his novel 'A Gothic Western,' and perhaps one should leave it at that, rather than trail him through Jungian symbolism or protests against technological civilization, for it looks as though Mr. Brautigan himself never quite decided where he was headed."

569. Anatomy of Wonder. A Critical Guide to Science Fiction. Third Edition. Ed. Neil Barron. New York: R.R. Bowker Co., 1987. 234.
"A pair of professional killers are hired to get rid of a monster created by an eccentric scientist. A funny variation of the Frankenstein theme, written in the author's typical mock-naive style, which works better here than in the hippie-utopia story Watermelon (1968)."

570. Anatomy of Wonder. A Critical Guide to Science Fiction. Second Edition. Ed. Neil Barron. New York: R.R. Bowker Co., 1981. 162.
"In a remote laboratory—house of prostitution in Oregon at the turn of the century, Professor Hawkline of Harvard combines chemicals that generate a powerful and dangerously mischievous life form. He is victimized by it. The twin Hawkline daughters hire professional killers, Greer and Cameron, to solve the problem. They do. A SF/fantasy hybrid by an enormously popular writer among American undergraduates—and many others. Very funny, with intimations of wisdom about the human condition as well."

571. Anonymous. "Books." *Playboy* 21 Sept. 1974: 22, 24.
"... [T]here is a real plot and a thread of continuity that runs through chunky, one-page chapters containing passages that run the gamut of style from [Edgar Allan] Poe to Zane Grey, from Ian Fleming to George V. Higgins. This is certainly Brautigan's most simultaneously unified and eclectic work."

572. Anonymous. "Brautigan, Richard." *The Booklist* 15 Sept. 1974: 70.
"With just the right blend of cowpoke humor and touches of the macabre, Brautigan hilariously spoofs the traditional western as well as the classic horror tale."

573. Anonymous. "Brautigan, Richard." *Kirkus Reviews* 1 Jul. 1974: 695.
"More Brautigan: smug, clever, silly, short and sweet.... [O]ne of the most distinctive voices in contemporary fiction, here or anywhere, like him or not."

574. Bannon, Barbara A. "The Hawkline Monster." *Publishers Weekly* 16 Aug. 1976: 122.
Excerpts from 576.

575. -----. "The Hawkline Monster." *Publishers Weekly* 4 Aug. 1975: 59.
Excerpts from 576.

576. -----. "The Hawkline Monster." *Publishers Weekly* 5 Aug. 1974: 50.
"Maybe somebody could make a 'Blazing Saddles' wild movie out of this but its hard to see it as much of a book."

577. Barnes, Julian. "Kidding." *New Statesman* 4 Apr. 1975: 457.
"The watered style and paper-thin narrative leave so much of the mind free that it zooms hopefully around looking for possible allegory, symbolism or even (cutting its losses) straightforward hidden depth. One returns to base fatigued and empty-handed."

578. Barnett, Richard J., and Robert Manning. "Books Briefly." *Progressive* (39) Jan. 1975: 55.
"There ought to be a law against the exuberance of book jacket blurbs which describe relatively modest literary efforts as 'major novels.'... It has its moments but one is not likely to remember them. A pleasant hour of reading, it qualifies as a minor entertainment rather than a major work."

579. Cabau, Jacques. "Western dans un château hanté." *L' Express* 1 Aug. 1977: 17.
"One of the most original of the counterculture writers.... He makes little marvelous creations, half novel, half poem, little loafings of the imagination which give off a light perfume of hashish."

580. Contemporary Literary Criticism. Vol. 5. Ed. Carolyn Riley. Detroit: Gale Research Company, 1976. 67-72.
Excerpts from 567, 577, 595, and 605.

581. Contemporary Literary Criticism. Vol. 12. Ed. Dedria Bryfonski. Detroit: Gale Research Company, 1980. 57-74.
Excerpts from 584.

582. Contemporary Literary Criticism. Vol. 42. Eds. Daniel G. Marowski and Roger Matuz. Detroit: Gale Research Company, 1980. 48-66.
Excerpts from 603.

583. Cook, Bruce. "'A Gothic Western,' He Calls It, and He's Right." *The National Observer* 14 Sept. 1974: 23.
"... [W]ith Brautigan, texture is all. He can pull off some of the craziest, silliest stuff any writer ever attempted simply because he gives everything he writes a very firm basis in reality through his telling use of specific details, and also through his diction, which is flat, colloquial, and rock solid. All this has the effect of encouraging us to suspend our disbelief. Reading... [Monster] is like watching a movie: You believe it as long as it is happening."

584. Cunningham, Valentine. "Whiskey in the Works." *The Times Literary Supplement* 11 Apr. 1975: 389.
"When you take on the surreal you must clearly watch out for its... embarrassing neighbors, triteness and banality. Richard Brautigan is not, on the whole, half watchful enough.

585. Downing, Pamela. "On the Creation and Use of English Compound Nouns." *Language* Dec. 1977: 810-42.
Collects and analyzes "non-lexicalized compounds" (noun+noun combinations) from Trout and Monster. See also 487.

586. Grubber, J. {"The Hawkline Monster."?} *Vortex* [1(5)] May 1977: 47-48.

587. Kaye, Sheldon. "Brautigan, Richard." The Library Journal Book Review 1974. Ed. Janet Fletcher. New York: R.R. Bowker Company, 1976. 593.
Reprint of 588.

588. -----. "Brautigan, Richard." *Library Journal* Aug. 1974: 1980.
"This book is primarily fun to read and it has some substance besides. Recommended despite its shortcomings."

589. Kincheloe, Henderson "The Hawkline Monster." Masterplots 1975 Annual. Ed. Frank N. Magill. Englewood Cliffs, NJ: Salem Press, 1976. 144-46.
"Monster combines characteristics of classic Westerns, modern gothic romances, and symbolic tales of good and evil.... [It] should be read for fun. This it will provide, if the reader is not repelled by the repeated vulgarisms, or the occasional coarseness."

590. -----. "The Hawkline Monster." Survey of Contemporary Literature. Revised Edition. 12 vols. Ed. Frank N. Magill. Englewood Cliffs, NJ: Salem Press, 1975. Vol. 5, 3302.
Reprint of 590.

591. Lee. L.L. "The Hawkline Monster." *Western American Literature* 10(2) Summer 1975: 151-53.
"Monster is a fairy tale for delayed adolescents."

592. Major, Clarence. "Open Letters." *American Poetry Review* 4(1) Jan.-Feb. 1975: 29.
Reviews Abortion and Monster in the form of a letter to a friend. Says that in Monster, "Brautigan attempts to ram a sharp set of horns directly into the flesh of a literary notion of capturing Experience as We Know It. While doing this, Brautigan laughs a lot." See also 551.

593. Nordell, Roderick. "American Gothic Comes of Age." *Christian Science Monitor* 8 Nov. 1974: 10.
Says Monster "seems a thin example of Mr. Brautigan amusing himself."

594. Olderman, Raymond M. "American Fiction 1974-1976: People Who Fell to Earth." *Contemporary Literature* 19(4) Autumn 1978: 497-530.
Says Monster is a "literal mutant" that will "serve the function of a mutation" because it represents "possible directions of our future."

595. Prescott, Peter S. "Monster in the Cellar." *Newsweek* 9 Sept. 1974: 82-83.
Says Monster "is rather more of a pastiche, more of a parody than any of Brautigan's other fictions. It lacks the complexity, the many evanescent refractions of his best work, Trout, which taps a central metaphor of American literature and deserves to survive the time in which it was written."

596. Quintana, Juan. "Un Western Gotico." *Nueva Estafeta* (30) May 1981: 102-03.
Criticism from a Spanish perspective.

597. Sage, Lorna. "The Edge of Hysteria." *Observer* 6 Apr. 1975: 30.
"... disarmingly funny, crossbreeding two improbabilities to produce a bizarre, engrossing nonsense."

598. Sale, Roger. "Fooling Around, and Serious Business." *Hudson Review* 27 (Winter) 1974-75: 623-35.
"It's a terrible book, deeply unfunny, in no need of having been written."

599. Sarcandzieva, Rada. "Precistvastijat Smjah Na Ricard Brotigan. Cudovisteto Hoklan; Edno Sombrero Pada Ot Nebeto." [The Purifying Laugh of Richard Brautigan in Monster and Sombrero.] Sofia: Narodna Kultura, n.d.
Criticism from a Bulgarian perspective. See also 664.

600. Slethaug, Gordon E. "The Hawkline Monster: Brautigan's 'Buffoon Mutation'." The Scope of the Fantastic: Culture, Biography, Themes, Children's Literature. Eds. Collins, Robert A. and Howard D. Pearle, III. Westport, CT: Greenwood, 1985. 137-45.
A paper presented at the First International Conference on the Fantastic in Literature and Film. "The structure of Monster reinforces the role of the buffoon mutation with its comic parody and burlesque masking its thematically serious function, in effect also following the buffoon tradition by functioning as a social corrective.... By using the romance form Brautigan successfuly debunked an overly romantic view of life. His 'buffoon mutation' has a distinctly social and philosophical function with a sure message, even while it is a sheer delight to read."

601. Tani, Stefano. "L'Esperimento del Professor Hawkline: Case Stregate e Sogno Americano da Brown a Brautigan." *Miscellanea 5* 1984: 45-79.
Discusses the haunted house theme in American literature.

602. Turner, William O. "An Acid-Rock Western." *Seattle Post Intelligencer* 15 Sept. 1974: F10.
"Except in an ultratechnical sense, this book is NOT an example of the mestizo genre known as the gothic western.... [It] is an acid-rock fairy tale.... It is without substance as either fantasy or satire. Whimsy is probably as good a label for it as any. It is simply a takeoff point for a sometimes clever writer who has nothing to write about. Brautigan is like a musician who chooses a familiar melody as background for a demonstration of virtuosity that too often degenerates into mere finger exercises.... In this novel-length effort the author's limitations become all too apparent. He writes cleverly, but is hardly versatile and we find him repeating the same old irreverence and obscenity. He runs out, it might be said, of innovation."

603. Willis, Lonnie L. "Brautigan's 'The Hawkline Monster': As Big as the Ritz." *Critique* 23(2) 1981-1982: 37-47.

"... [I]nvestigates the failure of the American experience to harmonize expectation and reality, and it calls attention to illusions that have distorted the national vision.... Brautigan's reader, being aware that Professor Hawkline's dream is the dream of America will perceive how unlikely the prospect is of maintaining the harmony of expectation and reality when Hawkline monster's shadow falls between them."

604. Wordsworth, Christopher. "Cassandra Syndrome." *Guardian Weekly* 12 Apr. 1975: 21.

"Of the Brautigan who wrote Trout little is left by now, just a cute Cheshire-kitten smile and that ubiquitous monosyllable coyly dimpling every page. Not so much artless as pointless, and whatever it is that a cult figure has to do to embarrass the faithful, it has surely been done with a thud."

605. Yohalem, John. "Cute Brautigan." *The New York Times Book Review* 8 Sept. 1974, Sec. 7: 6-7.

"Richard Brautigan is a popular writer. He is clever and brief; he touches themes and myths close to the current fantasy without being too difficult or too long to complete and understand at a single sitting... . It's a merry little book, good for reading by flashlight to friends toasting marshmallows during the next energy crisis, or else to be picked up for 15 minutes in a bookstore. You'll enjoy that quarter hour."

Willard and His Bowling Trophies

606. Adams, Phoebe-Lou. "Willard and His Bowling Trophies." *Atlantic* Oct. 1975: 110.

"Mr. Brautigan strings together some outlandish episodes to demonstrate that the world is full of misdirected violence. He must have been reading the papers."

607. Anonymous. "Books." *Playboy* Oct. 1975: 32.

"Brautigan is again writing in a style that gives off heavy imitations of [Ernest] Hemingway—had Papa ever gotten around to blowing a lot of grass. The story is slim, but the nuances are all touching.... You'll find yourself liking his characters—and very often he makes you smile, which has to be worth something these days."

608. Anonymous. "Brautigan, Richard." *The Booklist* 1 Sept. 1975: 23-24.
"The brief paragraphs telling this madcap tale resemble a constantly interrupted but never the less comprehensive conversation with the evidently irrepressible Brautigan."

609. Anonymous. "Brautigan, Richard." *Kirkus Review* 15 July 1975: 791.
"When Brautigan is good he is pure magic. But when he is bad he is perverse.... Not the best Brautigan, just a facsimile thereof."

610. Anonymous. "Briefly Noted." *New Yorker* 10 Nov. 1975: 189-90.
"There are a few small anchors for all this whimsy, and they may be all that prevents the book from rising out of the reader's hands and floating, deadpan, out the window...."

611. Anonymous. "Paperbacks: New and Noteworthy." *The New York Times Book Review* 24 Apr. 1977: 49.
"The wild whimsy that carries Brautigan so triumphantly through short pieces and verse doesn't quite sustain him through the length of this short novel of unhappy sex and senseless murder along the San Andreas fault."

612. {Bannon, Barbara A.?}. "Willard and His Bowling Trophies." *Publishers Weekly* 7 Feb. 1977: 94.
"There is double perversity in this bizarre thriller. Both the eccentric characters and Brautigan himself sometimes shock, sometimes gently amuse."

613. Bannon, Barbara A. "Willard and His Bowling Trophies." *Publishers Weekly* 7 Jul. 1975: 80.
"Brautigan hasn't developed much as a writer, but he has an irresistible knack of catching his reader unaware and for the present at least, that's more than good enough."

614. Barnes, Julian. "No Picnic." *New Statesman* 21 May 1976: 685.
Says reading Brautigan leaves one with "vacant brainspace.... It's like following a strip cartoon... one step back for every two forward, terrific of course, for those with spaced-out memories."

615. Bedell, Thomas D. "Brautigan, Richard." The Library Journal Book Review 1975. Ed. Janet Fletcher. New York: R.R. Bowker Company, 1977. 611.
Reprint of 616.

616. -----. "Brautigan, Richard." *Library Journal* 1 Oct. 1975: 1844.
"Brautigan's whimsical style, his wildly imaginative similes, have served him well through five other novels. But here style and substance create an uneasy mix, the 'real' world... strangely intruding into what seems a gentle fantasy."

617. Blumberg, Myrna. "Fiction." *The Times* (London) 10 June 1976: 10.
"Mr. Brautigan's images are inimitable.... Humour is bang on!"

618. Brooks, Jeremy. "A Camera at the Crucifixion." *The Sunday Times* (London) 23 May 1976: 39.
"Whatever is good in the book—and there's a lot—is all unconnected detail."

619. Cartano, Tony. "Heritier de Melville." *Quinzaine* (278) 15 May 1978: 7-8.
Review from a French perspective comparing Brautigan to Herman Melville.

620. Cole, William. "Prides and Prejudices." *Saturday Review* 10 Jan. 1976: 58.
Says Willard is the "Worst Novel" of 1975. "Up to the author's usual standards: fey and wispy."

621. Contemporary Literary Criticism. Vol. 12. Ed. Dedria Bryfonski. Detroit: Gale Research Company, 1980. 57-74.
Excerpts from 625, 627, and 638.

622. Contemporary Literary Criticism. Vol. 9. Ed. Dedria Bryfonski. Detroit: Gale Research Company, 1978. 123-25.
Excerpts from 614.

623. Copps, Dale G. "Books in Brief." *Bookletter* 1 Sept. 1975: 2.
"Much of the book is silly and gives a distinct impression of a 'first draft.' Until suddenly a mellifluous note is sounded by a magical metaphor... and we're in Brautigan country where, for all the heavy and often hollow humor, we visit the perverse mysteries of human relationships, most delicately revealed. A semiprecious gem for Brautigan's expectant readership."

624. Davis, Hope Hale. "Off the Hook." *The New York Times* 5 Oct. 1975, Sec. 7: 50.
Letter commenting on Michael Roger's 14 Sept. 1975 review. See 638. "Stange how the most thoughtful writers can lapse in their practical thinking. After commenting wisely on Willard (Sept. 14), Michael Rogers ends his review with the remark that it's 'hard not to imagine that somewhere, Richard Brautigan is still standing, telephone in hand, waiting for a call.' If his phone is hooked up the usual way, he'll wait a long time."

625. Davis, L.J. "Willard and His Bowling Trophies: A Perverse Mystery by Richard Brautigan." *New Republic* 20 Sept. 1975: 30.
"What Willard is is anyone's guess; I think Mr. Brautigan wants it that way."

626. Fallowell, Duncan. "Trips." *Spectator* 29 May 1976: 30.
Says that Brautigan's writing can be "extraordinarily delicious" but rarely is in this work.

627. Frank, Sheldon. "Brautigan." *The National Observer* 11 Oct. 1975: 21.
"Another experiment in mixed genres.... [I]t is not flawless, but it is a very sad and very funny book.... [T]he story of Bob and Constance is the best writing Brautigan has ever done."

628. Fremont-Smith, Eliot. "Making Book on a Sentimental Season." *Village Voice* 15 Sept. 1975: 50.
"A nude viewing of Johnny Carson is enlivened by the theft of some bowling trophies and the presence of a large papier-mâché bird."

629. Gordon, Andrew. "Richard Brautigan's Parody of Arthur Miller." *Notes On Modern American Literature* 6(1) Spring-Summer 1981: Item 8.
"Behind Brautigan's whimsy is a serious sense of despair about the inevitable decay caused by the misguided American worship of money and success.... The story... contains a deliberate spoof of elements of another work about the tragic effects of the American cult of success, Arthur Miller's play, 'Death of a Salesman'."

630. Gougeon, Leonard. "Brautigan, Richard." *Best Sellers* 35(7) Oct. 1975: 202-03.
"... Brautigan has apparently been hoist on his own petard since he presents a meaningless novel. While there are those who might feel that there is some value in this, I would suggest that comic books are perhaps more adept in this regard, and certainly less costly."

631. Hepburn, Neil. "Spare and Strange." *Listener* 27 May 1976: 687.
"It is hard to describe exactly what meaning it communicates in the same way it is hard to describe the meaning of [Anton] Chekhov stories and plays... but it is not hard to say why it is so enjoyable, since the definitive words already exist in Gerard Manley Hopkins: 'counter, original, spare, strange'."

632. Le Vot, André. "Willard et Ses Trophées de Bowling." *Esprit* (6) {Date?} 1978: 141-42.
Criticism from a French perspective.

633. Mason, Michael. "Rootin', tootin' and shootin'." *The Times Literary Supplement* 21 May 1976: 600.
"Willard will probably disappoint British readers who have followed Richard Brautigan's activity as a prose writer since his debut in this country in 1970. Many of the qualities that

were remarkable and beguiling in the earlier works are missing."

634. Morrow, Patrick D. "Willard and His Bowling Trophies." *Western American Literature* May 1976: 61-63.

"Maybe Brautigan will someday return to creating instead of crafting and fulfill the promise of his lost or stolen vision."

635. Neely, Mildred Sola. "Brautigan's Next Novel Slated for Fall by S & S." *Publishers Weekly* 6 Jan. 1975: 35.

Announces that Brautigan "has just delivered the manuscript of his new novel [Willard] and Simon and Schuster reports it will be published in the fall."

636. O'Connell, Shaun. "American Fiction, 1975: Celebration in Wonderland." *Massachusetts Review* 17(1) Spring 1976: 165-94.

"Though [this novel] may or may not be set in the '60s, it has an ad hoc discontinuousness [sic] appropriate to our recollection of that decade."

637. Parra, Ernesto. "Cocinas de Placer." *Nueva Estafeta* 26 Jan. 1981: 100-02.

Criticism from a Spanish perspective.

638. Rogers, Michael. "The Gentle Brautigan & the Nasty Seventies." *The New York Times Book Review* 14 Sept. 1975: 4.

"Perhaps Brautigan should make a retreat from the novel form. Or perhaps that flat, almost banal, ingenuous style, that worked so well for wistful depictions of loves lost and gained, of good luck and bad luck and loneliness just isn't right for a long bleak gaze at unhappy sex and senseless violence."

639. Sage, Lorna. "Hell Hath No Fury." *The Observer* 23 May 1976: 31.

"... [A] grim and wistful tale about what happens to a perfectly normal marriage attacked by a plague of veneral warts.... Richard Brautigan is still pretty funny, but he seems more and more to be engaged in solitary contemplation of his own quintessence."

Sombrero Fallout

640. Ackroyd, Peter. "Whimsies." *Spectator* 2 Apr. 1977: 27-28.
    Says Brautigan's whimsy is "quaint but effective... because he has no central theme to push his narrative into shape, he hunts out those little moods and tiny moments which pass by conventional novelists desperate in their search for a story."

641. Adams, Phoebe-Lou. "Sombrero Fallout by Richard Brautigan." *Atlantic* Nov. 1976: 118.
    "The meaning of all this is oblique and the style is relentlessly clever. As the author himself points out, 'After a while non-stop brilliance has the same effect as non-stop boredom.' Reckless of him."

642. Anonymous. "Brautigan, Richard." *Choice* Jan. 1977: 1433.
    "Brautigan is a sort of last gasp of the Beat Generation who has managed to adapt himself to changing literary tastes and pose as one of the masked men of experimental writing. His virtues are a poetic imagination that is often sheerly stunning in its casual connections, and a whimsical offhandedness in dealing with heartache that is, quite probably, distinctively Californian. His latest novel [involves two plots]; reading the second plot as outcome of the first provides a sort of critical rationale."

643. Anonymous. "Brautigan, Richard." *The Booklist* 15 Sept. 1976: 120.
    "Absurdity plays against pathos to the chunky rhythm of blunt, declarative sentences... Brief, ingenuous, the novel seems to follow Brautigan's eccentric muse wherever she leads, with little show of resistance."

644. Anonymous. "Brautigan, Richard." *Kirkus Review* 15 July 1976: 805.
    "Mostly it's just a kind of sentimental seppuku [ritual Japanese suicide]...."

645. Bannon, Barbara A. "Sombrero Fallout: A Japanese Novel." *Publishers Weekly* 26 July 1976: 68.
    "An amusing trifle for Brautigan fans."

646. Beaver, Harold. "Dead Pan Alley." *The Times Literary Supplement* 1 Apr. 1977: 392.
"Fracture is the essence of Brautigan's craft: the separation of perceptions, chapters, ideograms.... [I]t is an art, as Nathanael West would have said, of 'the dead pan.' Each movement is arrested in breath, transformed into a metaphor."

647. Bednarczyk, A.J. "Brautigan, Richard." *Best Sellers* (36) Jan. 1977: 315.
"There is neither imagination in the words nor coherence in the story.... If for no other reason, the novel should be criticized as a disgraceful waste of paper and space. But that unfortunately is the least of what's wrong. The book has no reason for being nor, overlooking that, no interest to sustain its tenuous existence."

648. *Bookletter*.
"Sombrero may be the best novel Richard Brautigan has written." Quoted on the back cover of the Touchstone Edition (1976).

649. Brooks, Jeremy. "Eight of the Best." *The Sunday Times* (London) 3 Apr. 1977: 40.
"An expensive curate's egg for some, but a satisfying meal-in-itself, no doubt, for addicts."

650. Carr, Adam. "Mexican Hats Miss Their Mark." *The Times* (London) 30 May 1987: 19.
"... [H]e writes with a botched pseudo-Hemingwayesque brevity complicated by a point-blank refusal to put words in sensible order. 'Revolutionary' according to his publisher—also absolutely infuriating."

651. Casey, Charles. "A Zany, Three-Stage Plot Under One Sombrero." *St. Louis Post-Dispatch* 16 Jan. 1977: 4B.
"This novel... offers more than the traditional Brautigan entertainment. It offers a glimpse of the author as well... it's [sic] touchingly funny moments and it's [sic] interesting experimentation make it one of his best."

Reviews—Novels 145

652. Christgau, Robert. "Sombrero Fallout." *The New York Times Book Review* 10 Oct. 1976, Sec. 7: 4.
"One senses yet another artist who feels defeated by his audience and longs for simpler times."

653. Contemporary Literary Criticism. Vol. 9. Ed. Dedria Bryfonski. Detroit: Gale Research Company, 1978. 123-25.
Excerpts from 652.

654. Contemporary Literary Criticism. Vol. 12. Ed. Dedria Bryfonski. Detroit: Gale Research Company, 1980. 57-74.
Excerpts from 657.

655. Daum, Timothy. "Brautigan, Richard." The Library Journal Book Review 1976. Ed. Janet Fletcher. New York: R.R. Bowker Company, 1977. 619.
Reprint of 656.

656. -----. "Brautigan, Richard." *Library Journal* 1 Oct. 1976: 2084.
"... [T]here isn't a page that won't make you scratch your head, smile, or want to start it all over again."

657. Edwards, Thomas R. "Books in Brief: Five Novels." *Harper's* Oct. 1976: 100.
"As a [Donald] Barthelme-like exercise in discontinuous modes, lyrical, topical, and confessional, the book is amusing but somehow self-cancelling."

658. Glendinning, Victoria. "Enter, Pursued by a Bear." *The Observer* 3 Apr. 1977: 26.
"It is most unsubstantial and equivocal, not really very funny, not really very sad. But Sombrero is subtitled 'A Japanese Novel' and all the foregoing strictures could be made by the uninitiated about, say, a haiku."

659. Howard, Phillip. "Fiction." *The Times* (London) 14 Apr. 1977: 12.
"It is as clever and delicate as a masterpiece of origami."

660. Lingeman, Richard R. "Getting a Fix on Fall Books." *New York Times Book Review* 29 Aug. 1976, Sec. 7: 6-7.
"We can definitely report that the title of Richard Brautigan's new novel is Sombrero. Groovy."

661. *Los Angeles Times*.
"It is a Brautigan book... for those who enjoy intricacy, subtlety and poetry written as prose." Quoted on the back cover of the Touchstone Edition (1976).

662. *Milwaukee Journal*.
"It is structural like a prose poem, conveyed in machine gun bursts of theme whose imagery is frequently bright and innovative and sometimes outright stunning." Quoted on the back cover of the Touchstone Edition (1976).

663. Mount, Ferdinand. "The Novel of the Narcissus." *Encounter* June 1977: 51-58.
Says that Sombrero attempts to arrange "dreck" to make "a treasure out of trash."

664. Sarcandzieva, Rada. "Precistvastijat Smjah Na Ricard Brotigan. Cudovisteto Hoklan; Edno Sombrero Pada Ot Nebeto." [The Purifying Laugh of Richard Brautigan in Monster and Sombrero.] Sofia: Narodna Kultura, n.d.
Criticism of Brautigan from a Bulgarian perspective. See also 599.

665. *St. Louis Globe Democrat*.
"The novel ends with calm satisfaction, and an inexplicable sense of completion. It should be read for this serene earned wisdom." Quoted on the back cover of the Touchstone Edition (1976).

666. Stewart, Joan Hinde. "Sombrero Fallout, A Japanese Novel." Magill's Literary Annual. Ed. Frank N. Magill. Englewood Cliffs, NJ: Salem Press, 1978. 785.
"This new novel—where the inspiration is not always in evidence, where the fictional devices are sometimes both blatantly factitious and rather hackneyed, and where the asides are occasionally downright sophomoric—seems unlikely to make many converts.... It is as droll, as unconventional, as

understated, as eccentric as his previous works, and it affords in places the undeniable pleasure of recognition—recognition of familiar though unwonted attitudes, of miniscule feelings and of frames of mind which the reader has experienced, though of which he may have had only a threshold of awareness."

667. Treglown, Jeremy. "Kithflicks." *New Statesman* 8 Apr. 1977: 471.
"Brautigan's comic touch is predictably unerring and the hilarious narrative development is studded with wry surreal gags."

668. Walters, Ray. "Paperbacks: New and Noteworthy." *The New York Times Book Review* 15 Jan. 1978: 27.
"Clever in spots, but—our reviewer wondered—is the clan still there?"

669. *Washington Star*.
"You won't be disappointed. Because Brautigan is a very funny man." Quoted on the back cover of the Touchstone Edition (1976).

Dreaming of Babylon

670. Anonymous. "Brautigan, Richard." *Choice* Jan. 1978: 1494.
"Brautigan's latest is a spoof of [Dashiell] Hammett, [Raymond] Chandler, et al.: a period detective piece that takes place in the San Francisco of 1942.... [M]ore like a parody than sincere imitation; the whimsy is, by now, getting as tiresome as sixties' cant.... [I]t is time someone gave the Brautigan turntable a kick, it is beginning to stick in a most familiar groove."

671. Anonymous. "Brautigan, Richard." *Kirkus Review* 1 July 1977: 677.
"... [U]npredictable Richard Brautigan at his very breeziest.... The deceptively simple sentences, the two-page chapters, and the surface amusements generate about the fastest 220 pages you'll ever read—leaving lots of extra time to wonder what, if anything, it all meant."

672. Anonymous. "Dreaming of Babylon." *Miami Herald* 16 Oct. 1977: 7E.
"The Dick-and-Jane prose style is undistinguished, and the deadpan narration by the first person hero is humorless. I don't doubt that Brautigan had a good time writing this book, but I had a bad time reading it."

673. Bannon, Barbara A. "Dreaming of Babylon." *Publishers Weekly* 14 Aug. 1978: 68.
Excerpts from 674.

674. -----. "Dreaming of Babylon." *Publishers Weekly* 20 June 1977: 67.
"Brautigan tells his whimsical little tale in dozens of short chapters that will add up to something meaningful to those initiated into Brautigan land and lore."

675. Brein, Alan. "The Voice of Vile Bodies." *The Sunday Times* (London) 16 Apr. 1978: 41.
"Mildly funny, hardly ever thrilling, it is quite endearing in its eccentric, self-indulgent fashion but something of a let down [after] Trout."

676. Cawelti, John G. "Gumshoeing It." *Chicago Sun-Times* 28 Aug. 1977, Sec. 3: 8.
"[Dreaming] is a sleek but sophomoric parody, and that's about it."

677. Contemporary Literary Criticism. Vol. 9. Ed. Dedria Bryfonski. Detroit: Gale Research Company, 1978. 123-25.
Excerpts from 680, 684, and 694.

678. Contemporary Literary Criticism. Vol. 12. Ed. Dedria Bryfonski. Detroit: Gale Research Company, 1980. 57-74.
Excerpts 689.

679. Contemporary Literary Criticism. Vol. 42. Eds. Daniel G. Marowski and Roger Matuz. Detroit: Gale Research Company, 1980. 48-66.
Excerpts from 687.

Reviews—Novels

680. Davis, Rick. "Dreaming of Babylon." *West Coast Review of Books* 4(1) Jan. 1978: 33.
"The only resemblance to a private eye story circa 1942 begins and ends with a P.I. and a beautiful girl.... All in all, a book to forget."

681. Desruisseaux, Paul. "Brautigan's Mad Body-Snatcher." *San Francisco Examiner* 18 Dec. 1977, This World [section]: 60.
"This is the author's fifth consecutive 'genre' novel.... [W]orking in these modes is like doing the crossword: it might be kind of fun, but it isn't writing."

682. Disch, Thomas M. "Dumber Than Dumb." *The Times Literary Supplement* 14 Apr. 1978: 405.
"Mini-chapter by mini-chapter the mindless tale advances with resolute pointlessness and a total mastery of anticlimax.... The book is a vacuous daydream.... Such, Brautigan suggests, are the pleasures of fiction, and probably life."

683. Feinstein, Elaine. "Fiction." *The Times* (London) 11 May 1978: 10.
"... Babylon dosen't hold us."

684. Flaherty, Joe. "The Sam Spade Caper." *The New York Times Book Review* 25 Sept. 1977, Sec. 7: 20.
"What Brautigan has done is to impose a 60s mentality on what he supposes to be a 40s form.... His editor should have served him better. Instead of encouraging him on this caper, he should have sent Brautigan off fishing somewhere in America."

685. Fletcher, Connie. "Brautigan, Richard." *The Booklist* 15 Nov. 1977: 525.
"... [U]pends the conventional private eye novel. It also wreaks havoc with the line between fantasy and reality.... A masterful comedy mixed with pathos."

686. Grimaud, Isabelle. "Stranger than Paradise." *Caliban* 23 1986: 127-35.
Says that an opaque, illusory uncertainty pervades Dreaming.

687. Grimes, Larry E. "Stepsons of Sam: Re-Visions of the Hard-Boiled Detective Formula in Recent American Fiction." *Modern Fiction Studies* 29(3) Autumn 1983: 535-44.

Compares Jules Feiffer's Ackroyd, Brautigan's Dreaming, and Thomas Berger's Who Is Teddy Villanova?.

688. Grove, Lee. "An Alas and Alack for This Babylon." *Boston Globe* 6 Nov. 1977: A32.

"Brautigan seduces us into believing that the detective's hijinks may come into a potentially disastrous head-on collision with what seems to be the stuff of a murky film noir. He invokes the sinister and then, unfairly, turns it into sausage."

689. Hope, Mary. "Dreaming of Babylon." *Spectator* 22 Apr. 1978: 24.

"There is not much point in parodying a style unless there is a valid alternative statement to make; this is just a thin idea, made thinner by the disparity between the master's theme and the pupil's variations."

690. Krim, Seymour. "Brautigan's Mythical Trip into Bogart Country." *Chicago Tribune Book World* 25 Sept. 1977, Sec. 7: 3.

"Brautigan takes off on the private-eye myth in... his usual unpredictable way: the story is told with dead-pan straightforwardness even when the incidents are so outrageous that they could only exist in a dream. You might even call his work dream-realism to try and pin down its elusive flavor."

691. Lee, Hermione. "Curtains." *New Statesman* 14 Apr. 1978: 500.

"This winsome pastiche of [Raymond] Chandler only makes one yearn for Chandler's own solidity of plot and complexity of characters, attributes which a freewheeling minimalist fiction cannot afford."

692. Lemontt, Bobbie Burch. "Dreaming of Babylon." *Western American Literature* 13(3) Fall 1978: 302.

"... [A]n amusing concoction of convention and imagination.... Brautigan's extravagant tomfoolery with language ingeniously parodies the 'hard-boiled' school of detective fiction. Both mystery enthusiasts and the uninitiated alike can find this novel entertaining and fast paced reading."

693. Petticoffer, Dennis. "Richard Brautigan." *Library Journal* Aug. 1977: 1674.

"Like previous efforts by the author, this is an entertaining, provocative fantasy which should delight and intrigue a whole range of readers."

694. Steiner, George. "Briefly Noted." *New Yorker* 21 Nov. 1977: 230-36.

"Richard Brautigan has mastered all the forms of children's fiction... and children's fiction for adults is what this pretty skimpy book is all about."

695. Thwaite, Anthony. "Sour Smell of Success." *The Observer* 16 Apr. 1978: 27.

"Here we have the whimsical old drawler at it again, spilling out a trail of goofy inconsequences about a man who plays at being a private detective.... For those who delight in this author's strenuously ingratiating facetiousness, another welcome offering; for the rest of us, another piece of inexplicable cultism."

696. Winks, Robin W. "Robin W. Winks on Mysteries." *New Republic* 26 Nov. 1977: 34-37.

"Much of the parody is hard boiled.... But I don't think that Brautigan is likely to come this way again."

The Tokyo-Montana Express

697. Ackroyd, Peter. "From the American Playground." *The Sunday Times* (London) 12 Apr. 1981: 43.

"Brautigan's vision of life is of some random and uncontrollable practical joke; the general sense is one of time passing, leaving a trail of empty days, faded memories, and the occasional wreckage of human beings who have tried to move against the flow.... What we get is Brautigan's literary personality spread thinly across the pages—he presents himself as whimsical, whacky, sensitive.... We are implicitly invited to read the book in a similarly light spirit... but Brautigan's writing leaves a sickly feeling in my mouth."

698. Ancola, Jim. "Crete Stop for Brautigan." *Lincoln* (Neb.) *Journal/Star* 9 Nov. 1980: 15TV [special entertainment section].
"[Express] clearly defines Brautigan's Weltanschauung, which is a view worth knowing as America plunges into the 1980s."

699. Anonymous. "Brautigan, Richard." *Kirkus Review* 15 Aug. 1980: 1093-94.
"... [A] few genuine delights amid the crackerjacks, and sheer pleasure for unquestioning, longtime Brautigan fans."

700. Anonymous. "The Tokyo-Montana Express." *People* 1 Dec. 1980: 16.
"... [T]his assortment of essays and short stories is like a photo album of Brautigan's annual journeys between his favorite city, Tokyo, and his home, Montana's Paradise Valley.... [The] funny, fast-paced reading is worth the fare."

701. Bannon, Barbara A. "The Tokyo-Montana Express." *Publishers Weekly* 11 Sept. 1981: 71.
Excerpts from 702.

702. -----. "The Tokyo-Montana Express." *Publishers Weekly* 19 Sept. 1980: 144-45.
"The vignettes are, for the most part, self-indulgent, lackadaisical, uninspired."

703. Berry, John D. "Taking a Ride with Richard Brautigan." *Washington Post Book World* 19 Oct. 1980:14.
"Brautigan spends most of his time describing things, and it is his unusual descriptions that catch our attention. But the interest lasts only as long as his descriptions stay fresh; after that we look beyond them for something more permanent. In Express the descriptions wilt after a while, and there is nothing behind them."

704. Brosnahan, John. "Brautigan, Richard." *The Booklist* 1 Oct. 1980: 181.
"Scenes from Brautigan's life relayed in a laid-back autobiographical novel prove that the author's funky brand of

countercultural charm is still alive and well.... [A] distinctive if round about and idiosyncratic journey of the imagination."

705. Carpenter, Don. "Brautigan Writing at His Peak." *San Francisco Examiner* 2 Nov. 1980: 6.
"Not since Ernest Hemingway has anyone paid so much attention to the sentence. His little chapters, poems and stories are hand grenades of compressed American English.... Express is Brautigan writing at the peak of his powers."

706. Clark, Jeff. "Brautigan, Richard." The Library Journal Book Review 1980. Ed. Janet Fletcher. New York: R.R. Bowker Company, 1981. 596.
Reprint of 707.

707. -----. "Brautigan, Richard." *Library Journal* 15 Nov. 1980: 2430.
"Here again is Brautigan in his inimitable buffet style, serving up a diverse feast of life—outer and inner—through a gentle, probing intelligence."

708. Contemporary Literary Criticism. Vol. 42. Eds. Daniel G. Marowski and Roger Matuz. Detroit: Gale Research Company, 1980. 48-66.
Excerpts from 703, 711, 715, and 733.

709. Daily, Robert. "The Tokyo-Montana Express." *Saturday Review* Oct. 1980: 87.
"... [H]as nothing to do with trains. Nor is it really a novel. Sadly, Brautigan's long-awaited ninth 'novel' is as craggy and uneven as the Montana landscape he evokes."

710. Greenwell, Bill. "Lobster Eating." *New Statesman* 8 May 1981: 21.
"I guess collections of writing like this are like shoals of lobster, each one I say I like instinctively."

711. Halpern, Sue M. "A Pox on Dullness." *The Nation* 25 Oct. 1980: 415-17.
"Express is not a novel. It is a collection of vignettes held together by contrivance.... The vignettes are not bad or boring, although many of them are.... All these pieces being

equal, however, it is apparent that Brautigan does not know when he is good and when he is insipid. If someone was keeping score, it would be clear that good would not win out in the end."

712. Harper, Cathy. "Brautigan, Richard." *VOYA* [*Voice of Youth Advocates*] Apr. 1981: 30.
"Express (a metaphor for Brautigan's physical and mental wanderings) is appropriately named. Few of the 'stops' along its path are sufficiently thought-provoking to make the reader want to stop. The book is comprised of anecdotes and observations that aim... to express something profound in a few words and images. Unfortunately, too many of the pieces are either overly sentimental or flat. Even YAs [young adults] who enjoy reflective prose will probably tire of this quickly."

713. Jones, Lewis. "Amis of Industry." *Punch* 25 Aug. 1982: 292.
"... Mr. Brautigan is laid-back and mellow and appears to be into Zen. His taste for the inconsequential is highly developed.... He writes very well about chickens."

714. Kline, Betsy. "'Express' Takes Readers on Journey That Rambles Through Author's Mind." *Kansas City Star* 21 Dec. 1980: 1, 12D.
[His] "prose is like a fishing expedition. Bobbing amid the vignettes of his tranquil life are some prize catches of life frozen in time.... [T]he reader ends the expedition feeling content but unlucky: happy for the catches and wondering wistfully about the ones that got away."

715. McCaffery, Larry. "Keeping Off Track." *San Diego Union* 2 Nov. 1980, Book Section: 5.
"... [W]hen Brautigan is at his best, his book is home-folks wise.... [W]e see the world as Brautigan does—a place so special, so magical that the most trivial, commonplace aspects of life shimmer with meaning and incandescence."

716. McEnroe, Colin. "Brain Candy for Literary Sweet Tooth." *Hartford Courant* 19 Oct. 1980: G8.
"... Brautigan's collection of pointless vignettes... represents some of the most... half-hearted drivel... bound between hard covers."

Reviews—Novels 155

717. Mason, Michael. "The Pancakes and the President." *The Times Literary Supplement* (London) 1 May 1981: 483.
"The book amounts... to a coherent meditation or investigation: united by a vision of things which is melancholy and alienated, and which is seeking an assuagement of these feelings.... Brautigan's mode is simply questioning, a proposed 'different way of looking'."

718. Mellors, John. "Trick or Treat?" *Listener* 14 May 1981: 652.
"Richard Brautigan produces verbal doodles rather than short stories, and many readers will surely agree with the narrator-author when he says that his mind 'is changing into a cranial junkyard.'... He seems to be promising the profundity of a Bertrand Russell translated into the easy-to-read chit-chat of a Nigel Dempster. Trick? Or treat?"

719. Milazzo, Lee. "Journey into the Fantastic." *Dallas Morning News* 23 Nov. 1980: 4G.
"Is Brautigan putting us on? ...We're not sure what it all adds up to, but it does mean fun reading—sometimes."

720. Mitgang, Herbert. "Home on the Range." *The New York Times Book Review* 26 Oct. 1980, Sec. 7: 59.
Brautigan talks about Express. "The novel is arranged like a train trip. There are stops along the way, and the 'I' in the story is the voice of the stations along the tracks.... Each chapter is separated by a photo of a medallion of the last coal-burning train that I saw in the transportation museum in Tokyo." About his travels between Montana and Tokyo Brautigan says, "I find a kinship between Montana and Japan; the people are dynamic in both places."

721. Pintarich, Paul. "Brautigan's Talents Lost in Gimmickry." *Oregonian* 26 Oct. 1980: C4.
"... Brautigan seems to have become a bulletin board whose personal advertisements for his own cleverness obscure the fact he has any talent at all. This is unfortunate... for devoted fans... initiates... and for Brautigan himself, who should know the time for gimmickry is over."

722. Ponicsan, Darryl. "'Tokyo-Montana' Line Runs on Uncoupled Ideas." *Oregonian* 16 Nov. 1980: C4.
Reprint of 723.

723. -----. "Brautigan Engineers a Train of Uncoupled Empty Thoughts." *Los Angeles Times Book Review* 9 Nov. 1980: 1.

    "The best that can be said for these wee snippets is that they are harmless and inoffensive, occasionally even cute.... [T]he worst [is that they] are probably too lightweight to register on even the most aerated of consciousnesses."

724. Rimer, Thomas. "A Ride on Brautigan's Very Remarkable Train." *St. Louis Globe-Democrat* {Date?} Dec. 1980: {Page?}.

    "If you care at all for this most genial of the old flower children, who can interject a happy dose of self-mockery on the path to self-enlightment, you will enjoy his invitation to step aboard this peculiar but very remarkable train."

725. Sage, Lorna. "Travelling [sic] Light." *The Observer* 19 Apr. 1981: 32.

    "This is a parody travel-book—the whole point about Richard Brautigan being that in most important senses he hasn't moved at all since Trout in the 1960s. As a student of space, he's terrific on time, an expert in the art of sitting still, and this collection of pieces is a loving, if slightly dismayed tribute to the places he has sat in over the past 10 years or so."

726. Sinclair, Andrew. "Fiction." *The Times* (London) 9 Apr. 1981: 12.

    "Express has come off the rails. It is the diary and jottings of an uncoupled mind.... Mr. Brautigan gives off a faint and disordered smell of the writer he was.... He is too talented not to try to put his head together again."

727. Skorupa, Joseph. "Brautigan, Richard." *Best Sellers* Dec. 1980: 309.

    "[Brautigan's] greatest problem is subject matter. The more a reader identifies with the subject of his mini-essays the better he or she will enjoy them, but why waste writing talent and reading time on umbrellas, spiders, spaghetti, rubber bands, light bulbs, sunflower seeds, snake dung, and an entire paragraph of 'Thank yous'? Express is an idiosyncratic hodgepodge that reveals Brautigan to be an uncompelling eccentric personality. It derails the reader's interest right after the first station stop."

728. Story, Jack Trevor. "Cult Express." *Punch* 29 Apr. 1981: 679-80.

"Express is Richard Brautigan's allegorical train journey into his own soul or bowels.... [It] holds lots of commonsense, some good ideas for stories (which he himself can't be bothered to write), some neat insights and observations."

729. Stuewe, Paul. "The Joys of Jersey and Battlefield Notes from the Cola War." *Quill & Quire* Mar. 1981: 62.

"A grabbag of unconnected prose fragments masquerading as a novel, occasionally enlivened by whimsy but otherwise flattened by the author's inability to follow a train of thought for more than a few pages. Embarrassing."

730. Swigart, Rob. "The Tokyo-Montana Express." *The American Book Review* 3 Mar. 1981: 14-15.

"[Mixes] the hippy interest in the east with the Montana sky.... Brautigan's real strength is in these quick but detailed anecdotes of a writer surprisingly free of arrogance or conceit, surprisingly graceful."

731. Taylor, David M. Dictionary of Literary Biography. Yearbook: 1980. Eds. Karen L. Rood, Jean W. Ross, and Richard Ziegfeld. Detroit: Gale Research Co., 1981. 18-21.

Critical review which calls this book "a pastiche of... entries, several previously published, set primarily in Tokyo, Montana, and San Francisco. The entries, unrelated by plot, are held together tenuously by the metaphor of the train."

732. Thomson, Robert. "Brautigan's Express Trip Past 130 Stops." *Oakland Tribune* 11 Jan. 1981, Calendar Section: 1, 10.

"Through the... stops... we become aware of ourselves as life-travelers. The passenger disembarks, not with the travelogue reader's well-developed remembrances of places and names, but rather with a new taste for life's adventure and a fear that we can't really control the speed and path of our own express train."

733. Yourgrau, Barry. "An Uneasy Middle-Aged Soul." *The New York Times Book Review* 2 Nov. 1980, Sec. 7: 13.
"... I find myself exasperated by Brautigan's indirectness. For a writer who seems so intimate, he is really quite unrevealing and remote. He is now a longhair in his mid-40's, and across his habitually wistful good humor there now creep shadows of ennui and dullness and too easily aroused sadness."

734. Weinberger, Andy. "The Tokyo-Montana Express." *Los Angeles Herald Examiner* 9 Nov. 1980: F5.
"[Express] goes nowhere. And the sooner it does, the better."

735. Witosky, Diane. "Riding the Rails with Brautigan." *Des Moines Sunday Register* 28 Dec. 1980: 5C.
"... [A] train trip through life... [that] takes the reader on a thoughtful, thought-provoking trip."

So the Wind Won't Blow It All Away

736. Anonymous. "Brautigan, Richard." *Kirkus Review* 1 July 1982: 743-44.
"... Brautigan's pretentious, whimsical tendencies—sometimes sliding into cuteness—peek up here and there in this slight fable, along with a stray sermonette or two.... But the central images... add up to something sad and tender; and this little sonata on loss, loneliness, death, and nostalgia is Brautigan's most appealing work in some time."

737. Anonymous. "New & Noteworthy." *The New York Times Book Review* 12 Feb. 1984, Sec. 7: 34.
Calls this "a caustic, elliptical novel."

738. Anonymous. "So the Wind Won't Blow It All Away." *People* 25 Oct. 1982: 18.
"Brautigan... has written ten novels, nine volumes of poetry and one book of short stories. Rarely have the distinctions between the three genres been less clear—or more fascinating—than in this work."

739. Anonymous. "So the Wind Won't Blow It All Away." *Playboy* Oct. 1982: 30.
"[Brautigan's] latest, Wind, is a deceptive charmer.... [T]he story is deft, moving, almost elegant in its indirection. Add it to your collection, if not for old-time's sake, for quality's."

740. Atchity, Kenneth. "A Refrain Along Brautigan's Oddpath." *Los Angeles Times Book Review* 19 Sept. 1982: 8.
"What Brautigan refers to as 'the oddpaths of imagination' are not as odd, nor even as pathlike, here as they are in his best novels."

741. Bannon, Barbara A. "So the Wind Won't Blow It All Away." *Publishers Weekly* 25 June 1982: 108.
"... [A] flat, listless narrative, enlivened fleetingly by Brautigan's bizarre imagination, but pretentiously self-important and contrived."

742. Brosnahan, John. "Brautigan, Richard." *The Booklist* Aug. 1982:1482.
"... [Q]uiet, muted, and captivating... a treat for the writer's fans and for readers who prefer their Brautigan in small doses."

743. Campbell, Patty. "The Young Adult Perplex." *Wilson Library Bulletin* Dec. 1982: 334-35, 365-66.
Brautigan's "novels are puzzles pulled apart into little pieces and put back together in disjointed sections until the whole pattern emerges. For this reason [his novels] require a bit of literary sophistication from young readers—although sometimes [young adults] seem to have an easier time with non-linear narratives than older people."

744. Cohen, Joseph. "Fulfillment Elusive, Brautigan Reminds Us." *New Orleans Times-Picayune* 5 Sept. 1982, Sec. 3: 12.
"... like the Ancient Mariner.... Brautigan's story is both an act of explanation and a warning...."

745. Contemporary Literary Criticism. Vol. 42. Eds. Daniel G. Marowski and Roger Matuz. Detroit: Gale Research Company, 1987. 48-66.
Excerpts from 755, 758, and 759.

746. DeMarinis, Rick. "Brautigan's Stylish Touch Turns a Grim Story into a Fairy Tale." *Chicago Tribune Book World* 3 Oct. 1982, Sec. 7: 3.
"Wind is a lyrical meditation told in a warm, personal voice. As you read, you have the feeling of listening to a friend ramble on about serious things in a lighthearted manner as you both drive down an abandoned highway toward a grand little pond the world has forgotten."

747. Durrant, Digby. "So the Wind Won't Blow It All Away." *London Magazine* June 1983: 102-03.
"Brautigan's latest novel, in its familiar laconic fashion, sounds its usual plangent note of nostalgia for the loss of American innocence."

748. Hackenberry, Charles. "Walden Reworked." *Thoreau Society Bulletin* 165 (Fall) 1983: 3.
"... Wind, borrows frequently from Walden to help paint a quiet, muted portrait... [and]... serves to remind us that [Henry David] Thoreau's prose still has the power to stir the imagination of a modern writer who is working a very different vein of ore with very familiar tools."

749. Hunter, Timothy A. "Brautigan's Latest: 'Gentle, Brief, Slippery'." *Baltimore Sun* 5 Sept. 1982: D5.
"... [W]riters like Richard Brautigan, master of the one-sitting novel, turn out books that require no effort to read, but leave less impact on your consciousness than your neighbor's latest batch of vacation slides... His new novel is gentle, brief and slippery, there are, to say the least, less pleasurable ways to spend an hour."

750. Ives, George L. "Brautigan, Richard." *Library Journal* Aug. 1982: 1478.
"Confronting death, Brautigan successfully moves his readers to an awareness that life is not an outgrowth of pure randomness but the result of choices willfully made."

751. Kane, Jean. "Naive Tone Perfect for Brautigan Novel." *Indianapolis Star* 19 Sept. 1982: F4.
"As a child's tale, Wind is convincing and passably wrought; when it must support ham-handed social commentary, the parable breaks down."

752. Kenny, Kevin. "Brautigan, Richard." *VOYA [Voice of Youth Advocates*] Feb. 1983: 32.
"Richard Brautigan's latest work is a sometimes wandering, but always touching, salute to an era and way of life (particularly early life) forever gone.... [It] is both subtle and perceptive. At work at many levels, better readers, particularly at the high school level, should have the perspective necessary to enjoy this treat. For adults, it's a bittersweet must."

753. Kline, Betsy. "Gentle 'Wind' Stirs Up Tragic Boyhood Memory." *Kansas City Star* 29 Aug. 1982: 10L.
"Mr. Brautigan is in beautiful form in his latest novel. The barebones simplicity of his story telling... goes directly to the heart of the matter. Wind is an eloquent elegy for rustic simplicity, childish pursuits and harmless fantasy."

754. Lippman, Amy. "The New Brautigan: A Silly Pretension." *San Francisco Chronicle* 2 Sept. 1982: 55.
"Brautigan intends Wind to be an American Tragedy, but the novel is too inconsequential to make his design for it little more than a silly pretension."

755. Montrose, David. "Death of the Dream." *The Times Literary Supplement* 22 Apr. 1983: 399.
"... [T]he author's most substantial novel since Watermelon... [but] the novel is by no stretch of the imagination a profound or major work."

756. Morley, Patricia. "It may not be literature but it's still entertaining." *Birmingham News* 26 Sept. 1982: 6E.
"Brautigan's fiction blends meticulous exactitude with free-ranging imagination. The images are zany but right, sometimes memorable. Lyricism, humor, and a playful profundity work well together in Brautigan's 20th book."

757. Myerson, Jonathon. "So the Wind Won't Blow It All Away." *Books & Bookmen* Aug. 1983: 35.
"This delightful, gentle novel evokes memories almost, but not quite, out of reach.... It is... Brautigan speaking, Brautigan the Fantasist, regretfully summing up his childhood and his America."

758. Ottenberg, Eve. "Some Fun, Some Gloom." *The New York Times Book Review* 7 Nov. 1982, Sec. 7: 13, 47.
"Grim, caustic, overly sentimental, peppered with incomprehensibly mixed metaphors, this novel seems determined to deprive its characters of any shred of well-being."

759. Pfaff, William. "So the Wind Won't Blow It All Away." *New Yorker* 13 Sept. 1982: 172-73.
"Only Mr. Brautigan's fans will mistake its slightness for subtlety."

760. Ronald, Ann. "So the Wind Won't Blow It All Away." *Western America Literature* Aug. 1983: 164-65.
"As soon as I start to translate a Richard Brautigan novel into everyday prose, its words dissolve. When I try to pin down his imagery... it eludes me.... Like the fabled trout of his best-known work, sliding upstream just out of an angler's eager cast, the language of <u>Wind</u> floats transparently between Brautigan's imagination and mine."

761. Sage, Lorna. "Gone Fishing Again." *The Observer* 17 Apr. 1983: 32.
"The contemporary muse is notorious for playing around, so it is perhaps not entirely shocking that she seems to have supplied Richard Brautigan with the same plot for his 'new' novel that she produced for Kurt Vonnegut's a very short time ago. I mean the one about the narrator who shot someone by accident when he was 12 and has been trying to rewrite destiny ever since.... Brautigan's distinctive tone takes him off in his own direction, into the kind of exiguous lyricism that established him as the first of the Hippies—or was it the last of the Beats?"

762. Scharnhorst, Gary. "Brautigan Produces a Yawner." *Dallas Morning News* 5 Dec. 1982: 4G.
"I heartily recommend it to all insomniacs.... [T]he Brautigan cult may hurry to local bookstores to purchase this indulgence. I would rather wear a clove of garlic around my neck."

763. Strell, Lois A. "Brautigan, Richard." *School Library Journal* Nov. 1982: 105.
"Brautigan is often brilliant at capturing the moment in metaphor, but at other times, his writing drags. This novel is a mixture of imagination and overkill."

764. Stuewe, Paul. "The English in India... Entertaining Advice... Words to Wow With." *Quill & Quire* Nov. 1982: 29.
"The author's penchant for combining radically experimental techniques with equally mundane material has attracted a host of imitators, but he still holds the patent on the most effective blend of these ingredients. His latest novel [is] typical in its relentlessly straight-faced handling of the most nonsensical situations. This works for just as long as it takes a reader to begin anticipating the against-the-grain results, which in this case is most of the way through a slight but entertaining story."

765. Traub, Nancy. "Brautigan Writes It Down Before It Becomes American Dust." *Oakland Tribune* 1 Apr. 1984, Calendar Section: 7.
"It's as if the narrator is compelled to tell this story, to understand his part in it.... The reader brings his or her own meaning to the story; we benefit from Brautigan's search."

766. Wagner, Joe. "So the Wind Won't Blow It All Away." *Baton Rouge Sunday Advocate* 24 Oct. 1982 : 15-Mag.
"There is no argument that Brautigan can write, and write very well; only, it's time he began to write something worthy of his talent."

767. Warren, Eric. "Brautigan's Latest Novel." *Christian Science Monitor* 8 Aug. 1984: 28.
"In this book, Brautigan has uncovered a vivid memorable character who engages our sympathies in a way few of his

people have done before. His latest novel is surely one of his best."

SHORT STORIES
Citations Listed Alphabetically

Revenge of the Lawn: Stories, 1962-1970

768. Anonymous. "Brautigan, Richard." *The Booklist* 1 Jan. 1972: 380.
"Using a tone of sophisticated amusement Brautigan combines elements of autobiography with fictional characters and situations in a montage of slight but diverting pieces...."

769. Anonymous. "Brautigan, Richard." *Kirkus Review* 1 Aug. 1971: 824.
"This book is a sort of general sweeping up after the other books." [It could have been called] "Little Abortions since none [of the stories] really seems to come full-term even by the loose standard Brautigan sets. Okay so long as the fey inspiration lasts, but this is Brautigan at his most puppy-mannered and inconsequential."

770. Anonymous. "Novel in Brief." *The Observer* 16 July 1972: 30.
"Short pieces, some no more than stray clippings and pairings.... As in Trout, the mood is a fey free-wheeling in which old history, lost landscapes and the ghosts of writers as disparate as [Edgar Allan] Poe and [William] Saroyan float in iridescent bubbles that burst with a melancholy pop. There's dross too, for Brautigan can be tricksy as well as unique."

771. Anonymous. "Revenge of the Lawn." *The New York Times Book Review* 3 Dec. 1972: 78.
Reprint of 772.

772. Anonymous. "Revenge of the Lawn." *The New York Times Book Review* 4 June 1972: 24.
"Stories from 1962-1970 by the gentle poet of small souls in torment. 'The Brautigan magic' is a everywhere apparent as

his characters sink into a healing coolness in the face of outrages life inflicts upon them."

773. Blackburn, Sara. "American Folk Hero." *Washington Post Book World* 28 Nov. 1971: 2.
"Here is a collection of short stories to delight Brautigan fans and demonstrate why his status has changed from writer's writer to American folk hero.... If you haven't read him yet, this collection is a good place to start."

774. Broyard, Anatole. "Weeds and Four-Leaf Clovers." *The New York Times* 15 Nov. 1971: 39.
"At its worst, Revenge sounds simultaneously, like a clumsily written children's book and a pretentious piece of avant-garde impressionism."

775. Contemporary Literary Criticism. Vol. 1. Ed. Carolyn Riley. Detroit: Gale Research Company, 1973. 44-45.
Excerpts from 782.

776. Contemporary Literary Criticism. Vol. 12. Ed. Dedria Bryfonski. Detroit: Gale Research Company, 1980. 57-74.
Excerpts from 788.

777. Dietrich, Richard F. "Brautigan's 'Homage to the San Francisco YMCA': A Modern Fairy Tale." *Notes On Contemporary Literature* 13(4) Sept. 1983: 2-4.
"Brautigan's 'Homage to the San Francisco YMCA' is probably best categorized as a fairy tale.... But of course it's not the usual fairy tale... for only a fairy tale, that form of literature most held in contempt by our 'realistic,' 'down-to-earth,' 'practical and no-nonsense' business civilization, could capture the reality of our cultural schizophrenia, which invokes God while worshipping Mammon. As his protagonist pays knightly homage to that institution most aptly symbolic of the selling out of spiritual intentions, Brautigan ironically portrays this American prince as an individual bewitched by false values and self-entombed upon 'the throne' of a materialist obsession."

778. Duberstein, Larry. "Revenge of the Lawn: Stories, 1962-1970." *Saturday Review* 4 Dec. 1971: 43, 49-50.
"Revenge exhibits considerable range and variety.... Brautigan lays out a characteristically spare, almost hollow line, jarred from regularity by the odd, clinking similes with which he frequently punctuates a thought. Occasionally Brautigan's writing breaks down: stylistic ease borders on laziness, disarming wit slips into grating gimmickry, and the childlike tone simply sounds silly... [but this] is one of Brautigan's best books, and at his best he is a writer of surprising talent and vision."

779. {Erdosi, Elizabeth?}. "Revenge of the Lawn: Stories, 1962-1970." *Publishers Weekly* 9 Aug. 1971: 48.
"... [T]his book is like an album of snapshots... a delightful collection, simple, honest, and charming."

780. Farrell, J.G. "Brautigan Briefs." *The Listener* 13 July 1972: 57.
"Revenge is a collection of stories which mixes fantasy with autobiographical reminiscences. The reminiscences, whether imaginary or not, have a genuine ring to them and yet at the same time often defy reality with complete success.... Many of the pieces are extremely delicate in what they manage to convey, and leave you with the impression of having read a poem rather than a page or two of prose."

781. Galloway, David. "Richard Brautigan, 'The World War I Los Angeles Airplane.'" *Die amerikanische Short Story der Gegenwart: Interpretationen*. Ed. Peter Freese. Berlin: Schmidt, 1976. 333-39.
Festschrift article.

782. Hendin, Josephine. "Revenge of the Lawn." *The New York Times Book Review* 16 Jan. 1972, Sec. 7: 7, 22.
Compares Revenge to General, Trout, and Watermelon saying it "is not Brautigan's best book, but it has the Brautigan magic—the verbal wilderness, the emptiness, the passive force of people who have gone beyond winning or losing to an absolute poetry of survival."

783. Hornick, Lita. "Kulchur: Memoir." *TriQuarterly* 43 (Fall) 1978: 280-97.
Recounts the contents of *Kulcher* magazine saying that in *Kulcher* 13, "Richard Brautigan, then a relatively unknown writer, contributed a characteristic piece of fiction called 'The Post Offices of Eastern Oregon'."

784. Langlois, Jim. "Brautigan, Richard." *Library Journal* 15 Oct. 1971: 3344.
"... [B]eneath [the] surface artlessness [of these stories] is an awareness of the poetry of memory in which hard-edged images are awash with vibrations of dreams.... These stories suggest new dimensions in the forms of short fiction and substantiate both Brautigan's widespread popularity and his growing critical reputation."

785. Lottman, Eileen. "Revenge of the Lawn: Stories, 1962-1970." *Publishers Weekly* 27 Sept. 1971: 68.
"These are brief sketches from the notebooks of one of the most exciting writing talents now producing. One of these days Brautigan will emerge as a big seller; while this book isn't it, the growing readership will dig it."

786. Malley, Terence. Richard Brautigan. New York: Warner, 1972.
Chapter Two deals with Revenge.

787. Minudri, Regina U. "Brautigan, Richard." *Library Journal* 15 May 1972: 1886.
"Striking, breathtaking, and funny images in short-stories by a master novelist, whose relaxed and natural attitude toward life finds a responsive YA [young adult] readership."

788. Norman, Gurney, and Ed McClanahan. "Revenge of the Lawn." *Rolling Stone* 9 Dec. 1971: 66.
"... Brautigan... very softly invites you into his fictional world. But once inside, indeed, your heart may well be broken, because within these apparently delicate pieces are people up against the ultimate issues of love, loneliness, and death."

789. Sheppard, R. Z. "Easy Writer." *Time* 1 Nov. 1971: 114-15.
"All of his images, longings and humor eventually float free of their structural moorings and are kept aloft by the only thing in Brautigan that really counts—his special voice."

790. Shrapnel, Norman. "Peasant Power." *Guardian Weekly* 22 July 1972: 19.
"... [C]oncrete and at the same time mysterious, like prose poems or modern folk tales. They are curious fragments... Not quite surrealism, though far from plain fun, with a bit of pioneer larkishness and a preoccupation with cinema, dreams, and children."

791. Strothman, Janet. "Brautigan, Richard." *Library Journal* 15 Dec. 1971: 4207.
"Brautigan has a marvelous feeling for and command of language: his images are striking, breath-taking, funny and, YAs [young adults]—if not their parents—are sure to respond to his relaxed, natural attitude toward life and sex."

792. Toye, Robert James. Letter to the Editor. *The New York Times Book Review* 27 Feb. 1972, Sec. 7: 27.
Letter disputing Josephine Hendin's review (See 782). "There's just one way to approach Brautigan, and that's to float along with his prose. Don't waste your time trying to be involved—with what he does or doesn't do."

793. Uellenberg, Klaus. "Tradition und Postmoderne in Richard Brautigan's Revenge of the Lawn—Stories." *Literatur in Wissenscraft und Unterricht* (Kiel, West Germany) 17(1) 1984: 37-52.
Criticism from a German perspective.

794. Webb, W.L. "From the Spring Lists." *Guardian Weekly* Jan. 1972: 19.
"[S]hould allow doubters to make up their minds...."

795. Whittemore, Reed. "Revenge of the Lawn: Stories, 1962-1970." *New Republic* 22 Jan. 1972: 29.
Calls this book "the height of fashion right now."

COLLECTION
Citations Listed Alphabetically

Trout Fishing in America, The Pill Versus the Springhill Mine Disaster, In Watermelon Sugar

796. Anonymous. "Trout Fishing in America, The Pill Versus the Springhill Mine Disaster, In Watermelon Sugar." *The New York Times Book Review* 6 Dec. 1970: 102.
Reprint of 797.

797. Anonymous. "Trout Fishing in America, The Pill Versus the Springhill Mine Disaster, In Watermelon Sugar." *The New York Times Book Review* 7 June 1970: 2.
"Three works... of extraordinary comic perception."

798. Contemporary Literary Criticism. Vol. 12. Ed. Dedria Bryfonski. Detroit: Gale Research Company, 1980. 57-74.
Excerpts from 288, 801, and 803.

799. Contemporary Literary Criticism. Vol. 1. Ed. Carolyn Riley. Detroit: Gale Research Company, 1973. 44-45.
Excerpts from 801.

800. Davenport, Guy. "C'est Magnifique mais Ce N'est pas Daguerre." *Hudson Review* 23 (Spring) 1970: 154-61.
"These works show Mr. Brautigan is one of the most gifted innovators in our literature."

801. McGuane, Thomas. "An Optimist vis-a-vis the Present." *The New York Times Book Review* 15 Feb. 1970, Sec. 7: 49.
"Stylistically, his American next of kin is Kenneth Patchen; but the sunniness reminds the reader of not only people like [Henry David] Thoreau and W.C. Williams but the infrequently cited Zane Grey."

802. Morris, Desmond. "Trout Fishing in America, The Pill Versus the Springhill Mine Disaster, In Watermelon Sugar." *The Observer* 21 Dec. 1969: 17.
"The most extraordinary literary discovery of the year for me was a young San Francisco writer, Richard Brautigans [sic]...."

803. Norman, Albert H. "Energy and Whimsy." *Newsweek* 29 Dec. 1969: 54-55.
Trout "is not a book for sportsmen to get hooked on. Brautigan... explodes every simile, makes all the senses breathe. Brautigan's collected poems [Pill] are too uneven to be truly satisfying. He lacks the abstract depth of Wallace Stevens and the focus of William Carlos Williams. [Watermelon] is Brautigan at his best. Every page is gracefully complex. The characters in this naive allegory are as sweet as sugar. The writing melts in your mouth."

804. Shatkin, A.I. "Brautigan, Richard." Library Journal Book Review 1970. Ed. Judith Serebnick. New York and London: Sowker, 1970. 703.
Reprint of 805.

805. -----. "Brautigan, Richard." *Library Journal* 15 Apr. 1970: 1500.
"A good addition to large fiction collections."

806. Walters, Richard. Survey of Contemporary Literature. Revised Edition. Ed. Frank N. Magill. Englewood Cliffs, NJ: Salem Press, 1977. Vol. 2. 883-89.
Reprint of 807.

807. -----. "Trout Fishing in America, The Pill Versus the Springhill Mine Disaster, and In Watermelon Sugar." Masterplots 1970 Annual. Ed. Frank N. Magill. Englewood Cliffs, NJ: Salem Press, 1970. 56-62.
"Brautigan is not the promising young writer of the year.... He [does not take] his writing seriously.... He is artlessly irreverent... wildly funny.... He blasphemes the continuing traditions of American literature... defies the timeless enigmas of man, and shuns the proper, proven subjects and

characters.... So it is difficult to proceed, unarmed as we are, with no convenient facts to gird our loins, with little literary reputation to take up and guide our venture, with no syllabus for another school of humor...." Brautigan emerges as a humorist. "Brautigan, if he is hailed for anything, will be known for his comedy—pure and simple."

MYSTERIOUS AND ERRONEOUS CITATIONS

MYSTERIOUS CITATIONS

808. Poems. New York: Delacorte Press, 1971.
 Cited in <u>Chicorel Index to Poetry in Anthologies and Collections in Print</u>. (First Edition. Ed. Marietta Chicorel. New York: Chicorel Library Publishing Corp., 1974. Vol. 5B, 1166.) A collection of 98 poems, the titles of which are exactly the same as those included in <u>Pill</u>.

809. {Author & Title?} *New West* [1] 20 Dec. 1977: 88.

ERRONEOUS CITATIONS

810. "A Study in California Flowers." *Coyote's Journal* (5-6) 1966: 81.
 This citation, in <u>Index to Little Magazines, 1966-1967</u>. (Comp. Evelyn G. Lauer. Chicago: Swallow Press, 1970: 26) indicates this work is a poem. It is, in fact, a short story from <u>Revenge</u>.

811. Chentier, Thomas. "Escape through Imagination in 'Trout Fishing in America'." *Critique* 16(1) 1974: 25-31. Cited in Leary, Lewis. Articles on American Literature, 1968-1975. (Durham: Duke University Press, 1979. 48.) The actual author of this article is Thomas Hearron.

812. "Lemons, Lemons" and "All Watched Over by Machines of Loving Grace." The Ways of the Poem. (Miles, Josephine. Second Edition. Englewood Cliffs, NJ; Prentice-Hall, 1972. Cited in Chicorel Index to Poetry in Anthologies and Collections. (1979 Edition. Ed. Marietta Chicorel. New York: Chicorel Library Publishing Corp., 1978. Vol. 5, 84.) "Lemons, Lemons" is in fact a poem by Al Young. The correct Brautigan poems here are "Chinese Checker Players" and "All Watched Over by Machines of Loving Grace."

OBITUARIES AND EULOGIES

Citations Listed Alphabetically

813. Abbott, Keith. "When Fame Puts Its Feathery Crowbar under Your Rock." *California Magazine* Apr. 1985: 90-94, 102-108, 126.
    Subtitled "Reflections on the Life and Times of Richard Brautigan," this article recounts several experiences the author had with Brautigan in California and Montana.

814. -----. "Garfish, Chili Dogs, and the Human Torch: Memories of Richard Brautigan and San Francisco, 1966." *Review of Contemporary Fiction* 3(3) Fall 1983: 214-19.
    Contends that "there is only one way to become well-known in America as a writer. That is to have your work represent something sociological.... Brautigan's work was said to represent the [sociological] chaos [in San Francisco's Haight-Ashbury district in 1968]." Says Brautigan was catapulted to fame by the efforts of the media to find a writer who represented... the developing hippie philosophy.

815. Anonymous. "Bernard Brautigan." *Detroit Free Press* 29 Oct. 1984: 14F.
    "Bernard Brautigan, 76, is one surprised man. He only just learned he was the father of author Richard Brautigan after

Richard's apparent suicide last week. A retired laborer in Tacoma, Brautigan was divorced from his wife, Mary Lula Folston, who never revealed she was pregnant when the couple split. Brautigan got the news via his sister-in-law. Only the proof of birth records and confirmation from his ex-wife convinced him. Said a shaken Brautigan, 'I don't know nothing about him. He's got the same last name, but why would they wait 45 to 50 years to tell me I've got a son'."

816. Anonymous. "Body Discovered in California Is Believed to Be Brautigan's" *The New York Times* 26 Oct. 1984, Sec.2: 6
"A body discovered yesterday by the police in a house in Bolinas, Calif., was believed to be the remains of Richard Brautigan...."

817. Anonymous. "Brautigan." File 260: UPI News—April 1983-May 1987. Dialog Database. Palo Alto, CA: Dialog Information Service, Inc. Dateline: Bolinas, CA, Oct. 27, 1984. General news obituary.
"Writer Richard Brautigan was found dead in his home and apparently had committed suicide, but the coroner's office says it will not announce its findings until next week."

818. Anonymous. "Brautigan." File 260: UPI News—April 1983-May 1987. Dialog Database. Palo Alto, CA: Dialog Information Service, Inc. Dateline: Tacoma, WA, Oct. 27, 1984. General news story dealing with Bernard Brautigan, Richard's father.
"The death of author Richard Brautigan shocked a Tacoma man who learned for the first time he was the 49-year-old writer's father. Bernard Brautigan, 76, a retired laborer, discovered his relationship to the Tacoma-born writer Friday in a telephone call from his ex-sister-in-law, Evelyn Fjetland. At first he did not believe the story but he said he called his ex-wife, whom he has not seen in 50 years. Brautigan was formerly married to... Mary Lula Folston... who gave birth to Richard on Jan. 30, 1935. Folston... [said] her ex-husband asked 'if Richard was his son, and I said, no. I told him I found Richard in the gutter.' Bernard Brautigan said he knew nothing about his famous son.... 'I never read any of his books,' he said. 'When I was called by Evelyn, she told me about Richard and said she was sorry about his death. I said, 'who's Richard?' I don't know nothing about him. He's got

the same last name, but why would they wait 45 to 50 years to tell me I've got a son'?"

819. Anonymous. "Brautigan Death." File 259: AP News July 1983-April 1987. Dialog Database. Palo Alto, CA: Dialog Information Service, Inc. Dateline: Bolinas, CA, Oct. 27, 1984. General news obituary.

"Richard Brautigan, the author laureate of the hippie generation whose apparent suicide was discovered last week, had been preparing for death for some time and was wont to 'get drunk and shoot things,' friends said."

820. Anonymous. "Brautigan Death Called Self-inflicted." *Great Falls Tribune* 28 Oct. 1984: 3C.

"Richard Brautigan, a literary idol of the 1960s who eventually fell out of fashion, was found dead Thursday at his secluded house in Bolinas, Calif."

821. Anonymous. "Brautigan-Obit." File 260: UPI News—April 1983-May 1987. Dialog Database. Palo Alto, CA: Dialog Information Service, Inc. Dateline: Bolinas, CA, Oct. 25, 1984.

"Author Richard Brautigan, whose 1967 novel, Trout turned him from a unknown Haight-Ashbury poet to best selling author, was found dead in his home Thursday. He was 49."

822. Anonymous. "Brautigan-Obit." File 260: UPI News—April 1983-May 1987. Dialog Database. Palo Alto, CA: Dialog Information Service, Inc. Dateline: Bolinas, CA, Oct. 26, 1984.

"Author Richard Brautigan, whose 1967 novel Trout made him a literary hero of the 1960s counterculture, is dead, the apparent victim of suicide. He was 49."

823. Anonymous. "Brautigan-Obit." File 260: UPI News—April 1983-May 1987. Dialog Database. Palo Alto, CA: Dialog Information Service, Inc. Dateline: Bolinas, CA, Oct. 26, 1984.

"Author Richard Brautigan, an unknown poet who became a guru to the nation's hippies, was found dead of unknown causes in his home. He was 49."

824. Anonymous. "Brautigan, Richard (Gary) 1935-1984." Contemporary Authors. Ed. Hal May. Detroit: Gale Research Company, 1985. Vol. 113. 65-66.
"Poet and author Brautigan [was] eulogized by publisher and friend Seymour Lawrence as 'a true American genius in the tradition of [Mark] Twain and [Ring] Lardner,' [who] became a counterculture hero during the 1960s because of his ability to articulate with humor and imagery the growing disillusionment with the American Dream that characterized that era."

825. Anonymous. "Ferlinghetti." File 260: UPI News—April 1983-May 1987. Dialog Database. Palo Alto, CA: Dialog Information Service, Inc. Dateline: San Francisco, CA, Nov. 26, 1984.
General news article about Lawrence Ferlinghetti, poet-publisher whose City Lights Bookstore was the literary center of San Francisco's Beat Era during the late 1950s and early 1960s. Ferlinghetti says the writers of the Beat Generation: Kenneth Rexroth, Jack Kerouac, Allen Ginsberg, Neil Cassady, Kenneth Patchen, William Burroughs, Gary Snyder, Ken Kesey, and Richard Brautigan set the stage for the activists of the 1960s.

826. Anonymous. "Friends Find Author Brautigan Dead at His Home in California." *Billings Gazette* 26 Oct. 1984: B7.
"Author Richard Brautigan, who owned a ranch in Paradise Valley near Livingston, Mont., was found dead Thursday at his home in Bolinas, a beach community north of San Francisco, his publisher said."

827. Anonymous. "Obit-Brautigan." File 259: AP News—July 1983-April 1987. Dialog Database. Palo Alto, CA: Dialog Information Service, Inc. Dateline: Bolinas, CA, Oct. 26, 1984.
"Richard Brautigan, whose emotion-packed writing touched millions and made him a hero to the 1960s hippie generation, apparently shot himself in the head weeks before his decomposed body [was] found, authorities said Friday."

828. Anonymous. "Obit-Brautigan." File 259: AP News—July 1983-April 1987. Dialog Database. Palo Alto, CA: Dialog

Obituaries and Eulogies

Information Service, Inc. Dateline: Bolinas, CA, Oct. 26, 1984.

"Richard Brautigan, whose offbeat novels and poetry about love, death and empty lives captured the imagination of the 1960s hippie generation, was found dead at home, his publisher and friends said."

829. Anonymous. "Obits." File 260: UPI News—April 1983-May 1987. Dialog Database. Palo Alto, CA: Dialog Information Service, Inc. Dateline: Bolinas, CA, Oct. 26, 1984.

"Author Richard Brautigan, an unknown poet who became a guru to the nation's hippies, was found dead of unknown causes in his home. He was 49.... Brautigan was an unknown poet in San Francisco's Haight-Ashbury district until he published Trout in 1967. It sold 2 million copies.... Born in Spokane, Wash., Brautigan is survived by a daughter from his marriage to Virginia Dionne, which ended in divorce in 1970."

830. Anonymous. "Obituaries." *Chicago Tribune* 28 Oct. 1984, Sec. 4: 17.

"Richard Brautigan, 49, an author whose offbeat novels... made him a celebrated figure in the 1960s; his books blended comedy, satire, odd bits of information and outrageously freewheeling style; in the last years of his life, his work fell out of favor with critics, who considered it old hat; found Oct. 25 in his Bolinas, Calif. home."

831. Anonymous. "Obituary Notes." *Publishers Weekly* 9 Nov. 1984: 20.

"Trout was first published in 1967 by Four Seasons Foundation in San Francisco, where Brautigan distributed his poems in the streets of Haight-Ashbury and where his underground reputation had its start. Alerted to that reputation, literary agent Helen Brann offered Trout and two other books at an auction won by Seymour Lawrence, who published the three in one volume in 1970 and who has been Brautigan's publisher since. Although Brautigan's audience in the U.S. has declined in recent years, his works are particularly popular in Japan and France and have been translated into 12 languages."

180 *Richard Brautigan Bibliography*

832. Anonymous. "Poet-Novelist Richard Brautigan Found Dead." *Detroit Free Press* 27 Oct. 1984: 6B.
"Author Richard Brautigan, known best for his 1967 novel Trout, is dead, an apparent suicide. He was 49."

833. Anonymous. "Poet-Writer Brautigan Found Dead in Home." *Bozeman Daily Chronicle Extra* 31 Oct. 1984: 6.
"Richard Brautigan, vagabond poet, offbeat novelist and a part-time Paradise Valley dweller who became a literary cult figure in the 1960s, was found dead in his Bolinas, Calif., home Thursday, Oct. 25, by friends, an apparent suicide victim."

834. Anonymous. "Richard Brautigan." *The Times* (London) 27 Oct. 1984: 12.
"Richard Brautigan, the American novelist, short story writer and poet has died at the age of 51. [Note that other news sources give his age as 49.] There was a kind of quality, suppressed but evident, in those early books [of fiction] which promised much. But Brautigan seemed not to have been able to go beyond it, or to develop.... His poems received little critical attention.... In later years, feeling that he had been unfairly discarded by public and critics alike, he became depressed and began to drink heavily."

835. Anonymous. "Richard Brautigan." *Washington Post* 27 Oct. 1984: B4.
"Richard Brautigan, 49, the author whose 1967 novel Trout made him a literary hero of the 1960s counterculture, was found dead of a gunshot wound Oct. 25 at his secluded home in Bolinas, Calif. The Marin County Coroner's Office said his death was an apparent suicide. Mr. Brautigan, whose body was found by friends who were concerned because he had not been seen in several weeks, was an unknown San Francisco poet when he published Trout, which sold two million copies. Another work, General, gave voice to the hippie generation."

836. Anonymous. "Richard Brautigan." *Time* 5 Nov. 1984: 80.
"Novelist and poet Richard Brautigan, 49, who became a campus hero in the 1960s with his whimsical novel Trout; reportedly of a self-inflicted gunshot wound, at his home in Bolinas, Calif. His works, which included General and

Watermelon, blended satire, extended metaphors and odd bits of information in a free-wheeling style that came to symbolize the hippie era. Later Brautigan lost favor with American critics (though he remained popular in France and Japan) and spent his last years emotionally troubled."

837. Anonymous. "Richard Brautigan 1935-1984." *Poetry* Dec. 1984: 178.
A poem seemingly written as an obituary.
"We age in darkness like wood
and watch our phantoms change
   their clothes
of shingles and boards
for a purpose that can only be
   described as wood."

838. Anonymous. "The Talk of the Town." *New Yorker* 3 Dec. 1984: 39.
"My friend Richard Brautigan, the writer, who recently died, had a penchant for absurdity akin to the jolly-serious outrages cooked up by the young Dadaists of Paris in the early nineteen-twenties."

839. Anonymous. "Vintage Brautigan: A fresh perspective." *Bozeman Daily Chronicle* 26 Oct. 1984: 1.
A eulogy composed of quotations from Watermelon, Pill, Rommel, and Express dealing with death and the consolation of grief for a dead friend.

840. Blei, Norbert. "In Memoriam: Richard Brautigan." *Milwaukee Journal* 11 Nov. 1984: [E]9.
"... [H]e was a writer in his time who attracted considerable attention. [H]e was our [Guillaume] Appolinaire ([Charles] Baudelaire, [Arthur] Rimbaud) and then some. [e.e.] cumming's whimsy. [William] Saroyan's mustache. The shadow of [Maxwell] Bodenheim. Variations on [Kurt] Vonnegut. He was all your eggs in one basket.... Wizard of weird metaphor. Savant of smiling similes.... You won't rest in peace, Richard. Promise?"

841. Bond, Peggy Lucas. "Richard Brautigan 1935-1984." *St. Petersburg Times* 2 June 1985: 7D.
"Maybe his death can be best explained in his own words:
When dreams wake
Life ends.
Then dreams are gone.
Life ends."

842. The Chronicle Staff and the Associated Press. "Brautigan Dead." *Bozeman Daily Chronicle* 26 Oct. 1984: 1, 2.
Incorporates Associated Press material and quotes from Bozeman residents who knew Brautigan.

843. Condon, Garret. "Locals Remember Brautigan in '60s." *Hartford Courant* 3 Nov. 1984: D1, 8.
Three Hartford residents remember Brautigan.

844. Dawson, Patrick. "Appreciation Can Give a Meaning to Endings." *Great Falls Tribune* 28 Oct. 1984: 3C.
Talks about Brautigan's lack of literary appreciation in the United States saying his work was appreciated far more in "Japan and France... he became more of an ignored national resource.... Today, all we can say is thanks to Richard Brautigan, for giving us so much of himself, for helping us to laugh at ourselves and feel things a bit more keenly."

845. Folkart, Burt A. "Brautigan, Literary Guru of the '60s, Dies." *Los Angeles Times* 27 Oct. 1984, Sec. 2: 7.

846. Foote, Jennifer. "An Author's Long Descent; Richard Brautigan: The Troubled Cult Hero and His Path to Suicide." *Washington Post* 23 Jan. 1985: D8-D9.
"Reprinted from yesterday's early editions." Recounts Brautigan's literary career through the remembrances of friends.

847. Haslam, Gerald. "A Last Letter to Richard Brautigan." *Western American Literature* 21(2) May 1976: 48-50.
Eulogy written as a personal letter. "You took [life] seriously and helped us to accept its seriousness with your flashing, your unexpected words."

848. Hinckle, Warren. "The Big Sky Fell In on Brautigan." *San Francisco Chronicle* 27 Oct. 1984: 4.

"Richard Brautigan's life was divided into three parts: Tokyo, North Beach and the Big Sky Country of Montana. A friend believes the third part helped kill him.... Ken Kelly, the writer and *Playboy* interviewer who became Brautigan's friend in the last decade of the writer's life [said] 'Up there you had a bunch of artistic weirdos living in rancher country. And the artists seemed compelled to compete in macho terms against the cowboys, and then tried to out-macho each other.... It was the whole mental macho thing in Montana that I think really got to Richard,' Kelly said. 'The books he wrote up there, like "Hawkline Monster," where full of violence—nothing like in the earlier hippie novels'."

849. Lynch, Dennis. "Tribute to a Friend and the Books That Might Have Been." *Chicago Tribune* 12 Nov. 1984, Sec. 5: 1, 8.

"The unexpected death of a respected writer evokes our sadness for the loss of life and for the loss of books that might have been.... To do the seemingly impossible and to make it appear easy—'to load mercury with a pitchfork'—is the writer's job, Brautigan's work tells us and he was a master of that art."

850. McDowell, Edwin. "Richard Brautigan, Novelist, A Literary Idol of the 1960s." *The New York Times* 27 Oct. 1984, Sec. 1: 33.

"Richard Brautigan, a literary idol of the 1960s who eventually fell out of fashion, was found dead Thursday at his secluded house in Bolinas, Calif.... Mr. Brautigan...divided his time between San Francisco and a small ranch near Livingston, Mont. He never learned to drive, never owned a car and by his own admission was inept at almost everything but writing."

851. Polman, Dick. "A '60s Hero's Pained Soul Is Finally Bared, in Death." *Philadelphia Inquirer* 3 Dec. 1984: E1.

"... [T]here is something quite sad about an artist who bares himself so willingly for an unresponsive audience."

852. Roiter, Margaret. "Death of a Poet: String Was Cut Between Brautigan and the World." *Bozeman Chronicle* 31 Oct. 1984: 3.

Discusses experiences in Brautigan's creative writing class at Montana State University and his death: "In his last novel he wrote a passage that seems fitting to be among his last: 'If ever I got pneumonia, I wanted whoever was there to tie a very long string on my finger and fasten the other end of the string to their finger and when they left the room if I felt I was dying, I could pull the string and they'd come back. I wouldn't die if there was a long piece of string between us.' In the end, there must not have been a string between Brautigan and the world."

853. Seymore, James. "Author Richard Brautigan Apparently Takes His Own Life, But He Leaves a Rich Legacy." *People* 12 Nov. 1984: 40.

Comments by Brautigan's publisher. "He felt at peace [in Japan] in a way that eluded him in Bolinas, his hideaway just north of San Francisco, or at his streamside home in Montana's Paradise Valley, where he loved to fish, even in the snow.... So long, sensei, Arigato, pardner."

854. Shorb, Terril. "This Fisher of Words Had Many a Winning Catch." *Billings Gazette* 7 Dec. 1984, Sec. D: 4.

"With his supple sentences and fragrant phrases, Richard Brautigan could tie his shoes with rainbows, comb his hair with the cold blue teeth of wind. He could stitch a cloud to a cliff with crowfeathers and spider spit. He could gargle stars, carry a faded river folded up in his wallet, invite you to a picnic of insight on the dainty red tablecloth of a hummingbird's heartbeat."

855. Smith, Barb. "Friends Say Stories Sensationalize Brautigan's Life After His Death." *Bozeman Daily Chronicle* 7 Nov. 1984: 29.

Brautigan's Montana friends defend him against charges of a violent lifestyle made by Ken Malley in a *San Francisco Chronicle* story by columnist Warren Hinckle.

856. Synder, George. "Brautigan Prepared for Death Since Summer, Friend Says." *San Francisco Chronicle* 27 Oct. 1984: 1, 14.

"Writer Richard Brautigan, who was found dead Thursday in his Bolinas home, apparently committed suicide—and a close friend said yesterday that the author had been preparing for death for some time."

857. T.B. "Letter from the North." *California Magazine* Jan. 1985: 116.

Laments the loss of North Beach, California characters. Recounts a conversation with Herb Gold, "North Beach doyen," about Brautigan. Gold said, 'What happens to a writer who has no strong connections with people, with family, with anything? When you hit your forties, you have to have some connection with the past. Brautigan was isolated. He had only intermittent contact with his daughter. He didn't consider others important. He didn't want to talk about his family. He never dealt with his [absent] father. He could have done something moving....'"

SOURCES

Abstracts of English Studies. 30 vols. Calgary: University of Calgary Press, 1958-Dec. 1987. Vol. 17, 654, 669-70; Vol. 20, 42, 120, 243, 670; Vol. 27, 86, 99, 353; Vol. 30, 193, 337.

Access. Eds. John Gordon Burke, Kathy Hill, and Ned Kehde. Syracuse: Gaylord Professional Publications, 1977-1985. Vol. 2, 28, 327; Vol. 9, 372.

American Authors and Books, 1640 to the Present Day. Third Edition. Eds. W.J. Burke and Will D. Howe. New York: Crown, 1972. 75.

American Poetry Index. Great Neck: Granger Book Co., 1983. Vol. 1, 1981-1982.

American Short-Fiction Criticism and Scholarship, 1959-1977 A Checklist. Ed. Joe Weixlman. Chicago: Swallow Press, 1982. 86-87.

Annual Bibliography of English Language and Literature. Terre Haute: Modern Humanities Research Association, 1921-1987. 1971, 571; 1972, 550; 1973, 612; 1974, 677-78; 1975, 634; 1976, 632; 1978, 534; 1980, 624-25; 1982, 575; 1983; 588; 1984, 563.

The Annual Index of the Times 1906-1987. Vaduz: Fraus Reprint, 1968-1987. 1970, Vol. 1, 35; 1971, Vol. 1, 33; Jan.-Mar. 1973, 71; Apr.-June 1975, 47; Apr.-June 1976, 57; 1977, Vol. 1, 183; 1978, Vol. 1, 173; 1981, Vol. 1, 153; 1983, 151; 1984, 130; May 1987, 14.

Annual Index to Poetry in Periodicals, 1984. Great Neck, NY: Poetry Index Press, 1985. 50.

Articles on American Literature 1968-1975. Comp. Leary Lewis. Durham, NC: Duke University Press, 1970. 48-49.

Arts & Humanities Citation Index. Philadelphia: Institute for Scientific Information, 1982-1987. 1975-1979, Vol. 1, 3925-26; 1980, Vol. 1, 925; 1981, Vol. 1, 881.

Author Biographies Master Index. Second Edition. 2 vols. Eds. Barbara McNeil and Miranda C. Herbert. Detroit: Gale Research Company, 1984. Vol. 1, 174.

Bibliographic Index. 27 vols. New York: H.W. Wilson Company, 1945-1988. 1976, 57.

Biography and Genealogy Master Index Second Edition. 8 vols. Eds. Miranda C. Herbert and Barbara McNeil. Detroit: Gale Research Company, 1980. Vol. 1, 611.

Biography and Genealogy Master Index, 1981-85 Cumulation. 5 vols. Ed. Barbara McNeil. Detroit: Gale Research Company, 1985. Vol. 1, 430.

Biography Index. New York: H.W. Wilson Co., 1949-Feb. 1988. Vol. 9, 84; Vol. 10, 86; Vol. 12, 93.

Book Review Digest 1905-1987. 83 vols. New York: H.W. Wilson Company, 1905-1987. 1970, 174.

Book Review Index. Detroit: Gale Research Company, 1965-1988. 1965 Cumulation, [no page numbers]; 1968 Cumulation, 76; 1980 Cumulation, 61; 1981 Cumulation, 75; 1982 Cumulation, 73; 1983 Cumulation, 75; 1984 Cumulation, 97.

Book Review Index: A Master Cumulation 1969-1979. 7 vols.
Detroit: Gale Research Company, 1980. Vol. 1, 334.

Books in Print 1988-89. 3 vols. New York: R.R. Bowker Company,
1988. Vol. 1, 673.

Books in Print 1987-88. 3 vols. New York: R.R. Bowker Company,
1987. Vol. 1, 645.

Bower, David A. and Carol Campbell Strempek. Index to Evergreen
Review. Metuchen, NJ: Scarecrow Press, Inc., 1972. 21.

British Books in Print 1986. 4 vols. London: J. Whitaker & Sons,
Ltd. 1986. Vol. 1, 799.

BRS Information Technologies. Lathan, New York. Computer
database searched 20 Nov. 1987.

Chicorel Index to Poetry in Anthologies and Collections in Print. Ed.
Marietta Chicorel. New York: Chicorel Library Publishing
Corp., 1974. Vol. 5, 170-72.

Chicorel Index to Poetry in Anthologies and Collections in Print.
1979 Edition. Ed. Marietta Chicorel. New York: Chicorel
Library Publishing Corp., 1978. Vol. 5, 84.

Chicorel Index to Short Stories in Anthologies and Collections. Ed.
Marietta Chicorel. New York: Chicorel Library Publishing
Corp., 1974. Vol. 12, 261-64.

Contemporary Authors. 122 vols. Detroit: Gale Research Company,
1974. Cumulative Indexes: Vols. 45-48, 17; Vols. 53-56, 12;
Vols. 69-72, 17; Vols. 77-80, 18; Vols. 85-88, 19; Vols. 97-
100, 20; Vol. 102, 574; Vol. 104, 568; Vol. 106, 569; Vol.
108, 581; Vol. 110, 575; Vol. 112, 563; Vol. 113, 65-6;
Vol. 114, 516; Vol. 116, 548; Vol. 118, 565; Vol. 120,
469; Vol. 122, 534.

Cumulative Index to Periodical Literature. March 1959-February 1970.
7 vols. Princeton: National Library Service Corp., 1976.
Vol. 1, 904.

Current Book Review Citations. New York: H. W. Wilson Company, 1977-1983. 1976, 70; 1977, 98; 1978, 97; 1979, 78. 1981, 99; 1982, 83.

DIALOG Database. Palo Alto, CA: Dialog Information Services, Inc. Date of search: 2, 6 Nov. 1987 and 15 Dec. 1989. Databases:
Academic American Encyclopaedia
America: History and Life (1963-1987)
Associated Press News (July 1983-April 1987)
Associated Press News (May 1987-October 1987)
Biography Master Index A-L
Book Review Index (1969-1987)
1987 Conference Papers Index (1973-1987)
Dissertation Abstracts Online (1861-October 1987)
ERIC (Educational Resources Information Center)
Everyman's Encyclopedia
Language Abstracts (1973-September 1987)
Library and Information Science Abstracts
LC MARC (Library of Congress Machine Readable Cataloging)
Magazine Index (1959-March 1970 and 1973-October 1987)
Magills Survey of Cinema
Marquis Who's Who (1982-July 1987)
MLA Bibliography (1965-June 1986)
National Newspaper Index (1979-October 1987)
Philosopher's Index (1940-October 1987)
Religion Index (1949-April 1987)
REMARC (Retrospective Machine Readable Calaloging pre-1900—July 1986)
United Press International News (April 1983-October 1987).

Essay and General Literature Index. 14 vols. New York: H.W. Wilson Company, 1934-1986. Vol. 8, 171; Vol. 10, 205.

French Periodical Index 1973-1986. Westwood, MA: F.W. Faxon Company, 1974-1987. 1977, 96; 1983, 29.

Havlice, Patricia Pate. Index to Literary Biography. 2 vols. Metuchen Scarecrow Press, 1975. Vol. 1, 156.

Humanities Index. (Split from Social Sciences & Humanities Index in 1975) 14 vols. New York: H. W. Wilson Company, 1975-

Mar. 1988. Vol. 1, 52; Vol. 2, 81; Vol. 3, 87; Vol. 9, 102; Vol. 11, 113; Vol. 12, 128.

Index to Book Reviews in the Humanities. 27 Vols. Comp. Phillip Thomson. Williamson, MI: {Publisher?}, 1964-1985. Vol. 6, 1965, 49; Vol. 9, 196, 28; Vol. 10,1969, 38; Vol. 11, 1970, 37; Vol. 12, 1971, 33; Vol. 13, 1972, 38; Vol. 14, 1973, 45; Vol. 15, 1974, 43; Vol. 16, 1975, 45; Vol. 17, 1976, 45; Vol. 18, 1977, 47; Vol. 19, 1978, 46; Vol. 20, 1979, 44; Vol. 21, 1980, 46; Vol. 22, 1981, 47; Vol. 23, 1982, 43; Vol. 24, 1983, 45; Vol. 25, 1984, 47.

Index to Commonwealth Little Magazines 1968-1969. Comp. Stephen H. Goode. Troy: Whitston Publishing Co., 1970. 31.

Index to Little Magazines, 1956-1957. Comps. Eugene P. Sheehy and Kenneth A. Lohf. Denver: Alan Swallow, 1958. 17.

Index to Little Magazines, 1960-1961. Comps. Eugene P. Sheehy and Kenneth A. Lohf. Denver: Alan Swallow, 1962. 28.

Index to Little Magazines, 1962-1963. Comps. Eugene P. Sheehy and Kenneth A. Lohf. Denver: Alan Swallow, 1964. 25.

Index to Little Magazines 1964-1965. Comps. Evelyn G. Lauer, Sarah S. Ropes, and Eizenija B. Shera. Denver: Alan Swallow, 1966. 26.

Index to Little Magazines 1966-1967. Comp. Evelyn G. Lauer. Chicago: Swallow Press, 1970. 26.

Index Translationum. Paris: United Nations Educational, Scientific and Cultural Organization, 1975-1986. 25, 1972, 542, 546; 26, 1973, 578; 27, 1974, 49, 285, 312, 462; 28, 1975, 273, 422; 29, 1976, 186, 364, 497, 701; 30, 1977, 369, 524, 562, 833; 31, 1978, 69, 208, 434, 565, 601, 734; 33, 1980, 73, 316, 451; 34, 1981, 387.

Literary Criticism Index. Eds. Alan R. Weiner and Spencer Means. Metuchen: Scarecrow Press, 1984. 77-78.

Magill Books Index. Ed. Frank N. Magill. Englewood Cliffs: Salem Press, 1980. 36.

Magill's Literary Annual 1978. Ed. Frank N. Magill. Englewood Cliffs: Salem Press, 1978. 785.

MLA International Bibliography of Books and Articles on the Modern Languages and Literatures. New York: Modern Language Association of America, 1964-1987. 1971, Vol. 1, 143; 1972, Vol. 1, 154; 1973, Vol. 1, 156, 164; 1974, Vol. 1, 169; 1975, Vol. 1, 185, Vol. 2, 210; 1976, Vol. 1, 181; 1977, Vol. 1, 164; 1978, Vol. 1, 197, 224; 1980, Vol. 1, 228, 232, 264; 1981, Vol. 1, 204, 207; 1983, Vol. 1, 227, 241, 271; 1984, Vol. 1, 185, 225; 1985, Vol. 1, 200, 221; 1986, Vol. 1, 193, 225.

Monthly Periodical Index 1979. Princeton: National Library Service Company, 1980. 44.

New York Times Index. New York: R. R. Bowker and The New York Times Company, 1961-Jan. 1988. 1971, 204; 1972, 242; 1974, 251; 1975, 250, 276; 1976, 187; 1977, 161; 1979, 184, 192; 1980,180; 1982, 128; 1984, 223.

Newsbank Urban Affairs Library: Literature Index. New Caanan, CT: Newsbank, Inc. Cumulative Index 1977, 1980-1981.

Newsbank Urban Affairs Library: Name Index. New Caanan, CT: Newsbank, Inc. Cumulative Index 1973-1981.

OCLC (Online Computer Library Center). Dublin, OH.

The Official Washington Post Index. Woodbridge, Conn.: Research Publications, 1979-1987. 1980: 90.

Personal Name Index to the New York Times Index. 1851-1974. 25 vols. Succasunna, NJ: Roxbury Data Interface, 1977. Vol. 3, 220.

Personal Name Index to the New York Times Index. 1975-1979 Supplement. Succasunna, NJ: Roxbury Data Interface, 1984. 153.

Reader's Guide to Periodical Literature. 89 vols. New York: H.W. Wilson, 1944-1987. Vol. 29, 171; Vol. 30, 174; Vol. 31, 164; Vol. 32, 167; Vol. 34, 158; Vol. 35, 159; Vol. 38, 202; Vol. 39, 207; Vol. 41, 244; Vol. 44, 272; Vol. 45, 301.

Review of the Arts. Literature. New Canaan, CT: Newsbank, Inc. 1983-1988. July 1982-June 1983, 44; July 1983-June 1984, 41; July 1984-June 1985, 49.

Short Story Index. Supplement 1969-1973. Ed. Estelle A. Fidler. New York: H.W. Wilson Co., 1974. 64.

Short Story Index. Supplement 1974-1978. Ed. Gary L. Bogart. New York: H.W. Wilson Co., 1979. 78.

Short Story Index. Supplement 1979-1983. Ed. Juliette Yaakov. New York: H.W. Wilson Co., 1984. 93.

Social Sciences & Humanities Index. (Formerly International Index). New York: H.W. Wilson Company, 1966-1974. Apr. 1969-Mar. 1970, 54; Apr. 1971-Mar. 1972, 51; Apr. 1973-Mar. 1974, 59.

Survey of Contemporary Literature. Revised Edition. 12 vols. Ed. Frank N. Magill. Englewood Cliffs, NJ: Salem Press, 1977. Vol. 12, Author Index, III.

The Times Index. Reading, England: Research Publications Limited, 1960-1987. 1970, II, 35; 1971, I, 33; 1973, 71; 1975, 47; 1976, 57; 1977, 183; 1978, 173; 1981, 153; 1983, 151; 1984, 130; May 1987, 14.

TriQuarterly Cumulative Index 1964-1981 Issues 1-50. Comp. Michael McDonnell. {Evanston: Northwestern University Press, 1982?} 7.

Twentieth-Century Literary Criticism. 27 vols. Detroit: Gale Research Company, 1978-1987. Vol. 27, 440.

Twentieth-Century Short Story Explication. Third Edition. Comp. Warren S. Walker. Hamden, CT: The Shoe String Press, 1977. 72.

Twentieth-Century Short Story Explication. Supplement I to Third Edition. Comp. Warren S. Walker. Hamden, CT: The Shoe String Press, 1980. 25.

INDEX

This index attempts to access information about Richard Brautigan from as many directions as possible. It includes book titles, journal and article titles, authors' names, and some subject terms. However, because this is an index of bibliographic citations, and because the annotations for each citation are necessarily brief, specific subject terms do not appear frequently. The reader is advised to consult the Table of Contents, peruse this index, and read the annotations to discover possible leads for specific subject terms.

Book titles are underlined. Journal and newspaper titles are italicized. Poems and short story titles appear in quotation marks. All titles by Brautigan are shown in bold face.

Index numbers refer to citation numbers, not page numbers.

A

Abbott, Keith, 204, 339, 813, 814
"Abortion and the Mission Moral Center: Two Case Histories from the Post-Modern Novel," 536
Abortion: An Historical Romance, The, 208, 234, 241, 275, 278, 322, 343, 361, 525, 529, 532, 536, 542, 543, 544, 546, 549, 551, 552, 554, 557, 561, 563, 592
    Translations:
    Avortement, (French), 118
    L'Aborto, (Italian)119

Goyohan apeum, (Korean), 120
Die Abtreibung, (German), 121, 122
"Absorbing Chaos," 403
Academic American Encyclopedia, 244, 301
"Acid-Rock Western, An," 602
Ackroyd, Peter, 567, 640, 687, 697
Acton, Jay, 319
Adams, Phoebe-Lou, 525, 568, 606, 641
Adams, Robert, 241
"Adrenalin Mother," 29, 43
Advent Publishers, 210
"After Halloween Slump," 22, 60
"After the (Mimeograph) Revolution," 310
American Library Association (ALA), 234
"Alas, Measured Perfectly," 29
"Alas and Alack for This Babylon, An," 688
"Albion Breakfast," 22
"All Watched Over by Machines of Loving Grace," 17, 29, 30, 50, 51, 59
All Watched Over by Machines of Loving Grace, 16, 17, 18, 19, 20, 22, 29, 247, 251, 256, 399
Allen, Donald, 29, 94, 106, 314
Altman, Dennis, 369
"Altre Seduzioni, Trout Fishing in America di Richard Brautigan," 479
America, 544
American 1960s, The, 299
American Authors and Books, 209
American Book Review 730
American Civil Liberties Union, 234, 236
"American Fiction 1974-1976, People Who Fell to Earth," 594
American Fiction of the Sixties, 381
American Fictions 1940-1980, 295
"American Folk Hero," 773
"American Gothic Comes of Age," 593
American Literary Anthology, The, 33, 38
American Literary Scholarship: An Annual 1972, 293
American Literary Scholarship: An Annual 1973, 294
American Literature, 286, 313, 503
American Poetry Review, 551, 592
American Poets Since World War II, 251
"American Post-Modernism," 365
"American Submarine, The," 13
Amerikastudien, 372
"Amis of Industry," 713
"An Eye For Good Produce," 187
Anatomy of Wonder. A Critical Guide to Science Fiction, 569, 570

Index

Ancola, Jim, 698
Anderson Union High School, 234
Anderson, Patrick, 183
Annotated Bibliography, An, 219
Annotated Bibliography of California Fiction, 1664-1970, An, 447
Annual Obituary Index, 1984, The, 242
Another World: A Second Anthology of Works from the St. Marks Poetry Poetry Project, 46
Anthony, Gene, 245
"'Anyway, All I Ever Wanted to Be Was a Poet.' Said Leon Uris, with a Smile, as We Strode Together into the Vomitorium...," 423
Appolinaire, Guillaume, 840
"Appreciation Can Give a Meaning to Endings," 844
"April 7, 1969," 374
"April Ground," 11
Architectural Design, 62
Ardery, Peter, 33, 38
"Arithmetic," 115
"As Big as the Ritz," 603
"As the Bruises Fade, the Lightning Aches," 37, 45, 52
"Aspects of Americans," 565
"At the California Institute of Technology," 22
Atchity, Kenneth, 740
Athens Messenger, 411
Atlantic 246, 525, 568, 606, 641
"Auction, The," 172, 183
Aura Broadside Series, 60
Aura Literary/Arts Review, 60
Australian and New Zealand American Studies Association, 369
Australian Journal of French Studies, 391
Austrian Diner's Club Magazine, 204
"Author Goes to College—as a Teacher," 240
"Author Richard Brautigan Apparently Takes His Own Life, But He Leaves a Rich Legacy," 853
"Author's Long Descent; Richard Brautigan: The Troubled Cult Hero and His Path to Suicide, An," 846
Autobiography (Good-Bye, Ultra Violet), 57, 61
Autobiography of a Super-Tramp, 473
"Automatic Anthole," 29
"Automobile Accident, The," 123
Auwera, Fernand, 362
"Avant-Garde and After," 300

B

Baird, Newton D., 447
Baker, Roger, 531
Bales, Kent, 477
Baltimore Sun, 749
Bannon, Barbara A., 532, 574, 575, 576, 612, 613, 645, 673, 674, 701, 702, 741
Barber, John F., 200, 219
Barnes, Julian, 577, 614
Barnett, Richard J., 578
Baronian, Jean-Baptiste, 363
Barron, Neil, 569, 570
Barth, John, 246, 365, 376, 388
Barthelme, Donald, 226, 299, 328, 337, 365, 657
Baton Rouge Sunday Advocate, 766
Baudelaire, Charles, 393, 840
Beat, 457, 464, 761, 471,
Beat Generation, 642, 825
Beat Generation, The, 265
Beat Movement, 265, 299
Beatitude, 22
Beatitude Anthology, 13
Beatles' Lyrics, The, 199
"Beautiful Poem, The," 20, 22
Beaver, Harold, 646
Bedell, Thomas D., 615, 616
Bednarczyk, A.J., 647
Beh, Siew-Hwa, 314
Bellow, Saul, 376
Benoit, Claude, 364
Berg, Peter, 245, 314
Berger, Thomas, 687
Berrigan, Ted, 403
Berry, John D., 703
Best American Short Stories 1972, The, 184, 247
Best of California, The, 204
Best of TriQuarterly, The, 194
Best Sellers, 432, 529, 555, 630, 647, 727
"Betrayed Kingdom, The," 173, 183
"Betwixt Tradition and Innovation," 421
Bibliographical Introduction to Seventy-Five Modern American Authors, A, 215
Bienen, Leigh B., 450
"Big Sky Fell In on Brautigan, The," 848

Big Sur, 447, 456
Big Venus, 31
Billings Gazette, 826, 854
Biography Almanac, 248
Birmingham News, 756
Blackburn, Sara, 773
Blackwell, Earl, 254
Blake, Harry, 365
Blakeston, Oswell, 533
"Blazing Saddles," 576
"Bleak Choice," 474
Blei, Norbert, 840
Bloodworth, W., 249
"Bloomsbury Comes to Big Sky, and the New Rocky Mountains," 243
Blue Book: Leaders of the English Speaking World, 250
Blue Suede Shoes, 57
Blumberg, Myrna, 617
"Boat, A," 11
Bodenheim, Maxwell, 840
"Body Discovered in California Is Believed to Be Brautigan's," 816
Bogklub, Samlerens, 129
Bokinsky, Caroline G., 251, 392, 393, 396, 398, 400, 402, 412, 427, 438
Bond, Peggy Lucas, 841
"Boo, Forever," 29
"Book Censorship Increasing in Schools," 233
Book Week, 457
Bookletter, 623, 648
Booklist, The, 425, 431, 441, 527, 572, 608, 643, 685, 704, 742, 768
Books & Bookmen, 451, 475, 508, 533, 757
"Books Briefly," 578
"Books in Brief," 623
"Books," 401
Boston Globe, 688
Boundary, 307
Bourgois, C., 75, 83, 84, 109, 134, 139, 146, 151, 157
Boyer, Jay, 205
Bozeman Chronicle, 239, 852
Bozeman Daily Chronicle, 833, 839, 842, 855
Bradbury, Malcolm, 318
"Brain Candy for Literary Sweet Tooth," 716
Bramwell, Murray, 369
Brand, Stewart, 97, 478
Brann, Helen, 269, 314, 320, 361, 830
Brann-Hartnett Agency, 352
Brautigan, Bernard, 815, 818
Brautigan, Ianthe, 314
"Brautigan Briefs," 780

"Brautigan Dead," 842
"Brautigan Death Called Self-inflicted," 820
"Brautigan Discusses His Writing, Teaching," 237
"Brautigan Engineers a Train of Uncoupled Empty Thoughts," 723
"Brautigan in Montana," 255
"Brautigan, Literary Guru of the '60s, Dies," 845
"Brautigan Prepared for Death Since Summer, Friend Says," 856
"Brautigan Produces a Yawner," 762
"Brautigan Was Here," 241
"Brautigan Writes It Down Before It Becomes American Dust," 765
"Brautigan Writing at His Peak," 705
"Brautigan's 'Buffoon Mutation'," 600
"Brautigan's Express Trip Past 130 Stops," 732
"Brautigan's Funky Fishing Yarn," 501
"Brautigan's 'The Hawkline Monster': As Big as the Ritz," 603
"Brautigan's 'Homage to the San Francisco YMCA'," 777
"Brautigan's Latest Novel," 767
"Brautigan's Mad Body-Snatcher," 681
"Brautigan's Mythical Trip into Bogart Country," 690
"Brautigan's Next Novel Slated for Fall by S & S," 635
"Brautigan's 'Rommel Drives on Deep into Egypt'," 420
"Brautigan's Stylish Touch Turns a Grim Story into a Fairy Tale," 746
"Brautigan's Talents Lost in Gimmickry," 721
"Brautigan's 'Trout Fishing in America'," 315
"Brautigan's Wake," 314
"Break and Enter to Breakaway, Scotching Modernism in the Social Novel of the American Sixties," 307
"Breaking Bread at Big Sur," 78
Brein, Alan, 675
Brent, Jonathan, 194
Brick, Ann, 234
"Briefly Noted," 610, 694
Brock, Bill, 22
Brooks, Jeremy, 618, 649
Brosnahan, John, 704, 742
Brown, F. J., 451
Brownjohn, Alan, 403
Broyard, Anatole, 774
Bryfonski, Dedria, 261, 262, 394, 415, 439, 455, 485, 513, 540, 581, 621, 622, 653, 654, 677, 678, 776, 798
"Buffalo Gals, Won't You Come Out Tonight?," 123
Bulletin of Bibliography, 214
Burke, William Jeremiah, 209
Burroughs, William, 825
Busani, Marina, 479
Butts, Leonard Culver, 220
Butwin, Joseph, 534

C

Cabau, Jacques, 579
Cabibbo, Paola, 535
Cadogan, Lucy, 452
"Calendula," 23
Caliban, 686
California, 204
California Institute of Technology, 319
California Living Magazine, 48, 53, 57, 158
California Magazine, 813, 857
"California Native Flowers," 23
"Camera at the Crucifixion, A," 618
Camp de L'Arpa: Revista de Literatura, 389
Campbell, Patty, 743
"CandleLion Poem, A," 29
Cannery Row, 390
"Cantos Falling," 11
Cape, Jonathan, 27, 71, 80, 107, 117, 126, 138, 144, 155, 181
Cariage, Daniel, 253
Carpenter, Don, 314, 705
Carr, Adam, 650
"Carrots," 23
Carson, Johnny, 628
Cartano, Tony, 619
"Carthage Sink," 186
Casey, Charles, 651
Cassady, Neil, 825
"Cassandra Syndrome," 604
"Castle of the Cormorants, The," 11
"Cat," 11
Catalogue, 37
Catholic Library World, 562
Cawelti, John G., 676
"Celebration of Solipsism: A New Trend in American Fiction, The," 277
Celebrity Register, 254
Censorship, 233
"C'est Magnifique mais Ce N'est pas Daguerre," 800
Chaffin, Terrell, 221
Chandler, Raymond, 376, 670, 691
Change, 183, 257
Chappel, Steve, 255
Charyn, Jerome, 96
Cheatham, Bertha M., 234
Checklist, A, 213
Chekhov, Anton, 631

Chénetier, Marc, 206, 317, 366, 367, 368
Chicago Review, 296
Chicago Sun-Times, 676
Chicago Tribune, 830, 849
Chicago Tribune Book World, 325, 554, 690, 746
"Childhood Spent in Tacoma, A," 11
"Chinese Checker Players, The," 11, 29, 51, 58
Choice, 426, 436, 448, 528, 642, 670
Christgau, Robert, 652
Christian Science Monitor, 593, 767
Ciardi, John, 453, 480
City Lights Anthology, 55, 57
City Lights Bookstore, 825
City Lights Journal, 90, 91
City of Words, American Fiction 1950-1970, 504
Clancey, Laurie, 369
Clark, Jeff, 706, 707
Clark, Tom, 201
Clark, William Bedford, 536
Clayton, John, 481
Clear Creek, 57
Cleary, Michael, 482
"Cleveland Wrecking Yard, The," 94, 95, 98, 101
Clinton Street Quarterly, 204
Clockwork Worlds, 256
"Closets," 66
Coastlines, 397
Coats, Reed, 537
"Cocinas de Placer," 637
CoEvolution Quarterly, 57, 158
Cohen, Joseph, 744
Cole, William, 620
Coleman, John, 454, 483, 510
Collection of Over 125 Poems, A, 44
College Review Service, 538
Collins, Robert A., 600
"Comets," 22, 60
Commonweal, 499
Communication Company, The, 16, 18, 19, 20, 22, 245
Companion to California, A, 278
"Complicated Banking Problems," 169, 183
Condon, Garret, 843
Confederate General from Big Sur, A, 70, 208, 234, 241, 273, 278, 292, 299, 322, 327, 361, 375, 383, 406, 449, 450, 454, 459, 460, 461, 463, 464, 465, 466, 468, 469, 470, 520, 782, 835, 836
    Translations:

Il Generale Immaginario, (Italian), 72
Generaal In Grijs, (Dutch), 73
Biggu sâ no nangun shôgun, (Japanese), 74
La Général Sudiste de Big Sur, (French), 75
En Konføderat General frå Big Sur, (Norwegian), 76
Ein Konföderierter General aus Big Sur, (German), 77
Contemporary American Literature, 1945-1972, 279
Contemporary Authors, 824
Contemporary Authors Vols. 53-56, 257
Contemporary Literary Criticism, 404, 413, 414, 455, 485, 486, 511, 653, 678, 708, 799
Contemporary Literary Criticism, Vol. 1, 258, 775
Contemporary Literary Criticism, Vol. 3, 259, 511, 539
Contemporary Literary Criticism, Vol. 5, 260, 512, 580
Contemporary Literary Criticism, Vol. 9, 261, 513, 622, 653, 677
Contemporary Literary Criticism, Vol. 12, 262, 394, 415, 439, 540, 581, 621, 654, 776, 798
Contemporary Literary Criticism, Vol. 42, 263, 484, 541, 582, 679, 745
Contemporary Literary Criticism Yearbook 1984, 264
Contemporary Literature, 594
Contemporary Novelists, 344, 345, 346
Contemporary Poets of the English Language, 211
Contemporary Poets, 282, 283, 311
Cook, Bruce, 265, 583
"Cookie Baking in America," 560
Cooley, John, 313
Cooper, James Fenimore, 223, 501
Coordinates, 288
Coover, Robert, 185, 226, 337, 365
Copps, Dale G., 623
Corodimas, Peter, 98
Corona, 66
"Corporal," 170, 183
Correll, Richard, 15
"Counterculture 'Love Story', A," 553
Coyote, Peter, 314
Coyote's Journal, 164, 183
"Crab Cigar," 29
Crane, Stephen, 459
Creeley, Robert, 94, 428
"Crete Stop for Brautigan," 698
Critical Anthology of the Short Story, A, 101
Critical Survey of Long Fiction, English Language Series, 276
Critique, 218, 461, 492, 501, 506, 516, 542, 603
Crosby, Margaret, 234, 235

"Crow Maiden," 49, 57
Cuadernos del Norte, 364
Cuadernos Hispanoamericanos, 370
"Cult Express," 728
"Cult Figure in the 1960s, Brautigan Has Successfully Moved into a New Era, A," 298
cummings, e.e., 840
Cumulative Book Index, 212
Cunningham, Valentine, 584
"Curiously Young Like a Freshly-Dug Grave," 47, 57
Curley, Dorthy Nyren, 316
"Curtains," 691
"Cute Brautigan," 605
"Cyclops," 11

D

Dadaists, 838
Daily, Robert, 709
Dalhousie Review, 292
Dallas Morning News, 719, 762
Daum, Timothy, 429, 430, 655, 656
Davenport, Guy, 800
Davie, W.H., 473
Davis, Hope Hale, 624
Davis, Kenn, 7, 11
Davis, L.J., 625
Davis, Lloyd, 213
Davis, Rick, 680
Dawson, Patrick, 844
"Day They Busted the Grateful Dead, The," 29, 44
"Dazzling Landscapes," 407
de Angulo, Gui, 12
"Dead Pan Alley," 646
"Death Is a Beautiful Car Parked Only," 29
"Death Like a Needle," 42, 57
"Death of a Poet: String Was Cut Between Brautigan and the World," 852
"Death of a Salesman," 629
"Death of the Dream," 755
"December 24," 22, 29, 59
"December 30," 22
DeMarinis, Rick, 746
Dempster, Nigel, 718
"Des Fjords Pluvieux... Du Nordouest ...," 379
Des Moines Sunday Register, 735

Desruisseaux, Paul, 681
Detroit Free Press, 815, 832
Detweiler, Robert, 104
Dickey, James, 220
Dictionary of Literary Biography Vol. 2. American Novelists Since World War II, 322
Dictionary of Literary Biography Vol. 5. American Novelists Since World War II, 251, 392, 393, 396, 398, 400, 402, 412, 427, 438
Dictionary of Literary Biography Yearbook 1984, 320
Dictionary of Literature in the English Language from 1940 to 1970, A, 267
Die Ameriikanische Short Story der Gegenwart: Interpretationen, 781
Dietrich, Richard F, 190, 777
Dietsche Warande en Belfort:, 362
Diggers, 245, 314
Dillard, Annie, 313
Dingman, Tony, 314
Dionne, Virginia, 827
Directory of American Poets and Fiction Writers, A, 269
Directory of American Poets, A, 268, 269
Directory of American Writers, A, 270
Disch, Thomas M., 682
"Discovery," 29, 43
Disjunctive Writers, 306
Dissertation Abstracts International, 220, 223, 224, 225, 226, 227, 228
"Distinctive and Conjunctive Modes in Contemporary American Fiction," 306
"Distinguished Writer Joins MSU English Staff," 238
Ditsky, John, 271
"Dive-Bombing the Lower Emotions," 55, 57
Dixon, Kent, 185
"Dogs on the Roof," 160
Donner Party, 37, 45
Doss, John 314
Doss, Margot Patterson, 314
"Double-Bed Dream Gallows, The," 29
"Double with Christina, A," 273
Downing, Pamela, 487, 585
Downstream from "Trout Fishing in America," 204, 339
"Dream and the Pen, The," 505, 523
Dreaming of Babylon, 146, 322, 343, 364, 376, 672, 673, 674, 676, 680, 683, 686, 687, 689, 692
   Translations:
   Babylon o yume mite, (Japanese), 149
   Träume von Babylon. Ein Detektivromam 1942, (German), 153
   Un privé a Babylon, (French), 151
   Dectective en Babilonia: Novela Negra, (Spanish), 152

"Dropping Out: Spiritual Crisis and Countercultural Attitudes in Four
   American Novelists of the 1960s," 224
Duberstein, Larry, 778
Duerden, Richard, 12
Dugdale, Anthony, 62
Duke University, 238
"Dumber Than Dumb," 682
Dunn, Joe, 7
Dunn, Thomas P., 256
Durrant, Digby, 747
Dutton Review, 122, 123

E

Earth, 158
Earth, Air, Fire, & Water, 272
"Easy Writer," 789
"Echoes of 'Walden' in 'Trout Fishing in America'," 491
"Edge of Hysteria, The," 597
"**Education,**" 29
Edwards, Thomas R., 657
"Eight of the Best," 649
"El Mito Como Consumo: Richard Brautigan," 389
"El Regresso del Detective Privado [The Return of the Private Detective]," 364
"**Elbow of a Dead Duck, The,**" 37, 45
Emerson, Ralph Waldo, 207
Encounter, 663
Encyclopedia of Science Fiction and Fantasy Through 1968, The, 210
"End Papers," 456
"End-of-the-Novel and the Endings of Novels, The," 383
"Energy and Whimsy," 803
English in India... Entertaining Advice...Words to Wow With, The, 764
"Enter, Pursued by a Bear," 658
Epos, 1, 2, 9
Erdosi, Elizabeth, 779
Erlich, Richard D., 256
"Erotica II," 221
"**Escape of the Owl, The,**" 11
"Escape through Imagination in 'Trout Fishing in America'," 492
Esprit, 632
Esquire, 57, 158, 174, 183, 188, 464
"Ethics in Embryo-Abortion and the Problem of Morality in Post-War German
   Literature," 545
Etudes Anglaises, 383
Evergreen, 158

Index 207

Evergreen Review, 90, 93, 169, 173, 183, 197
Evergreen Review Reader, 1957-1967 A Ten Year Anthology, 95
"Experimental Fiction," 281
Exploded Form: The Modernist Novel in America, 315
Exploited Eden: Literature on the American Enviornment, 50, 399
"Exploration and Defense of the Humor in Young Adult Literature, An," 406, 465, 520
Exponent, 238
Exquisite Corpse, 204

F

"Faces of Fiction," 376
Falk, Peter, 8
Fallowell, Duncan, 626
Fantastic in Literature, The, 329
Fantastic Worlds: Myths, Tales, and Stories," 191
Farrell, J.G., 488, 514, 780
Fechheimer, David, 314
"Feel Free to Marry Emily Dickinson," 11, 31
Feiffer, Jules, 687
Feinstein, Elaine, 683
Feld, Michael, 273
Ferlinghetti, Lawrence, 55, 314, 825
"Ferris Wheel, The," 11
"Fever Monument, The," 12, 29, 32
"Fiction," 531, 617, 659, 683, 726
"Fiction: The 1930s to the Present," 294
Fiene, Donald M., 489
"15 Stories in One Poem," 5
"Finding Is Losing Something Else," 48, 57
"Finny Peculiar," 483, 510
First International Conference on the Fantastic in Literature and Film, 600
First Reader of Contemporary American Poetry, A, 32
"First Winter Snow, The," 29
"Fishing the Ambivalence, or, A Reading of 'Trout Fishing in America.'," 477
"Five Novels," 657
"Five Poems," 42, 57
"Five Poets," 433
Fjetland, Evelyn, 818
Flaherty, Joe, 684
Fleming, Ian, 571
Fletcher, Connie, 431, 685
Fletcher, Janet, 442, 587, 615, 655, 706
"Flowers for Those You Love," 18, 22

Foff, Arthur, 100
Foley, Martha, 184, 247
Folkart, Burt A., 845
Folston, Mary Lula, 815, 818
Fonda, Peter, 314
"Food for Thought in Richard Brautigan's Trout Fishing in America," 494
"Fooling Around, and Serious Business," 598
Foot, 12
"**Football**," 189
Foote, Jennifer, 846
"**For Fear You Will Be Alone**," 53, 57
"Forma Si Substanta Umorului la Richard Brautigan," 387
Formula Western, 249
Forum, 306
Foster, Edward Halsey, 207, 470
<u>Four New Poets</u>, 3
"**Fragile, Fading 37/A Poem**," 40
"**Fragment**," 11
Franco, Jean, 318
Frank, Sheldon, 627
Frankenstein, 331, 334, 376, 569
<u>Free City</u>, 35
Free You, 37
Freese, Peter, 781
Fremont-Smith, Eliot, 628
"Fresh Perspective, A," 839
"Friends Find Author Brautigan Dead at His Home in California," 826
"Friends Say Stories Sensationalize Brautigan's Life After His Death," 855
"From Breton to Barthelme: Westward the Course of Surrealism," 355
"From the American Playground," 697
"From the Spring Lists," 794
"Frontier Sensibility in Novels of Jack Kerouac, Richard Brautigan and Tom Robbins, The," 228
Frumkin, Gene, 397
"Fulfillment Elusive, Brautigan Reminds Us," 744
"Fun in Section Eight," 457
Furbank, P.N., 490, 515

G

<u>Galilee Hitch-Hiker, The</u>, 8, 213, 247, 251
Gallego, Candido Perez, 370, 371
Galloway, David, 781
Gangewere, Robert J., 50, 399
Gannon, Edward, 432

"Garden in the Machine: Three Postmodern Pastorals," The , 266
Gardner, John, 220
Gardner, Peggy C., 522
"Garfish, Chili Dogs, and the Human Torch: Memories of Richard Brautigan and San Francisco, 1966," 814
"Garlic Meat Lady from, The," 29
Gass, William, 365
"Gee, You're So Beautiful That It's Starting to Rain," 29
"Gendai Shosetsu No Ending: Pynchon, Barth, Brautigan," 388
"General Custer Versus the Titanic," 29, 32
Genesis, 517
"Gentle 'Wind' Stirs Up Tragic Boyhood Memory," 753
"Gentle Brautigan & the Nasty Seventies, The," 638
"Gentle Poet of the Young," 338
"Geometry," 11
Georgia Review, 271
Germanic Review, 545
"Getting a Fix on Fall Books," 660
"Gifts," 3
Gillespie, B., 274
Gilroy, Harry, 456
Ginsberg, Allen, 321, 369, 825
"Girl Who Stayed Behind," 563
Gleason, Patrick, 32
Glendinning, Victoria, 658
Gold, Arthur, 457
Gold, Herb, 857
Golding, William, 288, 550
"Gone Fishing Again," 761
"Good Luck, Captain Martin," 54, 57
"Good-Talking Candle, A," 22
Gordon, Andrew, 629
"'Gothic Western,' He Calls It, and He's Right, A," 583
Gougeon, Leonard, 630
Graddy, Julia Colomitz, 222
Graham, Paul, 252
"Grand Penny Tour: Brautigan's 'Rommel Drives on Deep into Egypt', The," 420
"Grasshopper's Mirror, The," 66
Great Falls Tribune, 240, 820, 844
Great Gatsby, The, 461
"Great Golden Telescope," 192
Greenman, Myron, 275
Greenwell, Bill, 710
Greenwood, Robert, 447
Greiner, Donald J., 251, 392, 393, 396, 398, 402, 412, 427, 438
Grey, Zane, 571, 801

Grimaud, Isabelle, 686
Grimes, Larry E., 687
Grogan, Emmett, 245, 314
Grossteste Review, 167
"Grotesquerie," 567
Grove, Lee, 688
Grubber, J., 586
Guardian Weekly, 474, 604, 790, 794
"Gumshoeing It," 676
"Gun for Big Fish, A," 188

H

Hackenberry, Charles, 542, 748
Haight-Ashbury, 299, 821, 827, 830
"Haiku Ambulance," 29, 391
"Hair Brained," 488, 514
"Half-Sunday Homage to a Whole Leonardo da Vinci, A," 91
Hall, H.W., 217
Hall, Sharon K., 264
"Halloween in Denver," 170, 183
Halpern, Sue M., 711
Hamilton, David Mike, 276
Hammett, Dashiell, 670
"Hang-Ups," 558
"Hansel and Gretel," 11
Hansen, Allen J., 277
Hanser, Carl, 81, 108
"Happier (but Not Holier) than Thou," 325
"Happy But Footsore Writer Celebrates His Driver's Block, A," 312
<u>Happy to Be Here</u>, 231, 230
"Harbor, The," 29
Harlequin, 401
"Harmonics on Literary Irreverence: Boris Vian and Richard Brautigan," 366
Harper, Cathy, 712
Harper's Magazine, 49, 57, 657
Harrison, Jim, 440
Hart, James David, 278, 326
Hartford Courant, 716, 843
<u>Harvard Guide to Contemporary American Writing</u>, 281
Harvard University, 238
Harvest Records, 203
Harvey, Nick, 47
Haslam, Gerald, 847
Hassan, Ihab, 279

Hawkins, Bobbie Louise, 314
Hawkline Monster, The, 124, 216, 217, 249, 322, 331, 334, 343, 350, 361, 376, 487, 551, 568, 574, 576, 583, 585, 589, 590, 591, 592, 593, 594, 595, 600, 664, 848
  Translations:
  Hawkline-ke no Kaibutsu, (Japanese), 127
  Det Kolde Hu i Ørken, (Danish), 128, 129
  Hawkline Monstret, (Swedish), 130
  Hawkline-uhyret, (Norwegian), 131
  Kartanon Peto: Kauhuromanttinen Lannenromaani, (Finnish), 132
  Het Monster in de Kelder, (Dutch), 133
  Le Mostre des Hawkline, (French), 134
  El Monstruo de Hawkline: Un Western Gotico, (Spanish), 135
  Das Hawkline Monster, (German), 136
Hayden, Brad, 491
Hearron, William Thomas, 223, 492
Hearse, 5, 6, 14
Hedley, Leslie Woolf, 3
Heliotrope, 37
"Hell Hath No Fury," 639
Heller, Joseph, 223, 376
Helterman, Jeffrey, 322
Hemingway, Ernest, 459, 607, 705
Henderson, Jeanne J., 308
Hendin, Josephine, 280, 782, 792, 281
Hepburn, Neil, 631
"Heritier de Melville," 619
"Herman Melville in Dreams, Moby Dick in Reality," 11
Hernlund, Patricia, 516
"Heroe y Estile en la Novela Norteamerican Actual," 371
"Heroine of the Time Machine," 42, 57
Hesse, Hermann, 361, 550
Hewitt, Geof, 282, 283
"Hey, Bacon!," 22
"Hey! This Is What It's All About," 22
Hicks, Jack, 284
Higgins, George V., 571
Hill, Susan, 543
Hinckle, Warren, 848, 855
"Hip Elect," 472
"Hippie Poet Laureate," 339
Hirschman, Jack, 433
"Historical Romance 1966 di Richard Brautigan, Ovuero L'aborto Dell'eroe, An," 535
Hodge, Richard, 314
Hoffman, Daniel, 281

Hoffmann, Gerhard, 372
Hogan, William, 458
Holden, J., 285
Hollow Orange, 21, 22
Hollywood, 22, 59
Holmes, Ken, 314
Holt, Patricia, 235, 236
"Homage to Charles Atlas," 48, 57
"Homage to the San Francisco YMCA," 177, 183, 190, 191, 777
"Home Again Home Again Like a Turtle to His Balcony," 48, 57
"Home on the Range," 720
Homer Babbidge Library, 202
Hoopes, Robert, 103
Hope, Mary, 689
Hopkins, Gerard Manley, 631
Hopper, Dennis, 314
Hornick, Lita, 783
"Horse Child Breakfast," 29
"Horse Race," 12, 29, 32, 39
"Horse That Had a Flat Tire, The," 3, 29, 58
Horvath, Brooke Kenton, 224, 286, 287
Horwitz, Carey A., 416, 417
"How Hippies Got Hooked on Trout Fishing in America," 317
Howard, Peter, 4
Howard, Phillip, 659
Howe, Will David, 209
Hudson Review, 419, 556, 598, 800
Hughes, Catherine, 544
Hulesberg, Richard A., 190
"Hunchback Trout, The," 92, 95, 98
Hunt, Robert, 288
Hunter, Timothy A., 749

I

"I Cannot Answer You Tonight in Small Portions," 29
"I Feel Horrible. She Dosen't," 29
"I Lie Here in a Strange Girl's Apartment," 22, 221
"I Live in the Twentieth Century," 29
"Icarus in Timbuktu," 391
Idaho Statesman, 335
Il Lettore di Provincia, 479
"I'm Haunted by All the Space That I Will Live Without You," 35
"Image of America as Reflected in the Works of Some Contemporary American Writers, The," 373

"Impasse," 48, 57, 61
"Impasse and Other Poems," 61
"In a Cafe," 11, 29, 32, 65
"In Her Sweetness Where She Folds My Wounds," 37, 45
"In the California Bush," 93
In the Singer's Temple: Prose Fictions of Barthelme, Gaines, Brautigan, Piercy, Kesey, and Kosinski, 284
In Trout Country, 98
In Watermelon Sugar, 105, 195, 516, 521, 796, 797, 807
   Translations:
     In Wassermelonen Zucker, (German), 108
     Sucre de Pasteque et La Peche a la Truite en Amerique, (French), 109
     In Watermeloensuiker, (Dutch), 110
     In Wassermelonen Zucker & Forellenfischen in Amerika, 111
     Melonin Mehu, (Norwegian), 112
     Suika-tô no hibi, (Japanese), 113
     Arbuusisuhkrus, (Estonian), 114
Indianapolis Star, 751
"Indirect Popcorn," 29
"Individual and Society in Contemporary American Fiction," 377
Inoue, Kenji, 373
Instructor's Manual for "The Art of Fiction, 3rd Ed.," 190
Interdisciplinary Science Reviews, 105
International Antiquarian Book Fair, 42
International Authors and Writers Who's Who, 289
International Who's Who in Poetry, 290, 291
"Introspection d'un Tubiste," 253
"Irishman at Large," 454
Irwin, Robert, 213
"It's Going Down," 22
"It's Raining in Love," 21, 22, 29, 33, 38
"It's Time to Train Yourself," 46, 57
"I've Never Had It Done So Gently Before," 29
Ives, George L., 750

J

j, 12
Jeffrey, David L., 292
Jeopardy, 183
Jones, Lewis, 713
Jones, Stephen R., 214
Journal of Reading, 406, 465, 520
"Journey into the Fantastic," 719
"Joys of Jersey and Battlefield Notes from the Cola War, The," 729

"Judge Advances Fight Against Brautigan Book Ban," 236
"Jules Verne Zucchini," 37, 45
June 30th, June 30th, 63, 251, 352, 353, 359
Just What This Country Needs, Another Poetry Anthology, 43
Justus, James H., 293, 294

K

"Kafka's Hat," 11
Kaleidoscope-Madison, 40
Kaleidoscope-Milwaukee, 171
Kandel, Lenore, 245
Kane, Jean, 751
Kansas City Star, 298, 493, 714, 753
Karl, Frederick R. 295
"Karma Repair Kit: Items 1-4," 16, 22, 29, 39
Kay, Ernest, 289, 290, 291
Kaye, Sheldon, 587, 588
Kazuko, Fujimoto 74, 88, 113, 127, 140, 145, 149, 182
Keele, A. F., 545
"Keeping Off Track," 715
Keillor, Garrison, 229, 230, 231
Kelly, Ken, 848
Kenny, Kevin, 752
Kern, Robert, 296
Kerouac, Jack, 390, 458, 468, 473, 825
Kerouac, Jan, 297
Kesey, Ken, 377, 825
Kherdian, David, 58, 327
"Kidding," 577
Killinger, J.R., 459
Kimberly, Nick, 31
Kincheloe, Henderson, 589, 590
"Kingdom Come," 9
Kinsman, Clare D., 257
Kirkus Review, 424, 435, 526, 609, 644, 671, 699, 736, 769, 573
"Kithflicks," 667
Kline, Betsy, 298, 714, 753
Klinkowitz, Jerome, 299, 300, 301, 302, 303, 304, 305, 328, 330
Klonsky, Milton, 52
Knapp, Daniel, 100
Knowles, Carrie J., 441
Kolin, Phillip C., 494
Koller, James, 202
Kolodziej, Christine, 218
"Kool-Aid Wino, The," 102, 104

Kosinski, Jerzy, 365
Kraft, Werner, 374
Kramer, Elaine Fialka, 316
Kramer, Maurice, 316
Krim, Seymour, 690
Kroll, Stephen, 546
Kulcher, 163, 183, 783
"Kulchur: Memoir," 783
Kyger, Joanne, 314

L

"La Nouvelle Fiction Contre le Consensus." 375
La Rhétorique du Pararéel Dans l'Oeuvre de Richard Brautigan," 368
La Valley, Albert J., 102, 115, 321
"**Lady, A,**" 22
Lahr, Anthea, 547
Langlois, Jim, 548, 784
Language, 585
Lardner, Ring, 824
Lask, Thomas, 549
"Last Letter to Richard Brautigan, A," 847
"**Last Music Is Not Heard, The,**" 12
"**Last of What's Left, The,**" 66
Last Whole Earth Catalog: Access to Tools, 97, 478
"**Late Starting Dawn,**" 37, 65
"**Lay the Marble Tea,**" 11, 213, 247, 251
Le Vot, André, 306, 375, 632
Leavitt, Harvey, 517
Lee, Hermione, 691
Lee, L.L., 591
"**Legend of Horses, A,**" 42, 57
Leitaker, J.D., 234
Lemontt, Bobbie Burch, 692
Lepper, Gary M., 4, 7, 17, 26, 35, 36, 70, 79, 106, 116, 125, 215
"L'Esperimento del Professor Hawkline: Case Stregate e Sogno Americano da Brown a Brautigan," 601
"**Let's Voyage into the New American House,**" 22, 29, 60, 62
"Letter from the North," 857
"**Lettuce,**" 23
Levin, Martin, 460
Levy, Margot, 242
Lewis, Paul, 376
L' Express, 579
Lhamon, W.T., 307

Library Journal Book Review 1970, The, 417, 804
Library Journal Book Review 1974, The, 587
Library Journal Book Review 1975, The, 615
Library Journal Book Review 1976, The, 655
Library Journal Book Review 1978, The, 442
Library Journal Book Review 1980, The, 706
Library Journal, 430, 443, 471, 537, 588, 548, 616, 656, 693, 707, 750, 784, 787, 791, 805
"Library, The," 123
"Lieux Américains: Richard Brautigan," 380
Life, 338, 553
"Life and Death of Richard Brautigan, The," 357
Lincoln Journal/Star, 698
"Linear Farewell, Nonlinear Farewell," 29
Lingeman, Richard R., 660
Lion, R.C., 183
Lippman, Amy, 754
Lish, Gordon, 186
Listener, The , 472, 490, 515, 543, 631, 718, 780
Listening to Richard Brautigan, 203
Literary and Library Prizes, 308
Literary Disruptions, 302
"Literary Extensions of the Formula Western," 249
"Literary Life in California, The," 1964," 170, 183
Literatur in Wissenschaft und Unterricht, 793
"Literature in an Apocalyptic Age, or, How to End a Romance," 292
"Literature of Exhaustion, The," 246
Litinger, Boyd, 195
"Little Memoirs: Three Tales by Richard Brautigan," 170
Livingston, Montana, 826, 850
"Loading Mercury with a Pitchfork," 46
Loading Mercury with a Pitchfork, 56, 57, 251
    Translation:
        At Laesse Kviksølv Med en Fork, (Danish), 57
"Lobster Eating," 710
"Locals Remember Brautigan in '60s," 843
Locklin, Gerald, 461
Lodge, David, 309
Loewinsohn, Ron, 310, 314
London Magazine, 39, 273, 410, 747
"Long Time Ago People Decided to Live in America, A," 193
Look, 550
Los Angeles Herald Examiner, 462, 734
Los Angeles Times, 253, 661, 845
Los Angeles Times Book Review, 723, 740
"Lost Chapters of Trout Fishing in America, The," 174, 183, 186

"Lost Tree, The," 68
Lottman, Eileen, 495, 785
"Loufoque Brautigan?," 363
"Love Poem," 19, 22, 59
"Lovers," 22
"Lucky Punch," 362
Lynch, Dennis, 311, 849

M

McCaffery, Larry, 328, 715
McCall, Cheryl, 312
McClanahan, Ed, 788
McClure, Michael, 245, 314
McCullough, Frances Monson, 272
McDowell, Edwin, 850
McEnroe, Colin, 716
McGuane, Tom, 314
McIlroy, Gary, 313
McKean, Lynn, 328
Mackintosh, Graham, 23, 24
McKuen, Rod, 321
McLellan, Joseph, 434
McMichael, James, 43
Mademoiselle, 54, 57, 158, 176, 183, 187
Magazine for the Study of English and American Literature, 388
Magazine Littéraire, 363
"Magic Box and Richard Brautigan, A," 225
Magill, Frank N., 276, 470, 489, 521, 589, 590, 666, 806, 807
Magill's Literary Annual, 666
Mahoney, John, 99
Major, Clarence, 551, 592
"Making Book on a Sentimental Season," 628
Makino, H., 193
Malley, Ken, 855
Malley, Terence, 208, 405, 418, 463, 496, 518, 552, 786
Manning, Robert, 578
Manske, Eva, 377
Manso, Peter, 314
"Map Shower," 29
Mark in Time: Portraits and Poetry / San Francisco, 47, 57
Marowski, Daniel G., 263, 484, 541, 582, 679, 708, 745
Marquis Who's Who, Inc., 348, 351, 352, 353, 354, 357. 349
Martins, Heitor 497
Mason, Michael, 633, 717

Massachusetts Review, 636
Masterplots 1970 Annual, 807
Masterplots 1975 Annual, 589
Masterplots II. American Fiction Series, 470, 489, 521
Masters Abstracts, 222
"Mating Saliva," 29, 52
Matuz, Roger, 263, 484, 541, 582, 679, 708, 745
"Mayonnaise," 292
"Meek Shall Inherit the Earth's Beer Bottles, The," 3
Meeter, Glenn, 104
Meldsted, Tamara, 57
Mellard, James M., 315
Mellors, John, 718
Melonin Mehu, 112
Meltzer, David, 45, 198
Melville, Herman, 619
Memories of Richard Brautigan and San Francisco, 1966," 814
"Menu, The," 197
"Mercy Killing, The," 232
Merkur, 374, 390
"Mexican Hats Miss Their Mark," 650
Miami Herald, 672
Michigan Academician, 266
"Mid-February Sky Dance, A," 22, 29, 52, 59, 60
"Mike," 12
Milazzo, Lee, 719
Miles, Josephine, 51
Milk for the Duck, 22, 59
Miller, Arthur, 629
Miller, Ellen K., 238
Milwaukee Journal, 662, 840
Minas Gerais, Suplemento Literário, 497
Minimalist, 295
Minnesota Review, 420
Minot, Stephen, 101
Minudri, Regina U., 787
Miscellanea, 601
Mitgang, Herbert, 720
Modern American Literature, 316
"Modern Fairy Tale, A," 777
Modern Fiction Studies, 275, 277, 332, 333, 336, 687
Modern Occasions, 347
Modern Short Story, The, 104
"Modernism, Antimodernism and Postmodernism," 309
Modular Theater, 253
"Monster in the Cellar," 595

Montana State University, 852
Montana State University Staff Bulletin, 237
Montrose, David, 755
"More than Meets the Eye," 554
Morley, Patricia, 756
Morrow, Patrick D., 634
Morton, Brian, 317
"Mortuary Bush, The," 3, 6
"Moth in Tucson, Arizona, A," 42, 57
Mottram, Eric, 318
Mount, Douglas, 553
Mount, Ferdinand, 663
"Move Over, Mr. Tolstoy," 549
<u>Mug Shots: Who's Who in the New Earth</u>, 319
Muggeridge, Malcom, 464
Mullen, Michael P., 320
"Multicolored Loin Cloths, Glass Trinkets of Words: Surrealism in <u>In Watermelon Sugar</u>," 522
Murphy, Rosalie, 211
"My Nose Is Growing Old," 22
Myers, Robin, 267
Myerson, Jonathon, 757

N

"Naive Narration: Classic to Post-Modern," 336
"Naive Tone Perfect for Brautigan Novel," 751
Nation, 711
National Endowment for the Arts, 289, 308
National Observer, 547, 583, 627
"Nature in the Selected Works of Four Contemporary American Novelists," 220
"Nature Poem, The," 12
Neely, Mildred Sola, 635
Negro Digest, 469
Nemoianu, Anca, 378
"New American Fiction," 450, 468
New American Review, 11, 12, 183
"New & Noteworthy," 611, 668, 737
"New Approaches in the Post-Modern American Novel: Joseph Heller, Kurt Vonnegut, & Richard Brautigan," 223
<u>New Consciousness, The</u>, 102, 115, 321
New England Review, 285
"New Fiction from Esquire," 186
"New from Africa," 452
"New in Paperbacks," 437

New Ingenue, 158
New Orleans Review, 158
New Orleans Times-Picayune, 744
New Republic, 566, 625, 696, 795
New Review, 309
New Statesman, 403, 452, 558, 577, 614, 667, 691, 710
"New Trend in American Fiction, A," 277
New Writing in the USA, The, 90, 94
New York Review of Books, 241, 468
New York Times, 69, 233, 456, 549, 624, 774, 816, 850
New York Times Book Review, 232, 460, 561, 605, 611, 638, 652, 660, 668, 684, 720, 733, 737, 758, 771, 772, 782, 792, 796, 797
New Yorker, 229, 610, 694, 759, 838
New Fiction, 275
Newsweek, 519, 595
Nice, 183
Nicholls, Peter, 331
"Night," 11, 55, 57
"Night Flowing River," 68
Nilsen, Allen Pace, 406, 465, 520
Nilsen, Don L.F., 406, 465, 520
"Nine Crows: Two Out of Sequence," 55, 57
"Nine Things," 22, 59
"1942," 12
"1692 Cotton Mather Newsreel," 176, 183
"1930s to the Present, The," 293, 294
"No Picnic," 614
"Nobody Knows What the Experience Is Worth," 57, 61
Non-lexicalized Compounds, 585
Nordell, Roderick, 593
Norman, Albert H., 803
Norman, Gurney, 788
"Note On Brautigan and Robbe-Grillet, A," 342
"Note on the Camping Craze That Is Currently Sweeping America, A," 93
"Notes d'un Ouvre-Boîtes Critique," 367
Notes on Contemporary Literature, 342, 629, 777
Notes on Modern American Literature, 287
"Notes on the Counter Culture," 369
Novak, Robert, 322, 323
"Novel in Brief," 770
"Novel of the Narcissus, The," 663
Novels and Novelists, 324
"November 3," 22, 29, 52
Now Now, 183
Nueva Estafeta, 596, 637
Nuovi Argomenti, 385

Nye, Robert, 466

O

Oakland Tribune, 732, 765
Oates, Joyce Carol, 195
"Obit—Brautigan," 827
"Obits," 829
"Obituaries," 830
"Obituary Notes," 831
Observer, 407, 454, 483, 510, 563, 597, 639, 658, 695, 725, 761, 770
Occident, 382
O'Connell, Shaun, 636
"Octopus Frontier, The," 11, 12
Octopus Frontier, The, 12-21, 213, 247, 251
O'er, 22
"Off the Hook," 624
O'Hara, J. D., 325
Ohnemus, Günter, 28, 77, 121, 142, 150
Ohnemus, Ilse, 77, 121, 142, 150
"Old Bus, The," 178, 183
"Old Folk's Home, The," 12
"Old Lady," 198
Olderman, Raymond M., 594
"On Pure Sudden Days Like Innocence," 47, 57, 61
"On the Creation and Use of English Compound Nouns," 487, 585
"On the Elevator Going Down," 63, 64
On the Road, 390
"1/3, 1/3, 1/3," 166, 183
"Open Letters," 592
"Oranges," 29
Oregonian, 721, 722
Ottenberg, Eve, 758
"Our Beautiful West Coast Thing," 22, 29, 32
"Out of Sight," 409, 524
Outside, 158, 160
Overland Journey of Joseph Francl, The, 158, 159
Oxford Companion to American Literature, The, 326
Oyez Review, 252

P

"Pacific Nursery," 490, 515
"Pacific Radio Fire," 176, 183

Packerm, Nancy Huddleston, 103
"Pancakes and the President, The," 717
"Paperbacks," 434
Paradise Valley, Montana, 826, 833, 853
Parallel, 183
Paris Review, 25, 201
Parkinson, Thomas, 467, 498
Parnassus, 423
Parra, Ernesto, 637
"**Parsley,**" 23
Patchen, Kenneth, 433, 801, 825
Pearle, Howard D., III, 600
"Peasant Power," 790
<u>Penguin Companion to American Literature, The</u>, 318
People, 243, 312, 700, 853
Percy, Walker, 224, 232
"Perverse Mystery by Richard Brautigan, A," 625
"Pescando Trutas na América com Richard Brautigan," 497
Peterson, Clarence, 554
Pétillon, Pierre-Yves, 379, 380
Petticoffer, Dennis, 442, 443, 693
Pfaff, William, 759
Philadelphia Inquirer, 851
Phillips, Al, 555
Piggins, Brenda G., 308
"Pilgrim at Tinker Creek and the Burden of Science," 313
"**Pill Versus the Springhill Mine Disaster, The,**" 796, 797, 807
<u>Pill Versus the Springhill Mine Disaster, The</u>, 3, 4, 7, 11, 12, 16, 17, 18, 19, 20, 22, 25, 29, 43, 44, 195, 208, 211, 213, 216, 234, 241, 247, 251, 282, 283, 290, 301, 310, 327, 339, 391, 400, 405, 406, 409, 418, 465, 520, 524, 839
  Translations:
  <u>Die Pille gegen das Grubenunglück von Spring Hill und 104 andere Gedichte</u> (German), 28, 29
"Pink and Fading, in Watermelon Ink," 561
Pintarich, Paul, 721
Playboy, 156, 158, 170, 183, 449, 571, 607, 739, 848
<u>Please Plant This Book</u>, 23-25, 247
Plimpton, George, 33, 38
PNW Conference on Foreign Languages, 355
Pocket Books, 550, 557
Poe, Edgar Allan, 571, 770
<u>Poems Here and Now</u>, 58, 327
"Poems Versus Jokes," 285
"Poet-Novelist Richard Brautigan Found Dead," 832
"Poet-Writer Brautigan Found Dead in Home," 833

Poetry, 34, 37, 395, 409, 433, 524, 837
"Poetry of Richard Brautigan, The," 323
"Poker Star," 29
"Polluted Eden," 476, 509
Polman, Dick, 851
"Pomegranate Circus, The," 22, 29, 32, 60
Ponicsan, Darryl, 722, 723
Popular Western, 249
Porter, Peter, 407
Portnoy's Complaint, 307
Portola Institute, 97
"Portrait of a Child-Bride on Her Honeymoon," 11
"Portrait of the Id as Billy the Kid," 11
"Post Offices of Eastern Oregon, The," 163, 183, 193, 299, 783
Postcard from the Bridge, A," 13
Postcard from Chinatown, A," 12
Postcard Poems, 65
"Postman, The," 12
Postmodern Fiction. A Bio-Bibliographical Guide, 328
Post-Modernism, 205, 336
"Postmodernism in the Fiction of Richard Brautigan," 227
Postmodernism, 227
"Potato House of Julius Caesar, The," 12
"Pox on Dullness, A," 711
"Precious Little: Richard Brautigan; The Abortion: An Historical Romance
    1966," 530
"Precistvastijat Smjah Na Ricard Brotigan. Cudovisteto Hoklan," 599, 664
"Prelude, The" (Wordsworth), 492
"Preparing for Ecclesiastes," 78
Prescott, Peter S., 595
"Prides and Prejudices," 620
Primitivist poetics, 296
Pritchard, William H., 419, 556
"Private Eye Lettuce," 12
Proceedings of the Conference on the Comparative Study of Chinese Ideal and
    the American Dream, 373
"Professionally Speaking," 562
Progressive, 578
"Promise, the Reality and the Hope, The," 69
"Propelled by Portals Whose Only Shame," 37, 45
"Psalm," 6, 10
Publishers Weekly, 235, 236, 445, 495, 532, 574, 575, 576, 612, 613, 635,
    645, 673, 674, 701, 702, 741, 779, 785, 831
"Pudding Master of Stanley Basin, The," 93
Puetz, Manfred, 382
"Pumpkin Tide, The," 12

Punch, 713, 728
"Punitive Ghosts Like Steam-Driven Tennis Courts," 46, 57
Pynchon, Thomas, 224, 376, 388

Q

"Quail, The," 12, 43
Quest/77, 63, 64
Quill & Quire, 729, 764
Quintana, Juan, 596
Quinzaine, 375, 619

R

Rabate, Jean-Michel, 383
Rabkin, Eric S., 191, 288, 329
Rahv, Phillip, 468
"Rain, The," 14
Ramparts, 166, 183, 500
Rand, Ayn, 288
Randall, Dudley, 469
"Rape of Ophelia, The," 12
"Reader's Report, A," 460
"Rebels in the War with Life," 458
Redbook, 192
"Refrain Along Brautigan's Oddpath, A," 740
"Regained Paradise of Brautigan's In Watermelon Sugar, The," 517
Reginald, R., 216
Rembrandt Creek, 186
"Rendezvous," 67
"Rest of the Iceberg, The," 473
Return of the Rivers, The, 4, 213, 251, 400
Revenge of the Lawn: Stories, 1962-1970, 165, 179, 183, 194, 195, 208, 232, 250, 284, 322, 349, 361, 771, 772, 774, 780, 782, 786, 778, 779, 782, 785, 788, 795
  Translations:
    Shibafu No Fukushu, (Japanese), 182
    Die Rache des Rasens. Geschichen 1962-1970, (German), 183
Review of Contemporary Fiction, 204, 814
"Re-Visions of the Hard-Boiled Detective Formula in Recent American Fiction," 687
Revue Générale des Publications Français et Etrangéres, 379, 380
Rexroth, Kenneth, 825
"Rhetoric in New Fiction," 226

"Richard Brautigan: A Working Checklist," 218
"Richard Brautigan and the American Metaphor," 252
"Richard Brautigan and the Modern Pastoral," 333
"Richard Brautigan and the Pastoral Romance," 222
"Richard Brautigan Looks at Common Responses to Death," 287
"Richard Brautigan ni tsuite," 386
"Richard Brautigan 1935-1984," 837, 841
"Richard Brautigan Piccolo Eroe Della Controcultura," 385
"Richard Brautigan: The Politics of Woodstock," 481
"Richard Brautigan, 'The World War I Los Angeles Airplane'," 781
"Richard Brautigan, Novelist, a Literary Idol of the 1960's," 850
"Richard Brautigan's Good Nib: Artistic Independence in 'Trout Fishing in America'," 482
"Richard Brautigan's Parody of Arthur Miller," 629
"Richard Brautigan's Search for Control Over Death," 286
"Richard Brautigan's Trout Fishing in America Notes of a Native Son," 503
"Ride on Brautigan's Very Remarkable Train, A," 724
"Riding the Rails with Brautigan," 735
Riedel, Cornelia, 384
Riley, Carolyn, 258, 259, 260, 404, 413, 414, 486, 512, 511, 539, 580, 775, 799
Rimbaud, Arthur, 840
Rimer, Thomas, 724
Ritter, Jess, 330
Ritterman, Pamela, 499
"Rivets in Ecclesiastes, The," 78
Robbins, Albert, 294
Robbins, Gwen A., 225
Roberts, Peter, 331
"Robin W. Winks on Mysteries," 696
Rogers, Michael, 638
Rohrberger, Mary, 521, 522
Roiter, Margaret, 852
Rolling Stone, 37, 183, 357, 788
Rollyson, Carl E., Jr., 470
"Romance and Parody in Brautigan's 'The Abortion'," 542
"Romantic Renegades," 62
"Romeo and Juliet," 37, 52
Rommel Drives on Deep into Egypt, 35, 198, 208, 213, 234, 250, 251, 278, 282, 283, 374, 405, 418, 421, 839
Ronald, Ann, 760
Rood, Karen L., 446, 731
"Room 208, Hotel Trout Fishing in America," 92, 95
"Rootin', Tootin' and Shootin'," 633
Rose, Kate, 420
Ross, Jean W., 320, 446, 731
Rosselli, Aldo, 385

Rosset, Barney, 95
Russell, Bertrand, 718
Russell, Charles, 332
Russo, Anthony, 314
Rutgers Daily Telegram, 557

S

Sage, Lorna, 597, 639, 725, 761
St. Louis Globe Democrat, 665, 724
St. Louis Post-Dispatch, 651
St. Petersburg Times, 841
Sale, Roger, 598
Saleh, Dennis, 43
Salinger, J. D., 254, 550
"Salt Creek Coyotes, The," 91
"Sam Spade Caper, The," 684
Sampson, Sally, 558
San Deigo Union, 715
"San Francisco," 22,
San Francisco, 61
San Francisco Arts Festival Commission, 15
San Francisco Arts Festival: A Poetry Folio: 1964, 15
San Francisco Beat Movement, 278
San Francisco Chronicle, 467, 498, 754, 848, 855, 856
San Francisco Examiner, 681, 705
San Francisco Examiner & Chronicle, 559
San Francisco Examiner Review, 255
San Francisco Express Times, 37
San Francisco Poets, The, 45, 198
San Francisco Public Library: A Publishing House, 37
San Francisco Review, 10
San Francisco Stories, 158
"San Francisco Weather Report," 24, 25, 29
San Quentin, 197
"Sand Castles," 176, 183
Sandberg, David, 7
Sarcandzieva, Rada, 599, 664
Saroyan, William, 458, 770, 840
Saturday Review, 421, 458, 534, 620, 709, 778
"Sawmill, The," 12
Scharnhorst, Gary, 762
"Scheherazade Runs Out of Plots, Goes on Talking," 337
Scheneck, Stephen, 500
Schmidt, Carol, 239

Schmittroth, John, 99
Schmitz, Neil, 333
Scholes, Robert, 288
"Schoo! Board Socked with ACLU Suit in Brautigan Book-Banning Incident," 234
School Library Journal, 234, 763
Schroeder, Michael Leroy, 226
Schulz, Charlie, 566
Schuster, Arian, 444
Science Fiction and Fantasy Literature, 216
Science Fiction Book Review Index, 1974-1979, 217
Science Fiction Commentary, 274
Science Fiction Encyclopedia, The, 331
"Science Fiction for the Age of Inflation: Reading Atlas Shrugged in the 1980s," 288
Science Fiction Source Book, 334
Scope of the Fantastic: Culture, Biography, Themes, Chidren's Literature, 600
Scott, Bryan, 252
"Sea: Its Science and Poetry, The," 105
Seattle Post Intelligencer, 602
Seattle Times, 408
Secolul, 378
Second Anthology of Works from the St. Marks Poetry Project, A, 46
"Second Kingdom, The," 1
Seib, Kenneth, 501
Self-Apparent Word, The, 304
"September California," 15
Serebnick, Judith, 417, 804
Serendipity Books 4, 7, 23
"Seven Pieces for Violin and Piano," 221
Seymore, James, 853
"Seymour Lawrence and ACLU Fight Ban on Brautigan Books," 235
Seymour-Smith, Martin, 324
"Shags and Poets," 419
Shake the Kaleidoscope: A New Anthology of Modern Poetry, 52
Shannon, L.R., 69
"Shasta Daisy," 23
Shatkin, A.I., 805
"She Was," 115
Shea, Edmund, 53
"Shenevertakesherwatchoff Poem, The," 29
Sheppard, R. Z., 789
Shorb, Terril, 854
"Short History of Religion in California, A," 165, 183, 185, 194, 195
Short Story, The, 103

Shrapnel, Norman, 790
"**Sidney Greenstreet Blues, The,**" 12, 29, 32
Siegel, Mark, 502
"**Silence of Flooded Houses, The,**" 199
Silliman, Ron, 328
"Silly Pretension, A," 754
"**Silver Stairs of Ketchikan, The,**" 29
Simony, Maggy, 343
Sinclair, Andrew, 726
"**Sit Comma and Creeley Comma,**" 12
"'60s Hero's Pained Soul Is Finally Bared, in Death," 851
Skorupa, Joseph, 727
Skow, John, 560
Slethaug, Gordon E., 600
Slusser, George E., 288
Smith, Barb, 855
Smith, Mason, 561
Snyder, Gary, 369, 825
Snyder, George, 856
"So the Wind Won't Blow It All Away," 738, 739, 741, 747, 757, 760, 766
<u>**So the Wind Won't Blow It All Away**</u>, 161, 162, 317, 739, 746, 748, 751, 753, 754, 759, 760
"Social Criticism and the Deformation of Man, Satire, the Grotesque and Comic Nihilism in the Modern and Postmodern American Novel," 372
Solotaroff, Theodore, 179
<u>**Sombrero Fallout**</u>, 142, 322, 361, 376, 641, 648, 652, 658, 660, 663, 664, 666
   Translations:
   Sonburero <u>Rakka Su</u>, (Japanese), 145
   Retombées <u>de</u> <u>Sombrero</u>, (French), 146
Sombrero Fallout: A Japanese Novel," 645
"Some Fun, Some Gloom," 758
"Some Montana Poems/1973," 55
"Some Novels for the Pastor's Study," 459
"Some Observations on a Confederate General from Big Sur," 461
Somer, John, 252, 330
"**Sonnet,**" 11
Sorrentino, Gilbert, 395
"Sour Smell of Success," 695
Southern Review, 369
"Spare and Strange," 631
Spectator, 473, 488, 514, 567, 626, 640, 689
Spector, Robert D., 421
"Speed Kills: Richard Brautigan and the American Metaphor," 252
Spencer Library, University of Kansas, 201
Spicer, Jack, 12
"**Spinning Like a Ghost on the Bottom of a Top,**" 35

"Spinning Like a Ghost on the Bottom of a Top," 35
Sports Illustrated, 98
Sprug, Joseph W., 562
"Squash," 23
Stand, 376
Stanford, 238
Stanford French Review, 366
"Star Hole," 22, 59
"Star-Spangled' Nails," 29, 41
Steaua, 387
Steele, Judy, 335
Steinbeck, John, 390
Steiner, George, 694
"Step Toward Perception, A," 397
"Stepsons of Sam: Re-Visions of the Hard-Boiled Detective Formula in Recent American Fiction," 687
Sterling Lord Agency, 349, 350
Stetler, Charles, 461
Stetler, Susan L., 248
Stevens, Wallace, 315
Stevick, Phillip, 337
Stewart, Joan Hinde, 666
Stickney, John, 338
"Still Loving," 566
Stone, Wilfred, 103
Stone Wall Book of Short Fictions, The, 185
Story, Jack Trevor, 728
Story: An Introduction to Prose Fiction, 100
Story: Fictions Past and Present, 195
"Stranger than Paradise," 686
"Stranger than Truth," 556
Streitfeld, David, 339
Strell, Lois A., 763
"Strolling Across the Bridge," 410
Strothman, Janet, 791
Studi Sulla Narrativa D'iniziazione, 535
Studies in Contemporary Satire: A Creative and Critical Journal, 494
"Study in California Flowers, A," 164, 167, 183
Stuewe, Paul, 729, 764
Stull, William L., 503
Stuttaford, Genevieve, 445
Sub-Stance, 300
Sugiura, Ginsaku, 386
Sum, 183
Summer of Love, The, 245
Sun Also Rises, The, 461

Sunday Times, 565, 618, 649, 675, 697
Sundel, Roger H., 190
Supplement, The, 340, 341
"Surgeon, The," 95
"Surprise," 12, 29
Surrealism, 265, 456, 790
Surrealist, 460, 522
Survey of Contemporary Literature, 590, 806
Survey of Modern Fantasy Literature, 502
Sweatt, Suzanne Mitchell, 227
"Sweet Alyssum Royal Carpet," 23
Swigart, Rob, 730
"Symbol, The," 12
Synder, George, 856
Syracuse News Times, 422

T

T.B., 857
Takahashi, M., 193
"Taking a Ride with Richard Brautigan," 703
"Talk of the Town, The," 838
"Talk Show," 171, 183
Tani, Stefano, 601
Tannenbaum, Earl, 471
Tanner, Tony, 317, 504, 505, .523
"Taste of the Taste of Brautigan, A," 48
Taylor, David M. 446, 731
Taylor, L. Loring, 387
"Teaching Vonnegut on the Firing Line," 330
Tel Quel 71/75, 365
"Ten Pamphlets," 395
"Ten Stories for Mr. Brautigan," 230, 231
"Ten Stories for Mr. Brautigan, and Other Stories," 229
Ten Year Anthology, A, 95
"That Girl," 13
Theology Today, 459
"They Are Really Having Fun," 48, 57
"This Fisher of Words Had Many a Winning Catch," 854
Thompson, Craig, 328
Thomson, George H., 342
Thomson, Robert, 732
Thoreau, Henry David, 207, 491, 506, 748
Thoreau Journal Quarterly, 491
Thoreau Society Bulletin, 748

"Three by Richard Brautigan," 66
"Three Poems," 39
"Three Stories by Richard Brautigan," 176
Thunder City Press Broadside Series, No. 5, The, 59, 60
Thwaite, Anthony, 563, 695
"Tigers Again, The," 115
Time, 401, 560, 789, 836
Times, 466, 505, 523, 531, 617, 650, 659, 683, 726, 834
Times Higher Education Supplement, 317
Times Literary Supplement, 476, 509, 530, 584, 633, 646, 682, 717, 755
"To England," 11, 29, 44, 52
"Tokyo and Montana," 68
Tokyo Montana Express, The, 157, 158, 159, 317, 343, 348, 354, 360, 698, 700, 701, 702, 703, 705, 709, 711, 712, 714, 720, 722, 726, 727, 728, 730, 734, 839
   Translations:
   Express, (French), 157
   Der Tokyo-Montana-Express, (German), 158
Tolkein, J.R.R., 361
Tont, Sargun A., 105
Totem, 22
"Toward the Pleasures of a Reconstituted Crow," 42, 57
Toye, Robert James, 792
"Tradition und Postmoderne in Richard Brautigan's Revenge of the Lawn—Stories," 793
Trainsong, 297
"Transcendentalism Revived," 382
Transcendentalists, 381, 382
Transition, 450
Traub, Nancy, 765
Traveler's Reading Guide, The, 343
"Travelling [sic] light," 725
Treglown, Jeremy, 667
Trema, 368
Trevor, Allen, 475, 508
"Tribute to a Friend and the Books That Might Have Been," 849
"Trick or Treat?," 718
"Trips," 626
TriQuarterly, 30, 77, 78, 158, 165, 183, 189, 310, 337, 783
Troubled Vision, The, 96
"Trout Death by Port Wine," 93
Trout Fishing in America, 91, 92, 93, 105, 195, 198, 205, 208, 211, 216, 217, 228, 233, 234, 241, 244, 247, 248, 255, 273, 274, 278, 290, 291, 292, 295, 299, 301, 302, 303, 307, 309, 310, 315, 317, 319, 322, 327, 339, 344, 361, 370, 371, 375, 390, 466, 476, 477, 478, 481, 482, 483, 487, 488, 489, 490, 491, 495, 496, 499, 500, 501, 502, 504, 505,

506, 507, 509, 510, 514, 515, 523, 585, 595, 604, 675, 725, 770, 782, 803, 807, 821, 822, 827, 830, 832, 835, 836
Translations:
Forellenfischen in Amerika (German), 81, 90
Sucre de Pasteque et La Pêche a la Truite en Amérique, (French), 83, 109
La Pêche a la Truite en Amérique, (French), 84, 89
In Wassermelonen Zucker & Forellenfischen in Amerika (German), 85
Taimenenkalastus Amerikassa, (Finnish), 86
Ørretfiske i Amerika, (Norwegian), 87
Amerika no masu Zuri (Japanese), 88
"Trout Fishing in America and the American Tradition," 506
"Trout Fishing in America di Richard Brautigan," 479
"Trout Fishing in America Terrorists," 99, 100, 102
"Trout Fishing Sampler (from Trout Fishing in America), A," 96
Tsurumi, Seiji, 388
Tuck, Donald H. 210
Turner, William O., 602
Twain, Mark, 223, 265, 459, 824
"Twelve Roman Soldiers and an Oatmeal Cookie," 3, 6
"Twenty-Eight Cents for My Old Age, The," 11
"23, The," 123
"Two Guys Get Out of a Car," 46, 57

U

Uellenberg, Klaus, 793
"Ultima narrative norteamericana [Ultimate North-American Narratives]," 370
"Un Western Gotico," 596
"Understanding New Fiction," 275
"Uneasy Middle-Aged Soul, An," 733
Unfortunate Woman, An, 237
University of Connecticut, Storrs, 202
"Unwanted Books—in Fiction and Fact," 564
Updike, John 220, 224
Updike and Brautigan, 193
UPI News, 817, 818, 821, 822, 823, 829

V

Valencia, California, 253
Van Vactor, Anita, 472
Vanderwerken, David L., 506
Vanity Fair, 314

"Vault of Language: Self-Reflective Artifice in Contemporary American Fiction," 332
"Very Natural and No Childbirth," 546
Vian, Boris, 366
"Vida," 124
Viking Press, The, 507
Village Voice, 628
Villar, Raso M., 389
Vinson, James, 211, 282, 283, 311, 344, 345, 346
Virginia Quarterly, 416
Vogler, Thomas A., 344, 345, 346
Vogue, 168, 172, 175, 177, 178, 183
"Voice of Vile Bodies, The," 675
Voice of Youth Advocates, 712
Vonnegut, Kurt, 223, 226, 288, 299, 320, 328, 361, 362, 550, 761, 840
Vonnegut in America, 305, 752
Vonnegut Statement, The, 330
Vortex, 586
Vulnerable People. A View of American Fiction Since 1945, 280

W

Wagner, Joe, 766
Wakeman, John, 356
"Walden Reworked," 748
Walden (Thoreau), 491, 748
Waldman, Anne, 46
Walker, Cheryl, 347
Walters, Ray, 668
Walters, Richard, 806, 807
Wanless, James, 218
Wanless and Kolodziej, 4, 7, 23, 29
Warren, Eric, 767
Warsh, Lewis, 409, 524
Washington Post, 835, 846
Washington Post Book World, 339, 546, 703, 773, 434, 437
Washington Review, 68
Washington Star, 669
In Watermelon Sugar, 208, 210, 216, 217, 241, 247, 273, 274, 299, 310, 317, 322, 331, 334, 339, 342, 344, 361, 370, 406, 409, 465, 476, 483, 488, 490, 509, 510, 514, 515, 516, 518, 519, 520, 521, 522, 523, 524, 569, 755, 782, 803, 836, 839
Waugh, Auberon, 473, 564
"Way She Looks at It, The," 29
Ways of the Poem, The, 51

"We Meet. We Try. Nothing Happens, but," 48, 57, 61
"We Were the Eleven O'Clock News," 57, 61
"Weather in San Francisco, The," 168, 183
Webb, W.L., 794
"Weeds and Four-Leaf Clovers," 774
Weinberger, Andy, 734
West, Nathanael, 646
West Coast Review of Books, 680
Western America Literature, 249, 591, 634, 692, 847, 760
"Western dans un château hanté," 579
Western Humanities Review, 477
"Westward the Course of Surrealism," 355
"Wheel, The," 12, 29, 32, 39
Wheeler, Elizabeth Patricia, 228
"When Fame Puts Its Feathery Crowbar Under Your Rock," 813
"Whimsies," 640
"Whiskey in the Works," 584
Whitman, Walt, 207
Whittemore, Reed, 795
Who Is Teddy Villanova?, 687
Who Was Who in America, 348
Who's Who in America, 349, 350, 351, 352, 353, 354
Who's Who in the New Earth, 319
"Whorehouse at the Top of Mount Rainer, The," 13
Wickes, George, 355
"Widow's Lament," 22
Wiegensten, Roland H., 390
Wiggen, Maurice, 565
Willard and His Bowling Trophies, 136, 250, 322, 351, 357, 358, 361, 376, 606, 612, 613, 620, 624, 625, 633, 634, 635
  Translations:
    Willard et ses Trophées de Bowling, (French), 139
    Tori No Shinden, (Japanese), 140
    Willard y sus Tofeos de Bolos, (Spanish), 141
    Willard und seine Bowlingtrophäen, (German), 142
Williams, Hugo, 410
Williams, Jonathan, 423
Williams, William Carlos, 296, 321, 803
"Williams, Brautigan, and the Poetics of Primitivism," 296
Willis, David, 391
Willis, Lonnie L., 603
Wilson, Robley, Jr., 101
Wilson Library Bulletin, 743
Windless Orchard, 323
Wingrove, David, 334
Winks, Robin W., 696

"Winos on Potrero Hill, The," 12, 43
"Winter Rug," 175, 183
"Witness for Trout Fishing in America Peace," 93
Witosky, Diane, 735
"Wood," 34
Woodress, James, 293
Woodstock, 254, 566
Wordsworth, Christopher, 474, 604
Wordsworth, William, 492
World, The, 57
World Authors, 1970-1975, 356
"World War I Los Angeles Airplane, The," 179, 183, 184, 193
"Worsewick," 91
"Wrapped in a Winter Rug: Richard Brautigan Looks at Common Responses to Death," 287
Wreden, W.P., 159
Wreden, William P., 158
Wright, Lawrence, 357
"Writer Sights in on Bozeman Life," 239
Writers Directory 1976-78, The, 358
Writers Directory 1980-1982, The, 359, 360
Writers Directory 1984-1986, The, 361

X

Xavier Review, 536
"Xerox Candy Bar," 29

Y

Yardley, Jonathon, 566
"Yes, the Fish Music," 11
Yohalem, John, 605
"You Will Have Unreal Recollections of Me," 48, 57
Young, Barbara, 240
Young Adult Cooperative Book Review Group of Massachusetts, 444
"Young Adult Perplex, The," 743
"Young Poet, A," 2
"Your Catfish Friend," 22
"Your Departure Versus the Hindenburg," 29
"Your Necklace Is Leaking," 29
Yourgrau, Barry, 733
"Youth Fishing in America," 347

Z

"Zany, Three-Stage Plot Under One Sombrero, A," 651
Zeitschrift für Anglistik und Amerikanistik, 377
Zen, 317, 713
Ziegfeld, Richard, 446, 731
Zur Dichotomischen Amerikakonzeption bei Richard Brautigan, 384
"Zweimal [Twice] Richard Brautigan: I. Ein Gedicht-scheinbar einfach [A Poem—Apparently Simple]," 374
"Zweimal [Twice] Richard Brautigan: II. Allerlei Geschichten—scheinbar verrückt [All Sorts of Poems—Apparently Mad]," 390